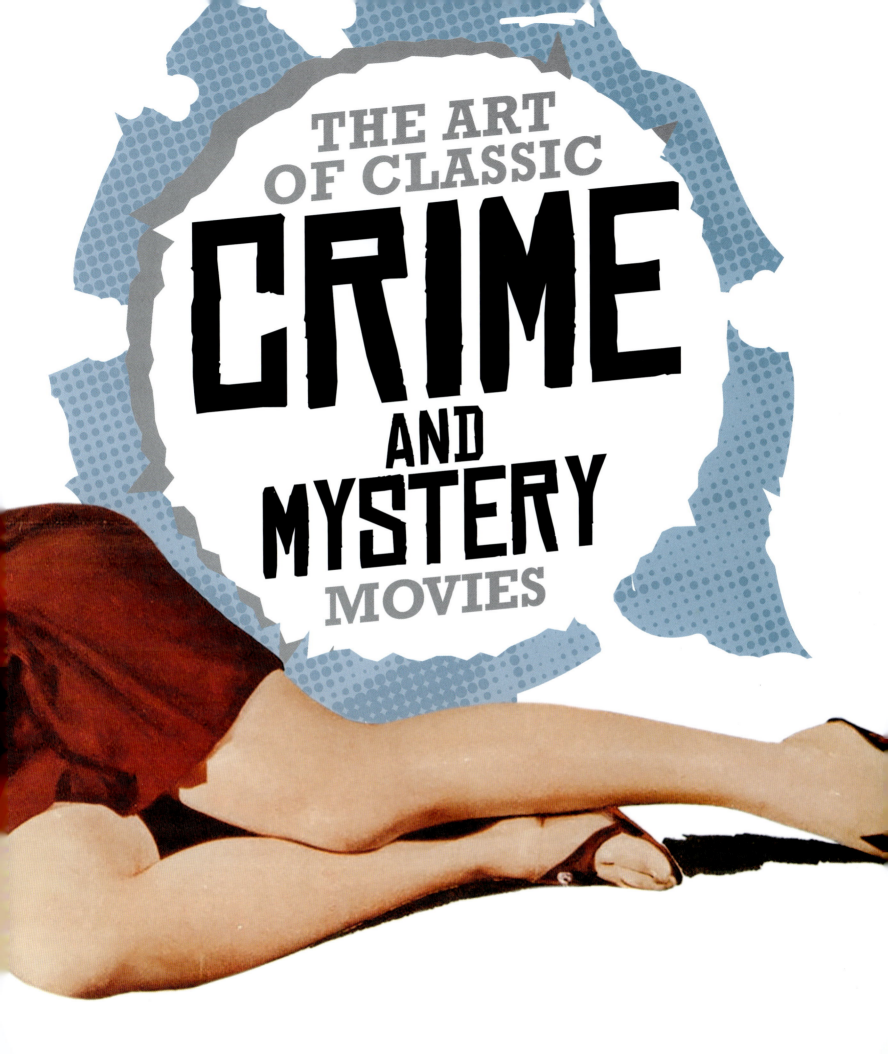

THE ART OF CLASSIC

CRIME

AND MYSTERY

MOVIES

Elephant Book Company Limited
Purcell, St. Mary's Hall
Rawstorn Road
Colchester
Essex, CO3 3JH
United Kingdom
www.elephantbookcompany.com

Editorial director: Will Steeds
Project manager: Tom Seabrook
Book design and cover artwork: Amazing 15

ISBN: 978-0-7643-6927-8
Printed in China

Published by Schiffer Publishing, Ltd.
4880 Lower Valley Road
Atglen, PA 19310
Phone: (610) 593-1777; Fax: (610) 593-2002
Email: Info@schifferbooks.com
Web: www.schifferbooks.com

For our complete selection of fine books on this and related subjects, please visit our website at www.schifferbooks.com. You may also write for a free catalog.

Schiffer Publishing's titles are available at special discounts for bulk purchases for sales promotions or premiums. Special editions, including personalized covers, corporate imprints, and excerpts, can be created in large quantities for special needs. For more information, contact the publisher.

We are always looking for people to write books on new and related subjects. If you have an idea for a book, please contact us at proposals@schifferbooks.com

PAGE 1: Poster art for *The Return of Sherlock Holmes* (Paramount, 1929), the first talking picture to feature Arthur Conan Doyle's great detective, and a substantial box-office success. British actor Clive Brook is pictured here; he reprised the role three years later in *Sherlock Holmes* (Fox Film Corp., 1932).

PAGES 2–3: The female crime victim pictured on the poster for *New Orleans After Dark* (Allied Artists, 1958). Marketed as one of the semidocumentary "exposé" films that were popular at that time, this low-budget noir was cobbled together from episodes of the short-lived TV series *N.O.P.D.* (1955), shot on location in the Big Easy.

ABOVE: The original, seldom-seen one-sheet designed for *The Thin Man* (M-G-M, 1934), the first of the popular series featuring sleuthing spouses Nick and Nora Charles. While marketing materials for big-budget M-G-M films typically revolved around one main image (referred to as "key art"), variant posters for *The Thin Man* bore completely different designs.

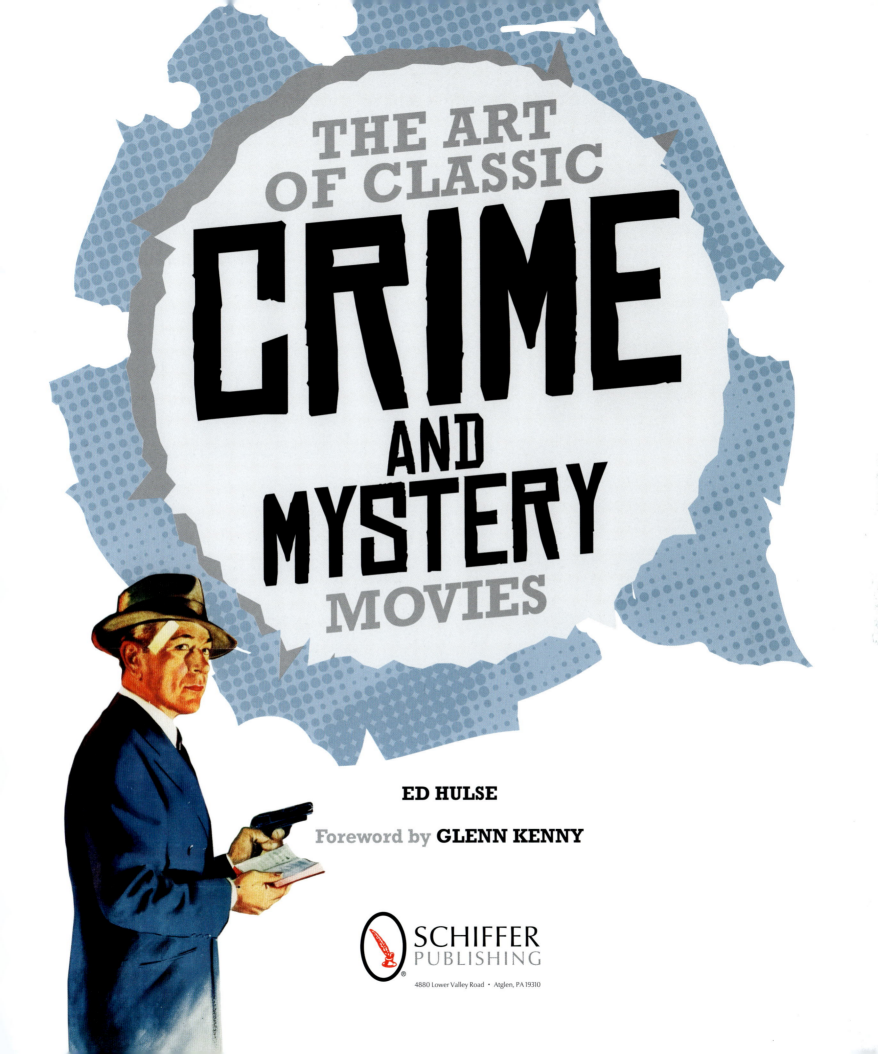

THE ART OF CLASSIC

CRIME

AND

MYSTERY

MOVIES

ED HULSE

Foreword by **GLENN KENNY**

SCHIFFER PUBLISHING

4880 Lower Valley Road • Atglen, PA 19310

CONTENTS

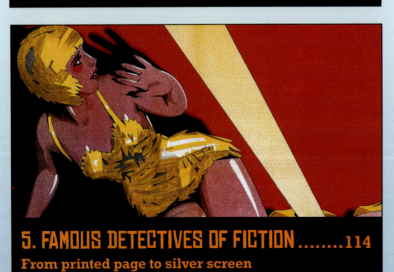

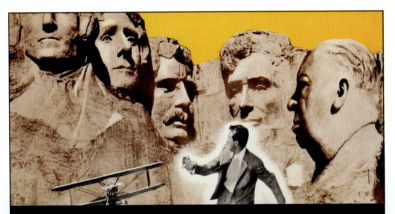

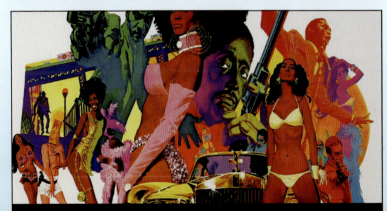

FOREWORD BY GLENN KENNY

T he world was a mess in 1971. The end of the 1960s was a disturbing spectacle of unrest and assassinations. The foment didn't bring about much meaningful change—the United States' involvement in Vietnam, which motivated much of the unrest, was still going strong. The country's president, a man of substantial intellect and unusual political gifts, was nonetheless nicknamed "Tricky Dick." A newly twelve-year-old movie nut possessing a scattered precociousness might have a hard time making sense of it all . . .

A grim face behind the long black barrel of a .44 Magnum Smith and Wesson revolver spoke to that kid—yes, it was me—in a way that was equal parts compelling and intimidating. The face belonged to Clint Eastwood, and the nearly psychedelically colored image of him pointing the gun out at the viewer, the black-and-yellow muzzle hovering right above a large hole sending cracks deep into a pane of glass, illustrated the poster for the winter 1971 release *Dirty Harry*.

I didn't pay much attention to the actual copy on the poster, placed in the white space of the hole in the window. Reading it now, it strikes me as trite, laughable, banal: "Detective Harry Callahan. He doesn't break murder cases. He smashes them." It was the image that worked on me. I knew Eastwood's face; I'd recently seen his three westerns with Sergio Leone in some combination of double features at my local suburban New Jersey movie house. His characters in those pictures were killers, sure, but they had a wry humor about them. Whereas *this* Eastwood character, a contemporary one, didn't look like he had any sense of humor at all, the near smirk on his face notwithstanding.

A dead serious carrier of lethal force—but to what end? As blunt as the image was, it was enigmatic, too. Was Harry Callahan here to save us, or to annihilate what was left of us? Never mind the reviewers (including Pauline Kael, who famously pronounced the Don Siegel–directed picture "fascist"); I had to see the picture myself to suss it out.

And that was the power of the poster. The one-sheet for the movie's sequel, *Magnum Force,* featured a full-body shot of Eastwood and his gun, with the gun

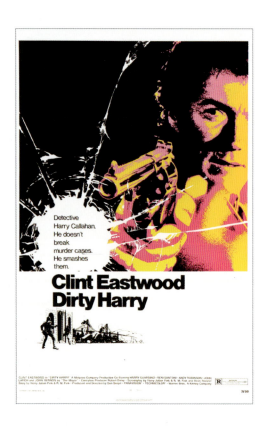

ABOVE: Although he had appeared in a few crime movies and war movies, Clint Eastwood in 1971 was best known as a star of westerns (especially the trio of "spaghetti westerns" in which he plays the Man with No Name) when he was cast as tough cop Harry Callahan in *Dirty Harry*, whose success greatly broadened his box-office appeal.

dwarfing him in the foreground of the image. Equally memorable, even if the movie itself wasn't a patch on *Harry*.

This splendid book walks us through a century of crime movie posters, and in this history, which also leads us into the more obscure corners of the genre, we see the dance between virtue and vice that the art of the crime movie has been stepping to. In early times, it's easy to tell the good guys from the bad guys, but by the same token, the bad guys aren't made to look unappealing—especially when the ballyhoo was for pictures made prior to the widespread adoption of the Production Code in the 1930s. Edward G. Robinson's steely gaze from behind a cigar in *Little Caesar*; Cagney getting ready to give Bogey a smack in *The Roaring Twenties*; Paul Muni dispatching his one-time boss in *Scarface*; these were not good guys, certainly not nice guys, but they sure were dynamic. But so too, in their way, were detectives Charlie Chan and Mr. Moto, not to mention Sherlock Holmes. A poster couldn't convey the deductive powers of these crime-solving powerhouses, but it could put across the inscrutability we sometimes associate with genius, just as the image of Humphrey Bogart as Sam Spade conveyed a hard-bitten toughness, or that of Ronald Colman as Bulldog Drummond put across the suavity of the "gentleman adventurer."

A good poster can lend an air of intrigue to the most ordinary picture, which of course was the artist's intention. Some posters, on the other hand, undersell the pictures they're flogging. *Phantom Lady*, with its central image of the ostensible title character coming to life on a book cover, is striking enough, but it doesn't come close to conveying the true delirium of the Robert Siodmak–directed noir excursion. With *Gilda* and *The Lady from Shanghai*, on the other hand, star Rita Hayworth (saddled with what many considered a disastrous haircut in the title role of the latter picture, as dictated by director Orson Welles) is enough to suggest complete worlds of lethal erotic misadventure. Putting male and female in the same frame also yielded potent results, the classic poster for Jacques Tourneur's definitive noir *Out of the Past*, for instance: the worried Robert Mitchum dragging on a cigarette in the upper half, right corner; an unusually demure-looking depiction of femme fatale Jane Greer on the left. Trouble is brewing in the present, clearly.

In the 1970s, ambiguity got more pronounced. A detective such as John Shaft was an unabashed good guy, but as the theme song in the first picture in the *Shaft* series puts it, "You say this cat Shaft is a bad mother?" (This question is shushed by the chorus, instructing composer/singer Isaac Hayes to "shut your mouth.") The poster images of him present a good guy who's also a badass. Similarly, Charles Bronson's Paul Kersey in *Death Wish* (1974) has no law enforcement affiliation. On the poster for the film, he's on some park stairs, aiming behind him at an unseen enemy; the yellow light suffusing the image makes us feel witness to a forbidden act. Al Pacino, hands on hips in the poster for *Godfather Part II*, would bring new specificity to the gangster as icon.

Charisma trumps morality. That's kind of what the crime movie's all about anyway. ✺

ABOVE: Mysteries emanating from "Poverty Row" studios generally had particularly eye-catching posters to help make them competitive with the major-studio fare playing at nearby theaters. *Strange People* (1933) was a cheapie shot at the Universal lot on the elaborate set built for the studio's *The Old Dark House* (1932) and rented by producer George Batcheller.

INTRODUCTION BY ED HULSE

Literary tales of crime date back to the Bible, beginning with Cain's murder of Abel. Virtually every civilization has engaged in storytelling of some kind, whether written or spoken, and serious transgressions by one human against another figure prominently in many recorded works of antiquity, including those carved on cave walls and stone tablets, and those scratched on parchment in ink . . .

A very specialized version of crime fiction emerged in the mid-nineteenth century, initially with the publication of Edgar Allan Poe's "The Murders in the Rue Morgue" (1841). That much-anthologized yarn featured as its protagonist an amateur sleuth named C. Auguste Dupin, who employs observational skills and deductive reasoning to solve the mystery surrounding a gruesome murder. "Murders" thus is considered the first modern detective story, although Poe never used the word.

In short order, popular fiction chronicling the investigation of crime proliferated in books and magazines. Charles Dickens's novels *Bleak House* (1853) and the unfinished *Mystery of Edwin Drood* (1870), along with Wilkie Collins's *The Moonstone* (1868) and Anna Katharine Green's *The Leavenworth Case* (1878), enthralled readers even as they established basic parameters for the nascent genre. The arrival on the scene of Arthur Conan Doyle's Sherlock Holmes, in *A Study in Scarlet* (1887), gave crime fiction its first "consulting detective" and inspired a legion of imitators.

For the next decade or so, the form was dominated by authors from the UK (Doyle, Arthur Morrison, R. Austin Freeman) and Europe (Maurice Leblanc, Gaston Leroux, Baroness Orczy). Despite the home-field advantage established by Poe, American fictioneers didn't make notable contributions to the literature — with the dubious exception of dime-novel detective Nick Carter — until the early years of the twentieth century, when Mary Roberts Rinehart invented the "had I but known" subgenre with *The Circular Staircase* (1908).

Several years later, Arthur B. Reeve created the first credible Yankee

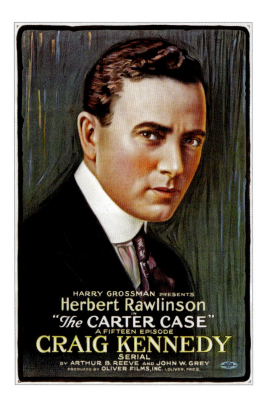

alternative to Sherlock Holmes, a "scientific detective" known as Craig Kennedy. By that time, a new storytelling form had seized the imaginations of American consumers: moving pictures. At first just a novelty—depicting parades, street scenes, even subway rides—this attention-grabbing technology soon was employed to present simple narratives. *The Great Train Robbery* (1903), often considered the first film to tell a complete story, was a straightforward depiction of crime, pursuit, and punishment. No investigations were necessary, no brilliant deductions required. The bandits are chased, overtaken, and brought to justice in a hail of gunfire.

Filmmakers gradually evolved techniques to facilitate their audience's understanding of plots dependent on visual presentation. (Narrative films sported explanatory title cards when necessary, but in the medium's early years these were perfunctory at best.) Audiences gathered to see these primitive celluloid dramas in crude theaters that were known as nickelodeons due to their five-cent admission charge. Until the advent of World War I, most of these venues exhibited new programs each day, offering sixty-to-ninety-minute compilations of short subjects individually ranging from five to twenty minutes in running time.

It wasn't practical to advertise in newspapers when the bill of fare changed that frequently, so exhibitors needed "point of purchase" marketing materials that would draw passersby to their box office. Even back then, there was nothing new about employing brightly colored, eye-catching posters to draw attention to special events or theatrical performances. In small towns and rural hamlets, they could be seen everywhere, advertising rodeos, circuses, and state fairs.

The first poster designed to promote a specific film—*L'arroseur arrosé*, a Lumiere Brothers short subject—used an illustration by French artist Marcellin Auzolle to draw patrons to a screening at the Grand Café in Paris on December 26, 1895. American moving-picture exhibitors were not so quick to grasp the poster's utility in attracting patrons to their venue, but eventually they caught on. The twentieth century was just a few years old when practically every "nickelodeon" in the country began promoting its celluloid attractions with colorful posters emblazoned with vividly illustrated scenes from those primitive one- and two-reelers. They were printed by lithography, a process that used flat surfaces—smooth-ground limestone and, after 1920, zinc plates—specially treated with oil-based inks that transferred to thin paper sheets.

Stone-litho posters had a unique textured look due to the grain that remained on the sanded-down limestone slab. The printing process was relatively simple. Artists created images on tracing paper, then transferred them to the stone with soft, waxy crayons and greasy paints. Carefully applied acid etched the artwork onto the slab, which was moistened with water in preparation for printing. Surface areas not protected by the greasy paints soaked up the H_2O. Next, oil-based inks were rolled onto the stone. The greasy surfaces absorbed the inks; the water-dampened sections did not. Sheets of poster stock were laid on the stone, and simple compression transferred ink to paper.

ABOVE: Matinee idol Herbert Rawlinson brought good looks and charisma to his characterization of Arthur B. Reeve's scientific criminologist Craig Kennedy in this 1919 mystery serial. Kennedy had previously appeared in three Pearl White chapter plays made several years earlier, impersonated by a somewhat dour Broadway actor named Arnold Daly.

Film-manufacturing companies made posters available in several configurations. The most versatile and therefore most frequently requested was the "one-sheet," which measured 27 × 41 inches. These were commonly displayed in front of theaters on large easels flanking the ticket booth, but also inside the lobby in glass frames along the walls. A "three-sheet" was just what the name suggested: three separate panels that, when properly aligned, formed one large poster of about 41 × 81 inches. Three-sheets primarily adorned bigger venues with wider sidewalks but could also be pasted to the sides of nearby buildings or wooden fences in the neighborhood. The same was true of a "six-sheet" (81 × 81 inches). Too large for easels, they were invariably pasted on walls or fences with wallpaper glue, which made them impossible to remove without shredding and therefore rendered them unusable for subsequent displays. The "twenty-four-sheet" (246 × 108 inches) was printed in twelve sections and designed for use solely on outdoor billboards. These were printed on heavier, more durable stock in anticipation of exposure to the elements for weeks (or, when advertising serials, months).

Smaller posters were printed on card stock. "Lobby cards" (11 × 14) came in sets of eight and pictured various scenes from each film. As the name indicates, they were typically displayed in theater lobbies, generally arrayed on the wall around a one-sheet. "Window cards" (14 × 22) carried similar designs to one-sheets but had a blank strip at the top or the bottom on which could be hand-lettered the local theater's name and the date of the film's engagement. They were intended for placement in the front windows of local retail establishments. "Inserts" (14 × 36, vertical) and "half-sheets" (22 × 28, horizontal) often combined painted images with photographs and were almost always part of extensive lobby displays.

Various printing firms scattered across the country produced posters for film production companies. Most of them were already involved in manufacturing posters for rodeos, circuses, state fairs, vaudeville houses, and theaters. Cincinnati-based Hennegan Show Print began supplying movie posters for Thomas A. Edison films shortly after the turn of the century. New York's United States Printing and Lithograph Company serviced early studios. Other New York firms specializing in posters included Acme Litho, Greenwich Litho, and the Joseph H. Tooker Litho Company of New York.

By the 1920s, three printing firms accounted for most of the major studios' posters: the aforementioned Tooker Litho Company and two Cleveland-based outfits, the Morgan Litho Company and Continental Litho. The latter was started in 1928 by a Morgan employee who not only left to start his own company but also managed to poach the Warner Bros. account on his way out.

Printers were forbidden from tampering with the original poster artwork supplied to them by film companies, except in extraordinary circumstances. All the major studios had fully staffed departments that turned out advertising and promotion materials. Several artists might be employed to produce a single poster: one might be assigned to paint the central image, whether the portrait of

ABOVE: The eerie artwork for this 1934 poster uses a visual device that was considered shopworn even back then: a handful of cast members portraying suspects under investigation for murder. *Secret of the Chateau* was just another B-grade whodunit of the type already familiar to Depression-era moviegoers — no better, no worse.

a star or the rendition of a scene; another might contribute background art, while a third hand-lettered titles, credits, and catchlines. These salaried employees worked anonymously; to this day, it's virtually impossible to identify movie poster artists. Some, such as Columbia's Glenn Cravath, occasionally signed their art, but, for the most part, they labored without recognition. (By the way, Cravath saved a number of his watercolor "prelims"—preliminary treatments submitted to studio art directors for approval—such as the hastily produced art for the 1940 Columbia serial *The Green Archer* shown here.)

The Poverty Row companies couldn't afford to maintain art departments and therefore farmed out poster design to small Hollywood ad agencies. These artists also went uncredited, even though their efforts often compared favorably with those of the major studios. Note that some of the most handsome '20s and '30s posters emanated from shoestring producers. This was no accident: since Poverty Row films couldn't compete with the major studios' product on the basis of star power or production quality, eye-catching posters were vital in attracting the attention of passersby who might see them outside theaters and be lured inside on the strength of the imagery.

Hollywood motion pictures were some of America's most profitable exports during the twentieth century's first four decades. Indeed, the major studios generated roughly 40 percent of their revenue from the international market. In 1940, with all of Europe plunged into war, the gravy train derailed. But once peace had been restored, the importation of American movies resumed.

In recognition of this, this book includes a number of foreign-produced posters advertising Hollywood films exhibited overseas. In some cases, approaches to poster design varied radically; nowhere is this more evident than in chapter 9, where we present four one-sheets designed in as many countries for Francois Trauffaut's *The Bride Wore Black*, an adaptation of Cornell Woolrich's classic mystery novel.

Particularly handsome movie posters were produced in Sweden, a hotbed of artistic experimentation during the late nineteenth and early twentieth centuries. The most graphically striking appeared during the '20s and '30s and reflected (if only in subtle ways) a variety of influences—cubism, art deco, modernism, surrealism, expressionism. One can even see a Gothic influence in the Swedish poster art for *The Bat* (1926, chapter 1), *The Cat and the Canary* (1927, chapter 1), and *The Cat Creeps* (1931, chapter 3). Rather than picturing the nineteenth-century mansions in which these films take place, the Swedish posters show medieval castles shrouded in darkness, strategically placed lights glowing from small windows in towers. The artists were prescient: covers of romance paperbacks had the same flavor, differing only in the presence of a female in the foreground, hurrying away from the darkened dwelling, casting a nervous glance backward at a solitary light in the attic or tower.

With a few exceptions, the following chapters are grouped more or less chronologically, enabling the reader to track the evolution of crime movie posters from the early silent era through the mid-1970s. At various points in

ABOVE: A watercolor "prelim" (preliminary) submitted to Columbia Pictures by prolific illustrator Glenn Cravath, who needed to secure approval from the marketing department's art director before starting work on the actual painting. You can see Cravath's finished poster for this 1940 thriller in chapter 9.

the text, we call attention to specific visual tricks used by artists to distinguish mystery film posters from those of other genres. But simply perusing the art page by page will give you a solid understanding of the techniques employed to create these underestimated marketing tools, which continue to fascinate us many decades after they served their original purpose. Vintage movie posters are now considered cultural artifacts and are avidly collected, with many of the most notable (including a fair percentage of those pictured in this book) selling at auction for tens of thousands of dollars.

You're about to take a crash course in an important segment of motion-picture history. But there won't be a test afterward, and you're guaranteed a passing grade. So enjoy yourself . . . ✪

ABOVE: A rare photo taken during production of *The Thin Man* (1934). Director W. S. "Woody" Van Dyke coaches costars William Powell and Myrna Loy, seated at the table, for the scene he's about to shoot. That's Oscar-winning cinematographer James Wong Howe leaning on the camera at left.

1

THE SILENT ERA

CRAVEN CROOKS, DARING DETECTIVES, BAFFLING MYSTERIES

BELOW: While not the first of the "old dark house" mysteries, Universal's *The Cat and the Canary* (1927) established the template used countless times by producers in years to come. Its central plot device — the reading of a wealthy decedent's will at midnight, with a murder-minded villain among the assembled greedy relatives — inspired three official remakes and countless imitations, some being unapologetic parodies.

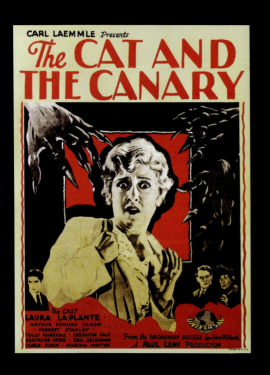

Even in its infancy, the American motion picture develops surprising variety in the types of stories it presents to nickelodeon audiences, many of whom return night after night to see the latest attractions and be absorbed, at least for a little while, into the make-believe lives of characters who flicker on the screens of storefront theaters. It doesn't take too many years for the venues to become larger and more comfortable, and for the stories to become more intricate and better acted. From the first, movie patrons are inexplicably attracted to narratives depicting crime and punishment . . .

The commission of crime was a regular feature in many early moving pictures, as the eternal struggle between good and evil provided conflict and generated suspense. The crimes themselves could be fanciful or prosaic; what mattered was how vividly they were dramatized in the new medium. One of the first feature-length films to achieve blockbuster status was 1913's *Traffic in Souls*, in which a brave young woman and her policeman boyfriend rescue her sister from white slavers, while an early one-reeler directed by D. W. Griffith, 1912's *Musketeers of Pig Alley*, anticipated the gangster film. There was no shortage of cinematic crime during the nickelodeon era.

The earliest example of sleuth as protagonist seems to have been *The Monogrammed Cigarette*, a 1910 short produced by the Yankee Film Company, a New Jersey–based independent. It revolves around plucky heroine Nell Pierce, described in an explanatory subtitle as "the fearless daughter of a famous detective." After her father is murdered while on a case, Nell decides to follow in his footsteps, apprehending the criminal and becoming a full-time private investigator herself. Beautiful young actress Elsie Albert played the Girl Detective in eight subsequent shorts, released in monthly intervals.

Other distaff crime fighters took up where Nell Pierce left off, the most famous being Ruth Roland, who starred in her own series of Girl Detective one-reelers during 1915, shortly before appearing in *The Red Circle*, a Pathé chapter play that put her—initially, at least—on the wrong side of the law. Ruth's success in

that episodic epic made her a Serial Queen second in popularity only to Pearl White, another Pathé star.

It was the serial, in fact, that pioneered several conventions of crime and mystery films. Pearl's *The Exploits of Elaine* (1914) and its two consecutively released sequels, *The Romance of Elaine* and *The New Exploits of Elaine* (both 1915), were the first serials to boast as their male hero a supersleuth imported from another medium. Arthur B. Reeve's scientific detective Craig Kennedy, then plying his trade in a series of short stories written for Hearst's *Cosmopolitan* magazine, enjoyed a reputation as "the American Sherlock Holmes," and readers were thrilled by his regular employment of technological marvels in the apprehension of criminals. *The Exploits of Elaine*, with its lurid

ABOVE: The cast and crew assembles on one of the sets for *The Cat and the Canary*. Seated at the table in the foreground are the picture's stars, Creighton Hale and Laura La Plante. Director Paul Leni has his hand on Hale's chair. The gent seated on the arm of a chair at far left is veteran Universal serial director Robert F. Hill, assigned to act as Leni's liaison with the crew because the German filmmaker spoke very little English.

ABOVE: A gag still taken during production of *Pearl of the Army* (Pathé, 1916), in which Warner Oland—later to play Charlie Chan and Fu Manchu—throttles an unconcerned Pearl White while her leading man, Ralph Kellard, appears to drive a dagger through the neck of Arnold Daly, Pearl's co-star on *The Exploits of Elaine.* Such candid photos were not often taken in those days, making this one particularly rare.

melodramatics common to early chapter plays, pits Kennedy (played by Broadway star Arnold Daly) against the silent screen's first true mystery villain, a masked malefactor known as the Clutching Hand for . . . well, you can guess what for by his name.

Two of Pearl's subsequent chapter plays, *Pearl of the Army* (1916) and *The House of Hate* (1918), also found her imperiled by mystery villains whose true identities were hidden from audiences until the final episode: the Silent Menace in the former, the Hooded Terror in the latter. Far more influential was *The Iron Claw* (1916), another of Pearl's starring vehicles. Its eponymous evildoer was known to viewers from the opening installment; this time around, the *hero's* identity was a secret. The Laughing Mask—who, um, wore a mask and laughed a lot—served as her protector for twenty action-packed episodes, his disguise just effective enough to fool moviegoers as well as the story's other characters. Scenario writer George B. Seitz planted clues to the Mask's identity at regular intervals; in the final chapter, David Manley, secretary to Pearl's father, admits to being the Laughing Mask.

Mystery men—on either side of the law—became fixtures in chapter plays, and with good reason. Serials faced a unique marketing challenge: they weren't a "one and done" proposition. At lengths of ten, fifteen, and even twenty episodes, they required careful scripting to draw theater patrons back week after week. Loosely plotted serials often saw moviegoers skipping multiple installments, if not abandoning the films altogether. But chapter plays with strong mystery elements—determining the identity of a hero or villain, solving a particularly baffling crime—stood a better chance of retaining their followers, who would be loath to pass up a single episode, lest they miss a vital clue.

During the 1910s, with the motion-picture serial at the height of its box-office potency, mystery and detective fiction in America was relegated largely to dime novels and pulp magazines. Crime stories often had out-and-out crooks for protagonists; "gentleman cracksmen" such as Jimmie Dale, Jimmy Valentine, Boston Blackie, and the Lone Wolf shared a chivalrous code of honor that prevented readers from finding them too objectionable—and, having attained loyal followings, they invariably reformed. All of them reached the screen too.

Conan Doyle's Sherlock Holmes and his many imitators, their stories rooted in deductive reasoning and more cleverly contrived than the average crime yarn, were popular in the States but not easily adaptable to the screen because complex ratiocination required too many explanatory subtitles to adequately convey. The mid-'20s craze for whodunits led Hollywood to attempt such films, but the results, as a rule, were desultory. And moviegoers still preferred their mysteries with strong visuals and melodramatic action, although that would change with the coming of talking pictures.

American crime and mystery films of the 1920s—especially those made late in the decade, with sound threatening to upend the entire industry—were dominated by two trends that developed more or less simultaneously: "old dark house" mysteries adapted from popular stage plays, and gangster movies reflecting the growth of organized crime in Prohibition's wake. Such spooky, stage-bound mysteries as *The Bat* (1926), *The Cat and the Canary* (1927), and *The Last Warning* (1929) relied heavily on visual effects such as low-key lighting, bizarre camera angles, and lengthy tracking shots to keep theater patrons on the edge of their seats. The latter two films were directed by German émigré Paul Leni, who infused them with his unique blend of Gothicism and expressionism.

Poster art for crime and mystery movies during the silent-movie years was often hard to distinguish from that illustrating other dramas; studio-employed artists had not developed an iconography for the genre. That began to change toward the end of the '20s, but it took several more years for the evolution in style to reach full flower, and therefore any discussion of the new look is better suited to discussion in chapter 3. ✧

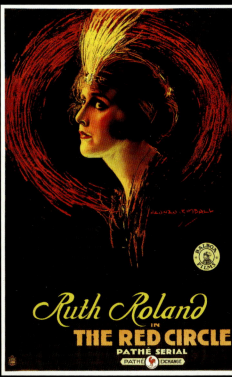

ABOVE: Pathé made the best crime serials, bar none. *The Iron Claw* (1916) was not only a big moneymaker but is also historically important for introducing the concept of a mystery *hero* whose identity is revealed in the final episode. *The Red Circle* (1915) introduced chapter-play fans to Ruth Roland, who would soon rival Pearl White in popularity.

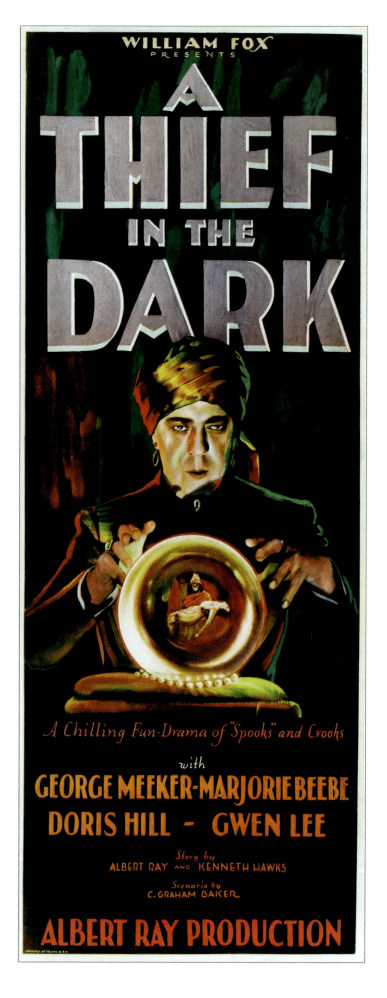

CRIME AND PUNISHMENT

Crimes depicted in American motion pictures of the embryonic silent era were fairly mundane, being routine stick-ups or commonplace swindles, with an occasional wallop to the head or, occasionally, a murder committed with gun or knife. As of yet, the supersleuth was unknown to picture audiences, and police were often depicted as ineffectual or blockheaded. Things began to change in the early 1910s, especially with the importation of European films such as Louis Feuillade's serialized exploits of master criminal Fantomas ("the Phantom") and costumed vigilante Judex ("Judge"). Such flamboyantly staged thrillers—very successful around the world—had a demonstrable impact on American filmmakers, who realized that baffling crimes, instead of being the byproducts of traditional melodrama, could be exciting events around which entire movies revolved. Producers also tumbled to the fact that while short subjects of one and two reels still dominated the marketplace, picture patrons found longer crime films sufficiently absorbing, as proved by the surprise success of Universal's *Traffic in Souls*.

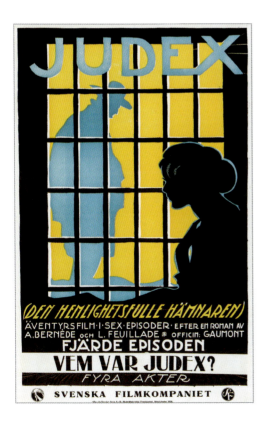

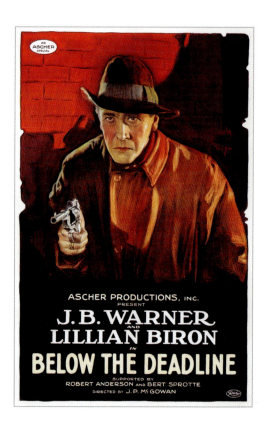

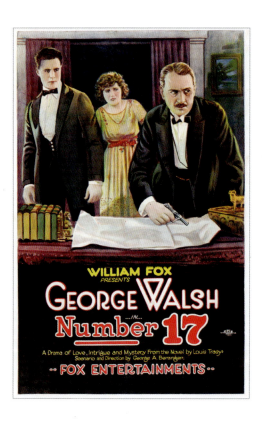

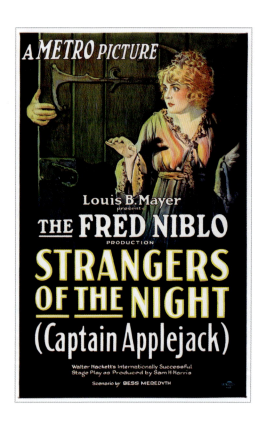

SIX REELS OF THRILLING REALITIES

TRAFFIC
IN SOULS
OR WHILE NEW YORK SLEEPS
A POWERFUL PHOTO-DRAMA OF TODAY

Morgan Litho Co

RUTH UNDER THE POWER OF WANG FOO AND MONSIEUR X.

FRANK G. HALL PRESENTS

THE CHAINED SOUL
EPISODE 9
OF

THE TRAIL OF THE OCTOPUS

WITH
BEN WILSON AND NEVA GERBER
THE MYSTERIOUS ADVENTURES OF A MASTER CRIMINOLOGIST
HALLMARK PICTURES
CORPORATION

CONSOLIDATED FILM CORP.
O.E.GOEBEL PRES.   LUDWIG G.B. ERB TREAS.
PRESENTS
MAURICE COSTELLO & Ethel GRANDIN
IN
THE CRIMSON STAIN MYSTERY
EPISODE Nº 3
"THE BROKEN SPELL"
PRODUCED BY ERBOGRAPH CO.

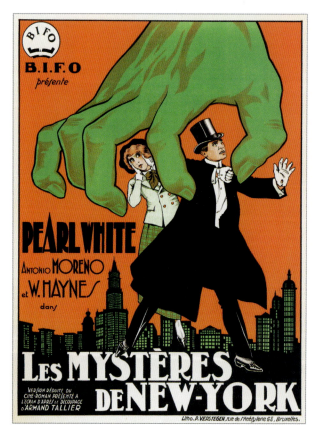

B.I.F.O

B.I.F.O
présente

PEARL WHITE

Antonio MORENO

et W. HAYNES

dans

LES MYSTÈRES DE NEW-YORK

VERSION RÉDUITE DU
CINÉ-ROMAN PRÉSENTÉ À
L'ÉCRAN D'APRÈS LE DÉCOUPAGE
D'ARMAND TALLIER

Litho. P. VERSTEGEN, rue de l'Hôtel, fene 68, Bruxelles.

CRIME SERIALS, PRE-1920

The motion-picture serial or "chapter play" doled out its chills and thrills in weekly installments of two reels, and during the 1910s it was not unusual for new episodes to be the feature attractions of nightly programs composed of shorts. Exhibitors found crime serials to be very good for business, holding audiences on the edges of their seats week after week. Regular attendees prided themselves on analyzing the myriad clues scattered throughout the four- or five-month continuities and correctly deducing a mystery's secret or a killer's identity. Because chapter plays presented violent and fast-moving action in addition to vividly depicted criminal activity, they rather predictably fell foul of educators, church groups, civic reformers, and other censorial local organizations. Under threat of having their products either restricted to adult viewing or banned altogether, serial producers after World War I toned down their products by omitting scenes calling for drug use, sexual menace, and graphic bloodletting. Faithful followers of these episodic epics weren't deterred or disappointed in the slightest, so long as their distressed damsels and handsome heroes continued to face Iron Claws, Clutching Hands, and Hooded Terrors.

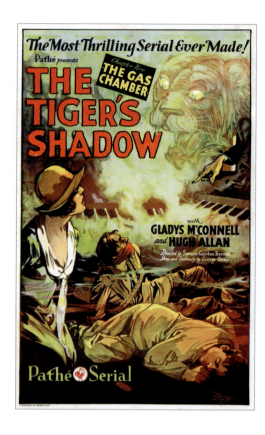

CRIME SERIALS IN THE 1920S

Chapter plays of the Roaring Twenties were more viscerally exciting and technically polished than their ancestors of the 1910s. Censors had succeeded in cowing producers, who voluntarily imposed bans on drugs, ethnic villains, and any suggestion of sexual molestation. Guns could be brandished and fired in self-defense, but lethal shootings became practically nonexistent. Action-hungry audiences were satisfied with lengthy fistic donnybrooks and daredevil stunting by male and female leads alike: leaps from rooftops, transfers from speeding airships to the tops of railroad trains, plunges from cliffs into roiling waters, and so on. But stunts alone could be missed without losing a story's thread; serials with strong mystery elements had to be followed religiously in order to have all the clues necessary to unmasking a villain or locating the long-lost papers in final chapters. Pathé made the best mystery serials during the 1920s, among them *The Green Archer* (1925), *The House without a Key* (1926), and *The Tiger's Shadow* (1928). But Mascot Pictures closed out the silent era with *The Fatal Warning* (1929), a spooky serial giving a meaty supporting role to pre-*Frankenstein* Boris Karloff.

LOUIS BURSTON presents

KING BAGGOT

WITH
Rhea Mitchell AND Grace Darmond
IN THE FIRST SERIAL DE LUXE

THE HAWK'S TRAIL

A 15 CHAPTER FEATURE PRODUCTION
DIRECTED BY W.S. VAN DYKE
EPISODE FIVE
"THE HOUSE OF FEAR"

A PATHÉ SERIAL

In the wake of the sinister
shadow came Ruiz's hand.

Ruth Roland
IN
"The Avenging Arrow"
BY ARTHUR PRESTON HANKINS
EPISODE 7
"THE DOUBLE GAME"

Produced by Ruth Roland Serials, Inc.
...At The Robert Brunton Studios, Inc...

A PATHÉ SERIAL

For once circumstances prove too
much for the resourceful Velvet.

GEORGE B. SEITZ
IN
VELVET FINGERS

WITH
Marguerite Courtot
EPISODE 5
"THE DESERTED PAVILION"

A DASHING SERIAL REPLETE WITH MYSTERY,
DARING AND THRILLING INCIDENT!

STORY BY
BERTRAM MILLHAUSER

PRODUCED AND DIRECTED BY
GEORGE B. SEITZ

MURDER AND MIRTH IN OLD DARK HOUSES

During the silent-movie years, some exhibitors strongly believed that murder mysteries were inherently stressful for theater audiences and that comic relief was essential for reducing tension between shootings and stabbings. Going a step further, producers in the mid-1920s inaugurated a cycle of thrillers that presented comedy and mystery in equal proportions. Most such films were adaptations of stage plays from earlier in the decade. The first of these, *The Bat* (1920) by Mary Roberts Rinehart and Avery Hopwood, was a Broadway smash that maverick producer/director Roland West brought to the screen in 1926, giving the picture a lavish production, designed by William Cameron Menzies with a nod to German expressionist cinema. But the apotheosis of these "old dark house" chillers—so named because they invariably unfolded in spooky old mansions—was *The Cat and the Canary* (1927), the stage production of which had charmed New York sophisticates five years earlier.

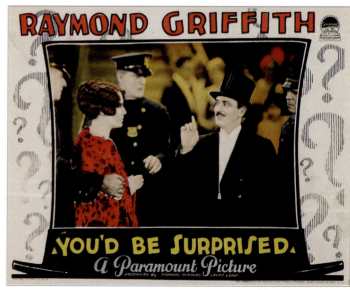

MYSTERIET
FLÄDERMUSEN

UNITED ARTISTS

LITO-SVENSK KONSTINDUSTRI

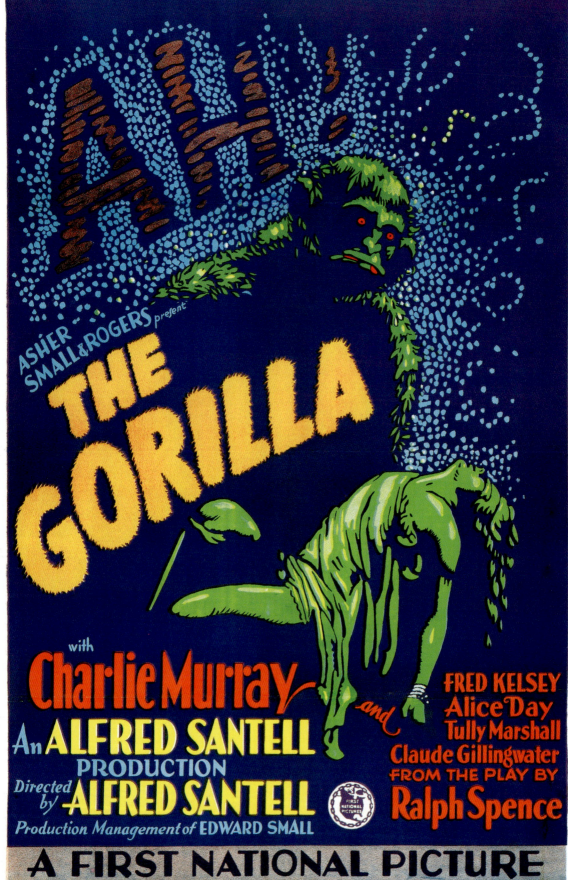

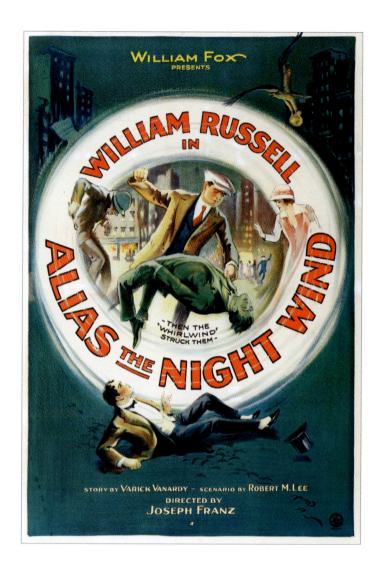

"MYSTERY" MEN FROM OTHER MEDIA

The simplistic plots that animated one- and two-reel films in the old nickelodeon days weren't enough for feature-length films, which proliferated after 1915 as more comfortable movie theaters began to spring up. Going to the "fillums" was no longer reserved primarily for uneducated working-class and immigrant audiences seeking temporary divertissement in the tenderloin districts of big cities. Picture patrons demanded more substantive entertainment, and producers responded by purchasing screen rights to novels and plays. O. Henry's reformed cracksman Jimmy Valentine, immortalized in a single short story, appeared in a handful of films, several of them adapted from Paul Armstrong's stage play. Jack Boyle's Valentine simulacrum, Boston Blackie, likewise appeared frequently on-screen in the person of several actors, including Lionel Barrymore. Musical/comedy stage star George M. Cohan brought his scintillating personality to a 1917 adaptation of *Seven Keys to Baldpate*, a novel written by Earl Derr Biggers—whose later creation, Charlie Chan, twice graced silent movies—for the second time in 1928's *The Chinese Parrot*, prior to becoming ensconced in talkies.

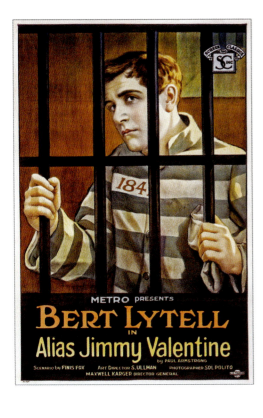

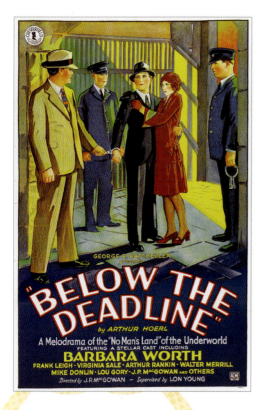

"Yes -- he was your father."

EARLY GANGSTER AND UNDERWORLD FILMS

The imposition of Prohibition—which forbade the sale, transport, and production of alcoholic beverages in America—gave rise to organized crime on a large scale as an entire industry sprang up solely to provide liquor to otherwise law-abiding citizens. It required the corrupting of police, politicians, and members of the judiciary. Gangsters who thus defied the foolishly ratified Eighteenth Amendment were considered folk heroes by many, and inevitably they were romanticized in a cycle of Hollywood movies. *Underworld* (1927), the first major picture of this type, wowed critics and audiences alike. Millionaire and dilletante producer Howard Hughes, willing to capitalize on the gangster craze without further glorifying organized crime, licensed Bartlett Cormack's stage hit *The Racket* (1928), whose brutal gang boss is limned as a despicable figure and receives his richly deserved comeuppance by film's end. The cycle weathered Hollywood's transition from silent movies to sound, not appreciably losing popularity until Prohibition's repeal in 1933 and the newly empowered FBI's subsequent crackdown on gangsters and racketeers.

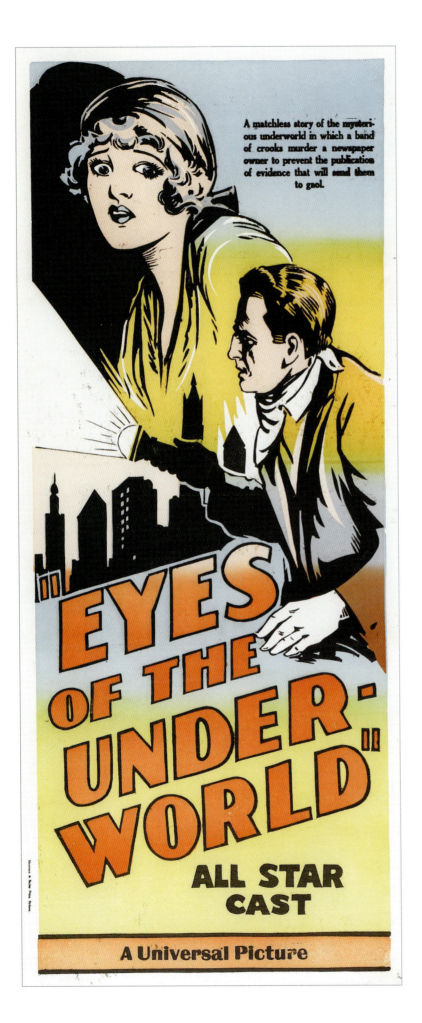

A matchless story of the mysterious underworld in which a band of crooks murder a newspaper owner to prevent the publication of evidence that will send them to gaol.

"EYES OF THE UNDER- WORLD"

ALL STAR CAST

A Universal Picture

"THE NIGHT RIDE"

Starring
JOSEPH SCHILDKRAUT

featuring EDWARD G. ROBINSON with BARBARA KENT
Story by HENRY LA COSSITT
A JOHN S. ROBERTSON PRODUCTION

Presented by CARL LAEMMLE
UNIVERSAL PICTURE

George Bancroft

in The DOCKS of NEW YORK

With BETTY COMPSON and BACLANOVA

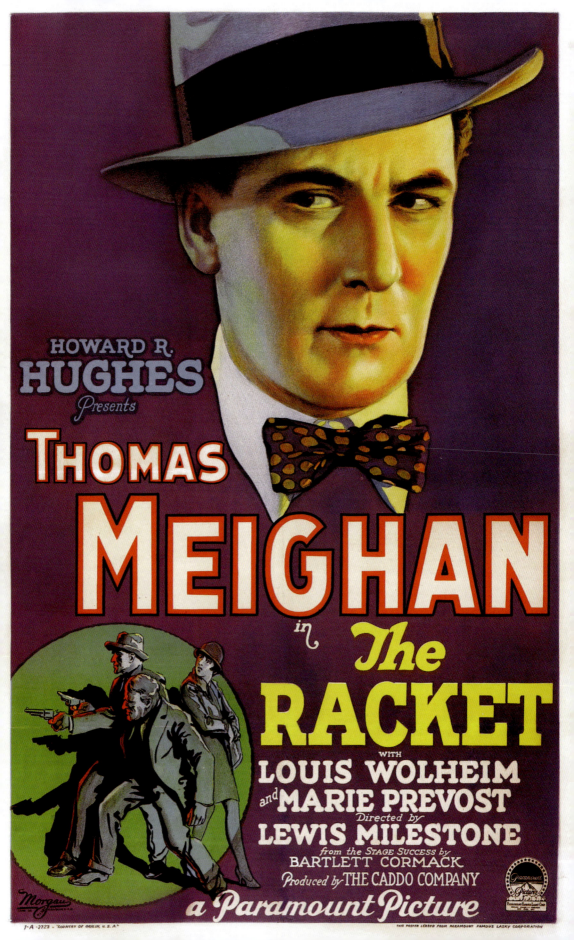

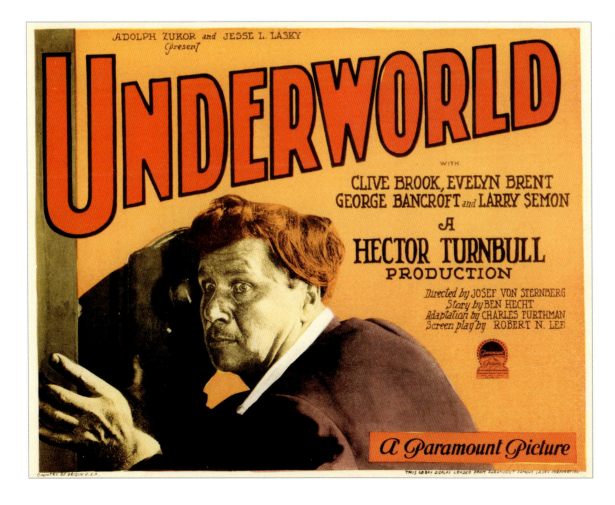

2

SHERLOCK ON THE SILVER SCREEN

"ELEMENTARY, MY DEAR WATSON!"

Of all the supersleuths who have flickered across the silver screen since the invention of moving pictures, one shines brighter than the rest, reflecting his exalted status in the pantheon of fictional crime fighters. Between 1900 and 2011, Arthur Conan Doyle's immortal Sherlock Holmes has accumulated more than 250 appearances on film and television, making him the most frequently portrayed fictional character in those mediums, according to the 2012 edition of *Guinness World Records* . . .

Cinematic adaptations of the Great Detective's exploits have varying degrees of fidelity to Conan Doyle's original stories but overall maintain a high entertainment average.

The 1887 issue of *Beeton's Christmas Annual*, a yearly magazine published by the London-based firm of Ward, Lock & Company, carried a short novel titled "A Study in Scarlet," which had been submitted to—and rejected by—numerous periodicals before finding a home in the *Annual*. Its author was a twenty-seven-year-old physician, Arthur Conan Doyle, who took up fiction writing when his private practice began to atrophy. Composed in just three weeks, "Study in Scarlet" was a mystery story whose protagonist, consulting detective Sherlock Holmes, operated out of a small flat at 221B Baker Street (a real London building, by the way), which he shared with another bachelor, Dr. John H. Watson. Holmes, who made uncanny deductions based on keen observational skill, was based on Joseph Bell, one of Doyle's medical-school professors and a pioneering forensic pathologist.

Awkwardly structured, with an anticlimactic second half, "Study in Scarlet" might have gone unnoticed but for Doyle's vivid characterization of the brilliant Sherlock Holmes. He continued writing about the character and eventually sold a series of twelve short stories to Britain's widely circulated *Strand Magazine*. Beginning with "A Scandal in Bohemia," the yarns ran in consecutive issues of the *Strand* from July 1891 to June 1892 and were collected in book form as *The Adventures of Sherlock Holmes*, published in October 1892 by George Newnes.

The dozen tales in *Adventures* familiarized readers with Holmes and Watson, with illustrations by Sidney Paget fixing their countenances in mind. It was Paget

ABOVE: When *The Hound of the Baskervilles* (1939) proved unexpectedly profitable, Twentieth Century-Fox wasted no time in signing Basil Rathbone and Nigel Bruce to reprise their roles in this handsomely produced sequel, which deals with the efforts of Professor Moriarty (George Zucco) to steal the British crown jewels from the Tower of London. This beautifully illustrated poster shows Holmes in his iconic deerstalker cap and Inverness cloak.

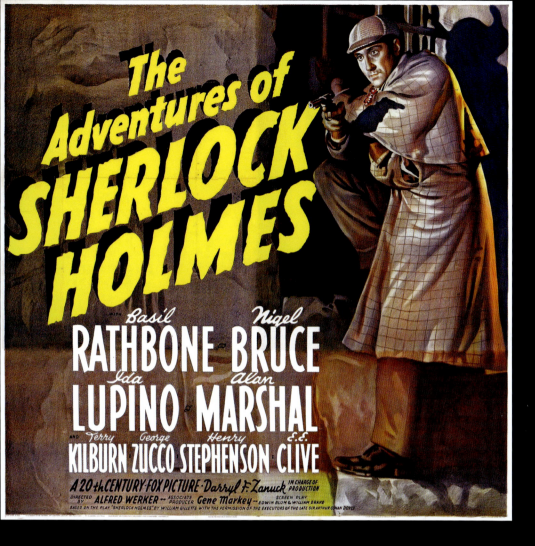

The Adventures of
SHERLOCK HOLMES

WITH

Basil   Nigel
RATHBONE BRUCE

Ida   Alan
LUPINO MARSHAL

AND Terry   George   Henry   E.E.
KILBURN ZUCCO STEPHENSON CLIVE

A 20th CENTURY·FOX PICTURE · Darryl F. Zanuck IN CHARGE OF
                                                PRODUCTION
DIRECTED   ASSOCIATE   SCREEN PLAY
BY   ALFRED WERKER —   PRODUCER Gene Markey — EDWIN BLUM & WILLIAM DRAKE
BASED ON THE PLAY "SHERLOCK HOLMES" BY WILLIAM GILLETTE WITH THE PERMISSION OF THE EXECUTORS OF THE LATE SIR ARTHUR CONAN DOYLE

who pictured Holmes wearing a deerstalker cap and tweed Inverness cape—articles not mentioned in Doyle's early stories but soon to become irreplaceable items that readers identified with him for decades to come.

The author, like many before and after him, eventually tired of his creation and killed him off in "The Adventure of the Final Problem" (the *Strand Magazine*, December 1893), the last of a second series of twelve short stories, collected between hard covers as *The Memoirs of Sherlock Holmes*. It pits the Great Detective against his nemesis, Professor James Moriarty, and concludes with the struggling men supposedly plunging from the top of Switzerland's Reichenbach Falls. Conan Doyle felt that readers would take comfort in losing their hero knowing he had disposed of "the Napoleon of crime."

The public outcry was immediate and overwhelming. The *Strand* office was deluged with angry letters and telegrams, and reportedly some twenty thousand readers canceled their subscriptions. The magazine's editor begged his star contributor to reconsider, but Doyle was determined to apply his talents to other literary endeavors, and he did so for the next eight years. Then, in 1901, he revived Holmes in what many believe to be his finest adventure.

The Hound of the Baskervilles, a book-length novel serialized in the *Strand* prior to its hardcover publication the following year, takes place before the events described in "The Final Problem." Its reception by the public was nothing short

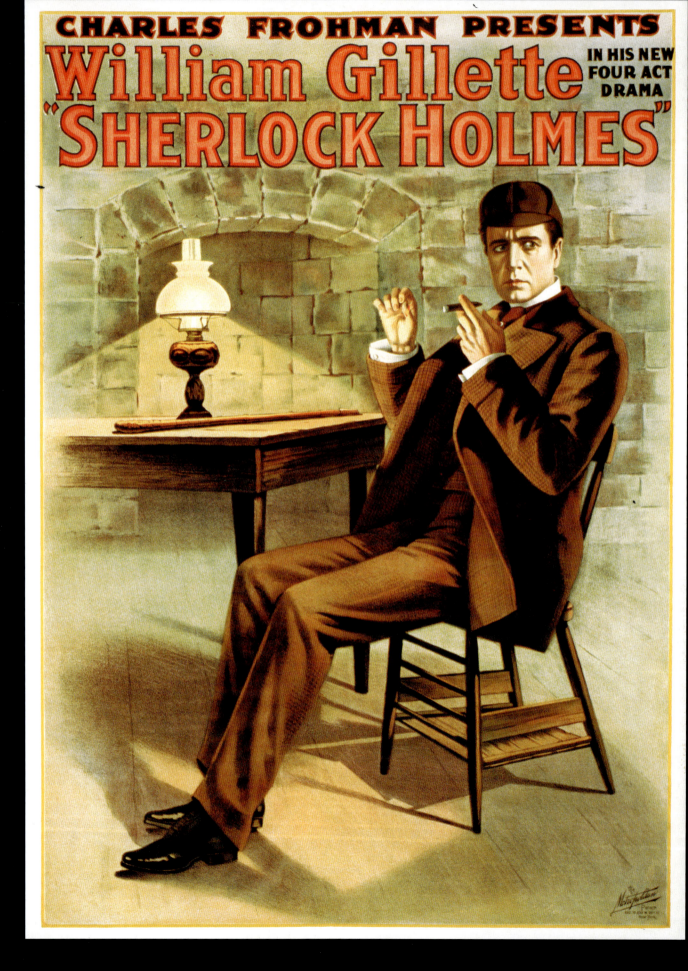

of rapturous, persuading the author to continue the saga. "The Adventure of the Empty House," published in the magazine's October 1903 issue, finds Holmes turning up unexpectedly and explaining to Watson that he did not perish at Reichenbach Falls but decided to let everyone believe he had, enabling the sleuth to evade his many enemies and travel around the world.

Finally resigned to the fact that he owed fame and fortune to Sherlock Holmes, Conan Doyle continued to chronicle the Great Detective's exploits until 1927. Ultimately, what Holmes devotees still refer to as "the canon" extended to four novels and fifty-six short stories, the latter collected in five books. Beginning in 1903, stories appearing first in the *Strand* were republished in a weekly American magazine, *Collier's*, with Frederic Dorr Steele illustrations that hewed closely to Sidney Paget's vision of the character.

The Sherlock Holmes canon has had a virtually incalculable impact on crime fiction, inspiring the creation of dozens of imitators, some of whom became quite popular in their own right. But none has duplicated the Great Detective's success in other media, particularly film. He appeared "live" for the first time in *Sherlock Holmes Baffled*, a thirty-second sketch filmed by the American Mutoscope Company in 1900, several years before *The Great Train Robbery*. This was followed by a 1905 Vitagraph short, *Adventures of Sherlock Holmes, or Held for Ransom*, which reportedly contained elements from an 1890 Holmes novel, *The Sign of Four*.

Testifying to the character's international appeal, Denmark's Nordisk Film Company produced thirteen Holmes shorts between 1908 and 1911. No fewer than five actors played Sherlock in these films, which might account for their failure to catch on with European audiences. In 1914, cliffhanger serial stars Francis Ford and Grace Cunard produced a two-reel version of *A Study in Scarlet* that greatly condensed the novel's events but maintained continuity nonetheless. Francis starred as Holmes, while his younger brother John, later to become one of Hollywood's greatest directors, played Dr. Watson.

The Great Detective graduated to feature-length films in 1916. That year, actor and playwright William Gillette starred in an adaptation of the Sherlock Holmes stage play he had written in 1899. The ruggedly virile Gillette didn't convey the character's intellectualism, coming off instead as a man of action, but film and stage audiences must have seen something in his Holmes, since he would play the character an estimated 1,300 times. Gillette's Holmes hit American theater screens just about the time British moviegoers were treated to an adaptation of *The Sign of Four* starring Harry Arthur Saintsbury, who had portrayed the detective hundreds of times in UK productions of Gillette's play.

The floodgates opened, figuratively speaking, in the early 1920s. On the following pages, you'll see posters from numerous Holmes films starring many notable actors, among them "Great Profile" John Barrymore, Eille Norwood, Clive Brook, Reginald Owen, Arthur Wontner, Peter Cushing, and Christopher Lee. But none had the staying power—or the cultural resonance—of Basil Rathbone, who took the role for the first time in 1939 and made it his own. ⬡

ABOVE: Actor/writer/director William Gillette as Holmes in the 1916 silent film based on his play, *Sherlock Holmes*. Although he achieved widespread public acceptance in the role, the erstwhile matinee idol didn't in the slightest resemble the character as depicted in Sidney Paget's original *Strand Magazine* illustrations.

OPPOSITE: In 1899, with the help of famous producer Charles Frohman, Gillette brought his play—reportedly, but not actually, the result of a collaboration with Arthur Conan Doyle—to the New York stage. It was an immediate hit, logging 256 performances in its original Garrick Theater run. Gillette revived the show numerous times and toured the country with it, ultimately playing Holmes onstage some 1,300 times over a thirty-year period.

EARLY HOLMES IMPERSONATORS

The first major actor to play Sherlock Holmes on film was American matinee idol William Gillette, whose self-written play featuring the character came to the screen in 1916. His drama also was the nominal source for a 1922 Holmes thriller starring "the Great Profile," John Barrymore. But Conan Doyle himself endorsed the characterization of Eille Norwood, a distinguished British actor who still holds the record for celluloid portrayals of the Great Detective, having appeared in forty-five short subjects and two feature films—all adapted directly from the canon—between 1921 and 1923. The first sound-era Sherlock was another Brit, Clive Brook, a stolid performer who projected intelligence but lacked charisma; he made three appearances as Holmes between 1929 and 1932. Perhaps the most offbeat casting was that of perennial character actor Reginald Owen, who essayed the role of Sherlock in *A Study in Scarlet* (1933) after playing Watson to Brook's Holmes the previous year!

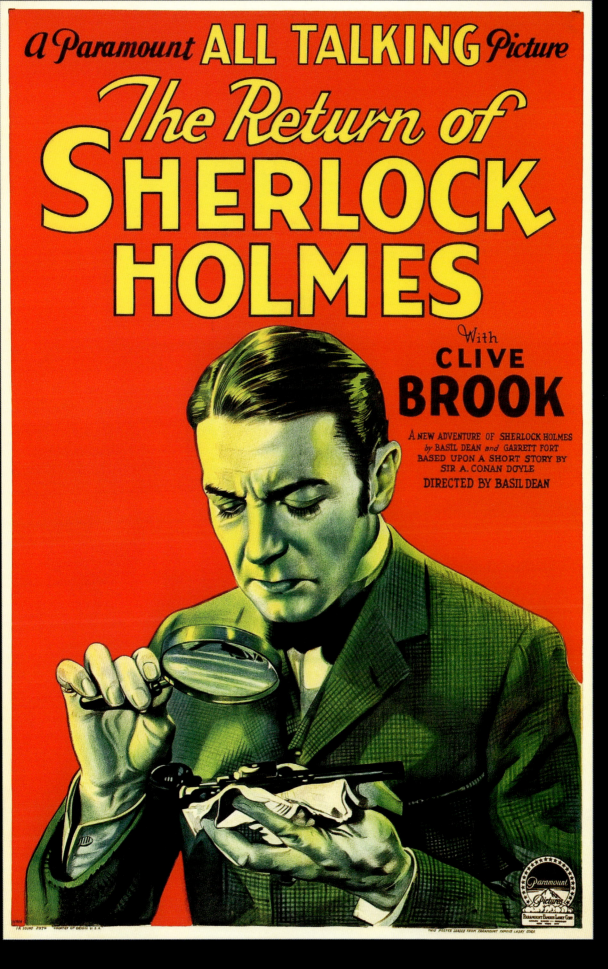

Two master minds meet at the precipice of Death

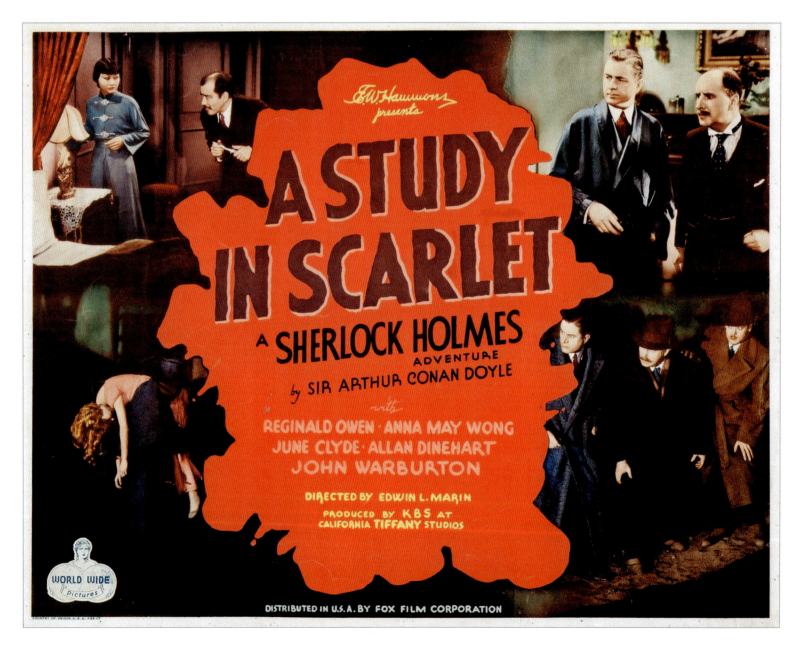

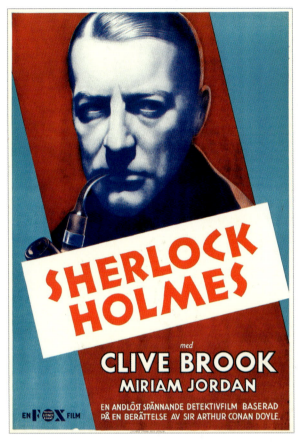

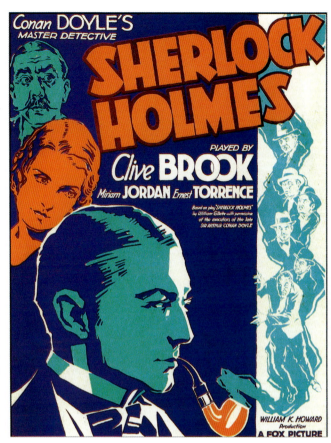

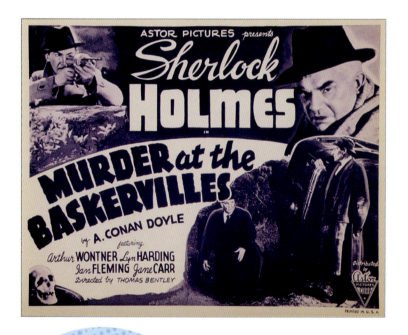

BRITAIN'S BEST HOLMES: ARTHUR WONTNER

Born in 1875, Arthur Wontner began his acting career at the age of twenty-two and made his film debut in 1916. Preferring stage to screen, he appeared in only a dozen or so motion pictures before assuming the role upon which his admittedly limited claim to movie immortality rests. The script for *Sherlock Holmes' Fatal Hour* (1931), the UK's first Holmes talkie, was cobbled together from two Conan Doyle short stories. Wontner appeared to have stepped out of a Sidney Paget illustration for the *Strand Magazine*, and he played the Great Detective soberly, studiously, and with great dignity. He reprised the role in *The Missing Rembrandt*, *The Sign of Four* (both 1932), *The Triumph of Sherlock Holmes* (1935), and *Silver Blaze* (a.k.a. *Murder at the Baskervilles*, 1937). Unlike previous British-made Holmes films, Wontner's efforts were well received by American audiences, and his might well have been regarded as the definitive characterization, had not one more actor worn the deerstalker cap in 1939 . . .

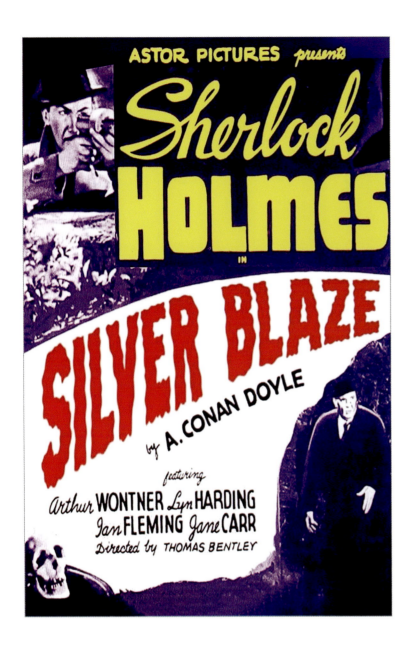

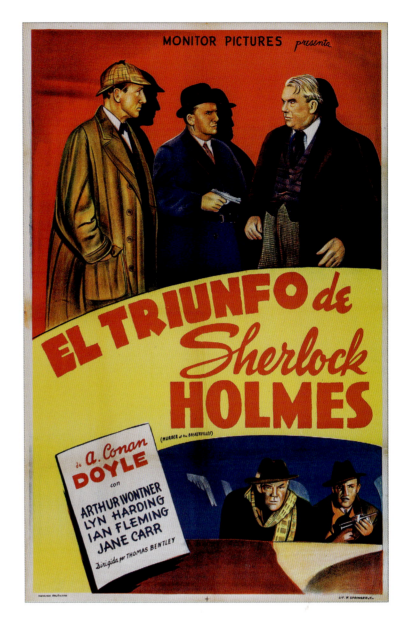

RATTERS AND WILLIE

British actors Basil Rathbone and Nigel Bruce had already worked in dozens of major Hollywood films when, in late 1938, they were cast as Holmes and Watson, respectively, for Twentieth Century-Fox's production of *The Hound of the Baskervilles*. The 1939 picture was intended to boost the career of up-and-coming Richard Greene, who as the Baskerville heir got top billing. But Rathbone and Bruce (whose nicknames were "Ratters" and "Willie") proved so popular with filmgoers that studio head Darryl F. Zanuck ordered a sequel rushed into production. *The Adventures of Sherlock Holmes* was just as good, but Fox elected not to make additional Holmes films. The character rights were snapped up by Universal, which hired Rathbone and Bruce to reprise their roles in twelve stylishly made "B" pictures, released between 1942 and 1946. Ratters and Willie became closely identified as Holmes and Watson and spent years playing the characters on radio as well. Few actors have ever been as beloved in roles they so thoroughly dominated for so long.

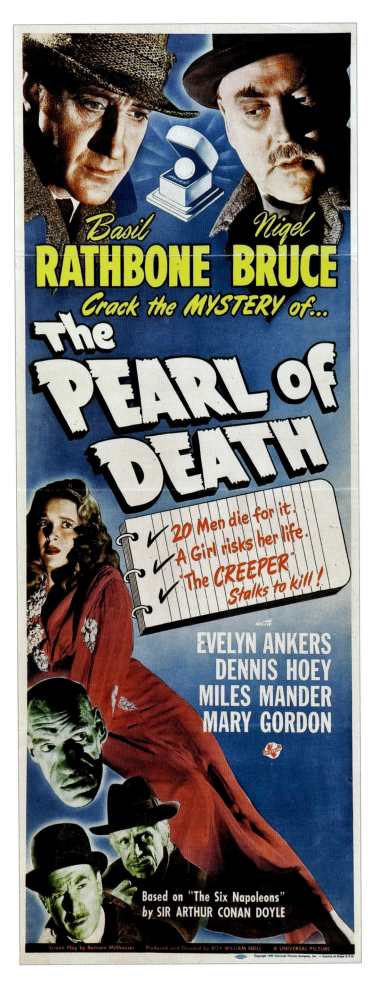

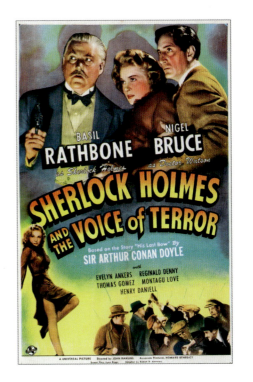

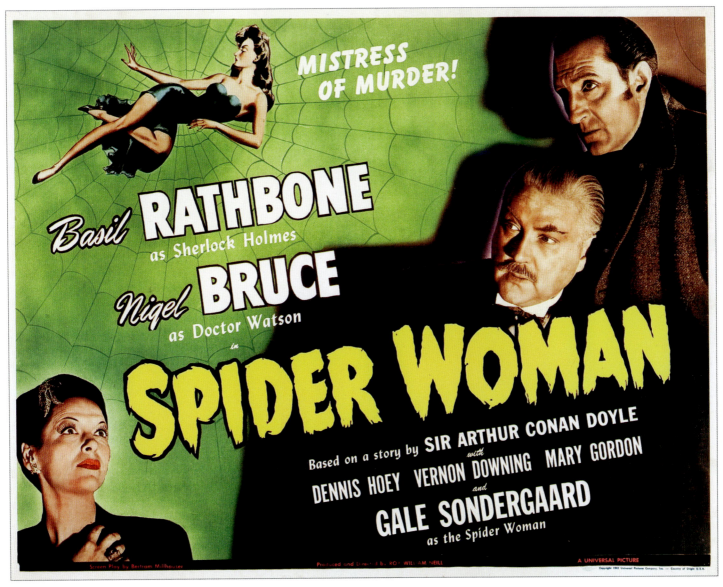

THE HOUND OF HELL

Many aficionados consider *The Hound of the Baskervilles* to be the Great Detective's finest novel-length exploit and one of the all-time best mystery stories. It certainly has appealed to filmmakers around the world, who have adapted the yarn for motion pictures and television programs some two dozen times over the last hundred years. Germany alone has accounted for five versions, and variations of the tale have been produced in India, Italy, Japan, Ukraine, and even the Soviet Union, as well as Britain, Canada, and Australia. But nearly everyone agrees that the 1939 Hollywood remake, which introduced Basil Rathbone and Nigel Bruce as Holmes and Watson, is the best of the bunch. (Fittingly, all of its posters employed the image of a silhouetted Holmes wearing his deerstalker cap and smoking a pipe.) Nearly all the adaptations have exploited the yarn's cinematic potential—the Gothic appearance of Baskerville hall and spooky, fog-shrouded night scenes taking place on the moor—and contained chapter 2's chilling last line, among the most memorable in crime fiction: "Mr. Holmes, they were the footprints of a gigantic hound!"

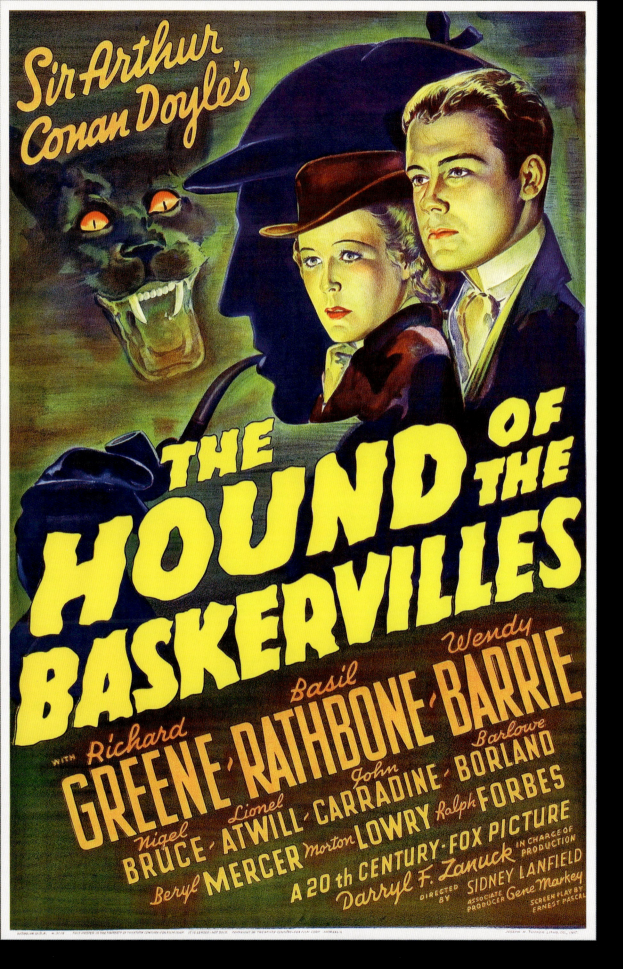

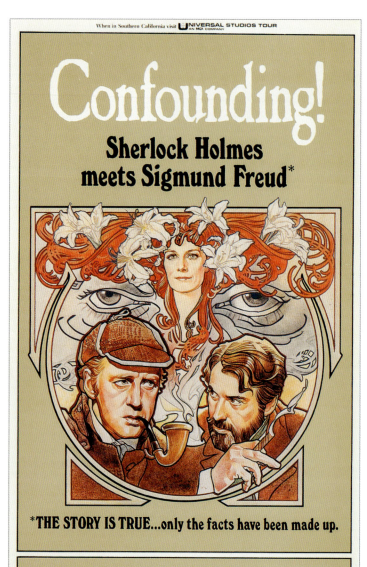

THE LATTER-DAY HOLMES

No fictional character can survive as long as Sherlock Holmes without inspiring parody, pastiche, and bald-faced revisionism. During the 1960s and '70s, filmmakers took all three approaches, with the resulting products vacillating between fairly entertaining and downright embarrassing. One of them, the British-made *A Study in Terror* (1966), had occasional flashes of dark humor but was generally a credible pitting of Holmes against Jack the Ripper. Unfortunately, its American release was sabotaged by an advertising campaign making the film seem indebted to the campy but wildly popular *Batman* TV show. *The Seven-Per-Cent Solution* (1976), which had Holmes consulting Sigmund Freud for a method of shaking his cocaine addiction, turned out better but probably would have horrified Conan Doyle—as would *The Private Life of Sherlock Holmes* (1970), a legendary botch job that nearly tanked the career of renowned producer/director Billy Wilder. Another Wilder, comedic actor Gene, wrote, directed, and starred in *The Adventure of Sherlock Holmes' Smarter Brother* (1975), an out-and-out farce.

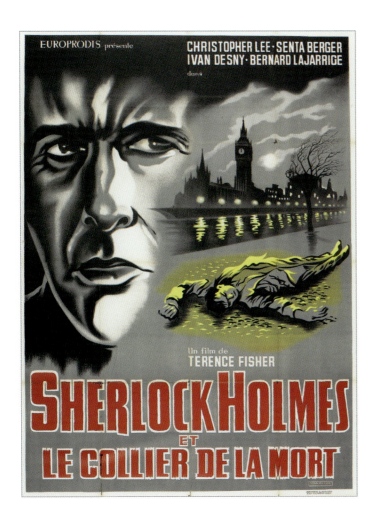

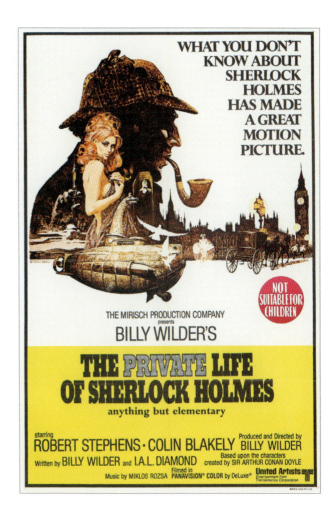

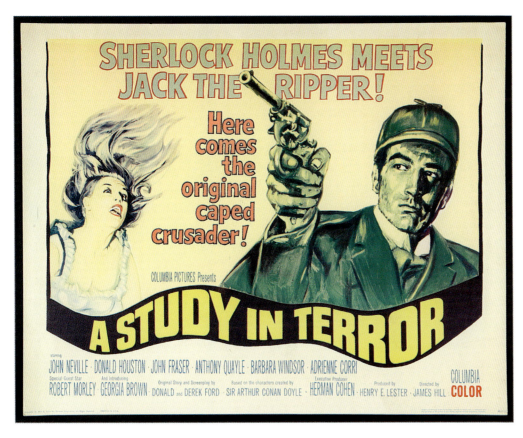

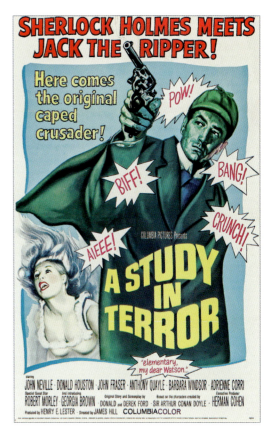

3

SLEUTHING FOR SOUND

HOLLYWOOD WHODUNITS COME OF AGE

Silent movies become an endangered species with the 1927 release of *The Jazz Singer*, a Warner Bros. drama that stars legendary stage performer Al Jolson and features several songs in addition to snippets of ad-libbed dialogue. Within a few short years, the film industry turns itself upside down to accommodate the new technology capturing the imaginations of American moviegoers. Murder mysteries, produced both from original screenplays and those adapted from wildly successful "whodunit" novels, delight audiences and become staples of studio release schedules . . .

The coming of sound more or less paralleled the burgeoning popularity of murder mysteries. This literary form of crime story—distinct from the thrillers of Edgar Wallace and E. Phillips Oppenheim—was pioneered by British authors, among them Agatha Christie, Philip MacDonald, Dorothy L. Sayers, and Margery Allingham. In America, the whodunit's rise to popularity began in the mid-1920s, kicked off by the 1926 American publication of Christie's *The Murder of Roger Ackroyd* and the initial appearances of Earl Derr Biggers's Charlie Chan (in *The House without a Key*) and S. S. Van Dine's Philo Vance (in *The Benson Murder Case*). These intellectually oriented puzzles—solved by dogged police detectives and gifted dilettantes alike—quickly supplanted other types of crime yarns as favorites of the reading public. Two of Van Dine's best, *The Greene Murder Case* (1928) and *The Bishop Murder Case* (1929), held fourth position in lists of the bestselling novels during their respective years of publication.

By that time, Warner Bros. had kicked off the sound revolution—initially in 1927, with Jolson's *Jazz Singer*, and the next year with *Lights of New York*, the first all-talking feature film. Next to the musical, no other genre was better suited to talking pictures than the whodunit. Films with lengthy and numerous interrogations of suspects, followed by often-windy reconstructions of crimes and climactic revelations of culprits' identities, were eagerly devoured by movie audiences mesmerized by the addition of talking to their filmgoing experience. Hollywood studios, accustomed to crafting scenarios that told stories visually, imported novelists and playwrights whose facility with dialogue earned them

ABOVE: *Broadway* (1929) went into production as a silent but was completed as a talkie. It might look like a musical, and there were big production numbers in it, but the underlying plot is a New York gangster story. Universal's extravagant film adaptation of George Abbott's hit 1926 play had Thomas Jackson reprising his stage role of a tough police detective. He would play similar characters for the next fifteen years.

as much as a thousand dollars per week. Highly regarded New York critic and playwright Herman J. Mankiewicz, shortly after arriving in Hollywood and settling at Paramount Pictures, sent a now-legendary telegram to his friend and fellow dramatist Ben Hecht: "Millions are to be grabbed out here, and your only competition is idiots. Don't let this get around."

But it *did* get around, and by the early 1930s, Tinseltown was swimming in writers, many of them working almost exclusively in narrowly targeted niches. Celluloid whodunits being just as popular as their printed-page counterparts, scribes who exhibited a talent for devising clever murder puzzles found themselves very much in demand. Studio executives feverishly optioned film rights to previously published detective stories and characters, but they also encouraged the creation of original screen sleuths whose adventures could be profitably produced without the added expense of licensing fees.

ABOVE: The decision to turn *Broadway* into a lavish musical drama cost Universal several hundred thousand dollars more than was originally budgeted. Some $75,000 went into the building of this huge crane, designed by director Paul Fejos to shoot the musical numbers with sweeping overhead shots. It greatly enhanced Universal's technical capabilities and would be used innumerable times thereafter.

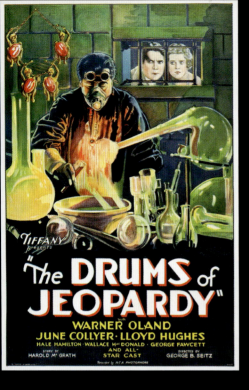

ABOVE LEFT: *Drums of Jeopardy* (1931) emanated from Poverty Row but was a sturdier production than most of its type, boasting a larger-than-usual budget and some inventive camerawork. An out-and-out thriller previously filmed ten years earlier as a silent, it was decidedly old-fashioned but proved quite entertaining to the undiscriminating audiences for which it was targeted. Note the poster's use of green and its eerie shadow effects in the foreground.

ABOVE RIGHT: Swedish American actor Warner Oland menaces costar Ernest Hilliard in *Drums of Jeopardy*. Warner's character in this one was named "Dr. Boris Karlov"!

Since primitive sound technology demanded camera immobility, early whodunits were generally stodgy affairs, with casts milling around in spacious sets and detectives conducting their investigations at a rather leisurely pace. Interminable questioning of suspects risked lulling audiences into somnolence, but during sound's earliest years the novelty of listening to actors talk, talk, talk was enough to keep theater patrons engaged, provided the dialogue was well crafted and the performances sufficiently lively.

In fact, the popularity of incessantly chatty murder mysteries proved a boon to Poverty Row filmmakers, perpetually short of funds and always looking for ways to turn out low-budget product that could grab patronage from the big, studio-owned theater chains. These scrappy, undercapitalized producers relied on rented studio space, and most whodunits could be staged on one or two standing sets that they could procure for limited periods at reasonable prices. A 1934 report on Poverty Row movies in the *Saturday Evening Post* related the story of an enterprising producer who rented a particularly impressive set for $2,500 per day; after being assured the space would be his exclusively for a *full* day, he assembled his cast and crew and worked for twenty-four hours straight, capturing nearly three hundred scenes on film—accounting for roughly 95 percent of the script—before dismissing his exhausted employees. Normally it would have taken four or five days to generate that much footage, even working at high speed.

Such practices, while certainly extreme, were not uncommon during the early days of the Depression, before the unions grew to wield supreme power and when Poverty Row actors and technicians were grateful for any work they could get. What's more, dialogue-heavy murder mysteries were tailor-made for stage-trained performers used to memorizing dozens of pages of speeches. And it wasn't just the cheapie producers who exploited the subgenre's growth: Tinseltown's "mini-majors," Universal and Columbia, ground out mysteries on an assembly-line basis, confident their respective sales forces would find venues for them among the thousands of independently owned theaters not affiliated with major studios. Most such productions were grade-"B" efforts that utilized the services of young, up-and-coming contract players determined to need seasoning before assuming roles in major pictures.

Although straight whodunits surged in popularity during the early and mid-1930s, gangster films and comedy-mystery thrillers of the "old dark house" variety were still very much in demand. Mob movies proliferated until 1934, when Hollywood's newly empowered censorial body, the Production Code Administration, complained they were glorifying organized-crime figures. It didn't help that talkie-era gangsters were played by such charismatic new performers as James Cagney, Paul Muni, Humphrey Bogart, and Edward G. Robinson. With Prohibition now a thing of the past, the studios deglamorized mobsters and cast tough-guy actors like Cagney and Robinson as "G-men"— the slangy designation given to Department of Justice agents by crookdom. Gangsters continued their cinematic depredations but always lost out to law enforcement by the film's end.

During this period, artists producing posters for crime films gradually found ways to identify mystery movies in visual terms. One was liberal usage of the color green, which has also been associated with horror. Green backgrounds and tints on faces became de rigueur on mystery-film posters in the late '20s and remained so throughout the '30s, especially when used in conjunction with deep shadows.

Another tipoff to a film's criminous content was the insertion of silhouetted figures, brandishing guns or knives and menacing the principals depicted in artwork. Often, these carefully limned characters could be seen reacting with fear or horror etched on their faces, enhancing the poster's unnerving effect and leaving little doubt as to the type of movie that audiences could expect upon forking over their dimes and quarters.

The prevalence of murder mysteries in Hollywood's Depression-era product mix led to a proliferation of detective series, mostly but not entirely built around characters from other media. We deal with series whodunits in subsequent chapters; the posters shown on the following pages almost exclusively illustrate stand-alone mysteries. ⬡

ABOVE: Paramount made some of the most interesting B-grade crime thrillers of the 1930s. *The Preview Murder Mystery* (1936), directed with great panache by Robert Florey, revolves around mysterious killings at a Hollywood studio and boasts some great shots of the Paramount back lot and soundstages, delighting movie fans interested in behind-the-scenes glimpses of filmmakers at work.

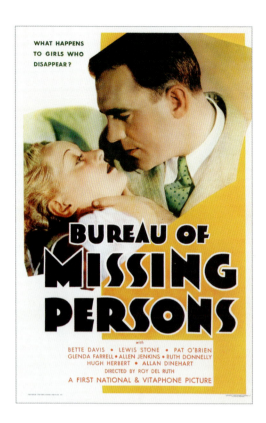

MAJOR-STUDIO MURDER AND MAYHEM

It's not an understatement to say that crime flourished during the 1930s. Not just the real-life kind (which in America intensified early in the decade, courtesy of Prohibition's lingering effects) but the celluloid variety as well. Talking pictures had moved past the novelty phase and were now firmly entrenched in the marketplace. The major producer-distributors—M-G-M, Fox, RKO, Warners, Paramount, and United Artists— manufactured murder mysteries, courtroom dramas, gangster pictures, and police procedurals on an assembly-line basis, particularly once the Depression-inspired demand for double features surged middecade. The public's appetite for such entertainments appeared to be insatiable, but the movie industry shoved crime pictures down viewers' throats, eager to restore the level of profitability the major studios had attained before the economy went south. Even class-conscious M-G-M, whose lavish, star-laden, sophisticated product had largely insulated it from declining revenues, saw the wisdom in feeding picturegoers a steady diet of cinematic murder and mayhem. Whoever said "crime does not pay" certainly wasn't thinking about Hollywood.

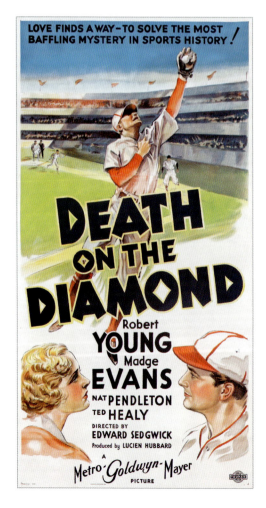

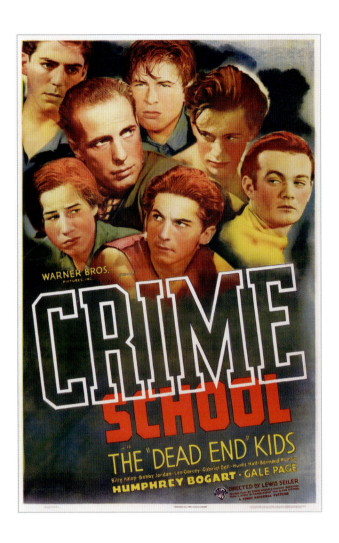

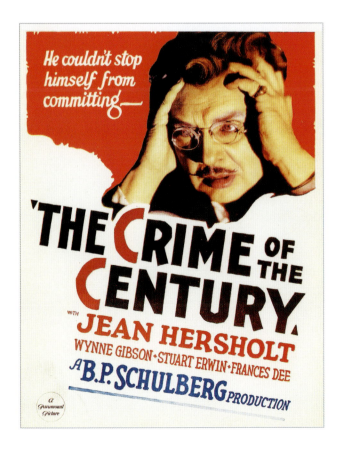

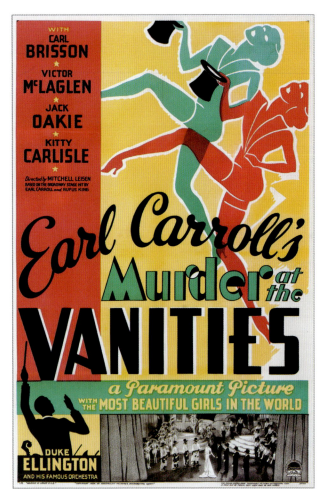

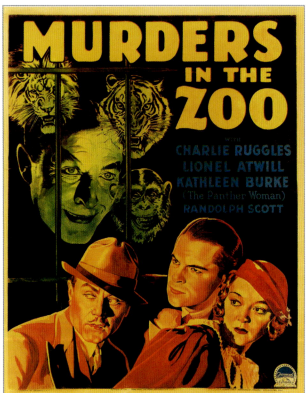

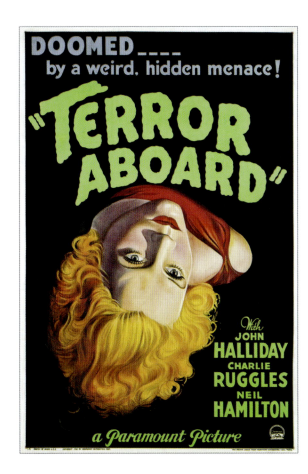

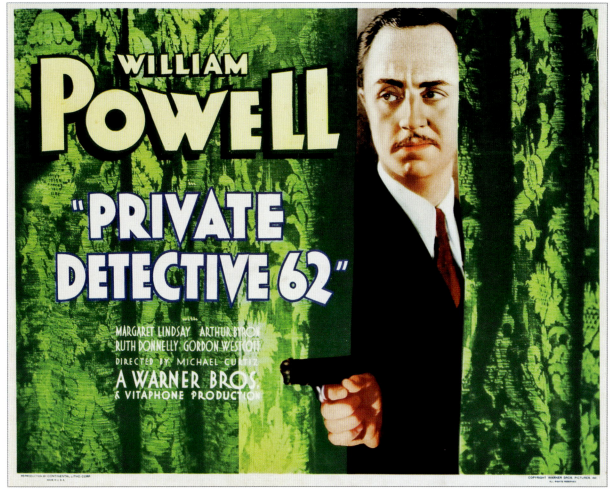

THE GOLDEN AGE OF
THE GANGSTER FILM

The late 1920s gangster-film cycle continued unabated throughout the
'30s. If anything, it was strengthened by the addition of sound, with spoken
dialogue enhancing the performances of charismatic players who had come
to Hollywood from the stage in the days following Al Jolson's prophetic
declaration "You ain't heard nothin' yet!" Edward G. Robinson got the decade
off to a rip-roaring start as *Little Caesar* (Warner Bros., 1930), the Al Capone–
inspired underworld ruler of W. R. Burnett's bestselling novel. The next year's
Public Enemy, another ultraviolent Warners gangster opus, made a star of
bantam badman James Cagney, instantly typecast after his unqualified success
as the titular terror. Paul Muni, one of the legitimate stage's most respected
stars, portrayed another ersatz Capone in *Scarface* (United Artists, 1932),
produced by Texas tycoon Howard Hughes and roundly condemned not
only for its violence but also for a non-too-subtle hint of incest between the
mobster and his younger sister (Ann Dvorak). Even screen heartthrob Clark
Gable played a gang leader in *Manhattan Melodrama* (1934).

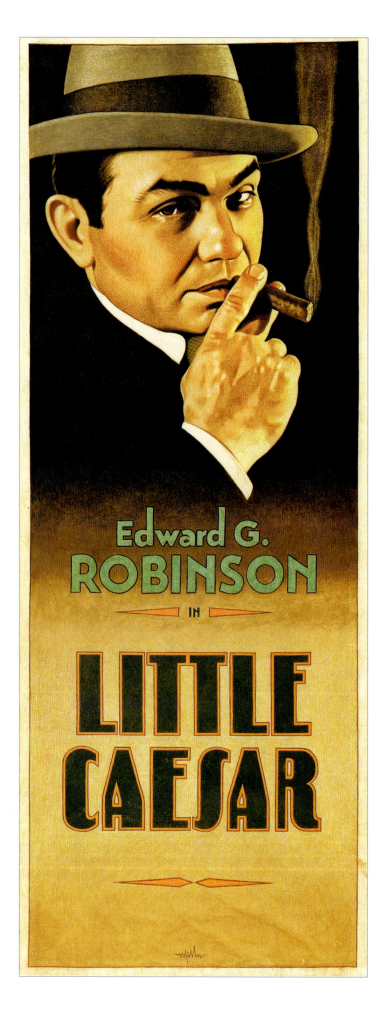

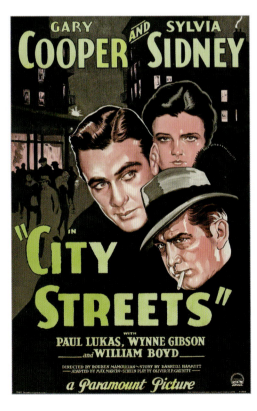

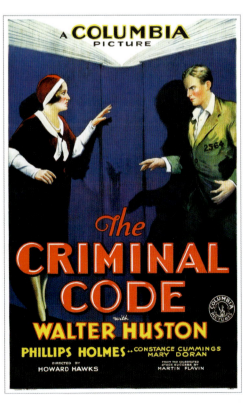

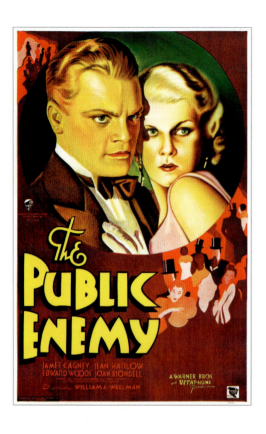

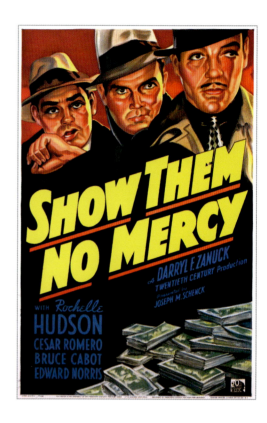

MURDER ON POVERTY ROW

Small independent production companies that flourished during the silent era had fallen on hard times with the Depression's advent, but the rapidly growing popularity of crime movies gave them a new lease on life, especially because murder mysteries in particular could be filmed cheaply—an important advantage for parsimonious producers. Hurriedly renting sound equipment to compete with major studios once talkies became the rage, the denizens of Poverty Row worked feverishly and helped flood the market. Their whodunits, rarely surpassing an hour in length, were shot in days, not weeks; their casts were budding thespians on the way up or, just as likely, silent-movie veterans on the way down. Since their product lacked big-name stars and major-studio production values, the indie producers invested a good chunk of their meager resources in poster art. Mysteries such as *The Phantom* (1931), *The Shadow Laughs* (1933), and *Rogues' Tavern* (1936) might have been made for peanuts, but their posters were just as eye-catching as those manufactured by Fox, Warners, or Paramount.

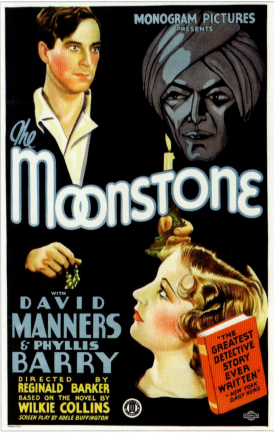

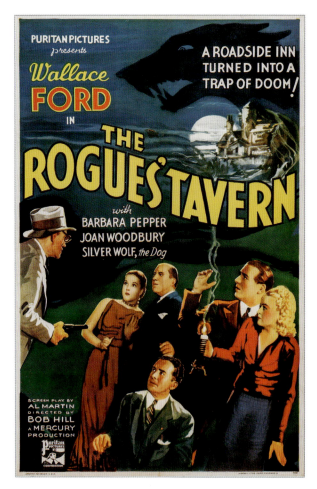

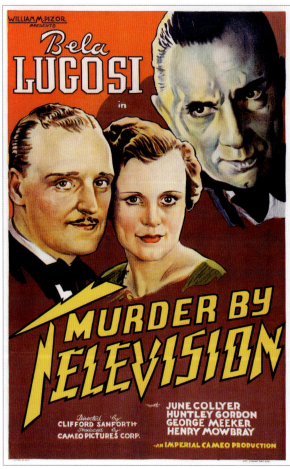

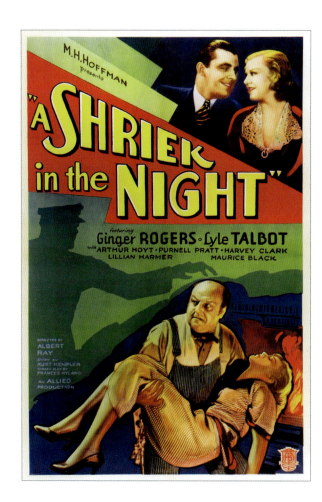

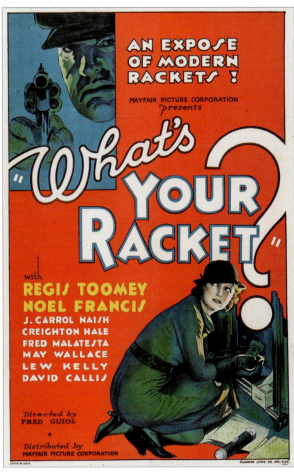

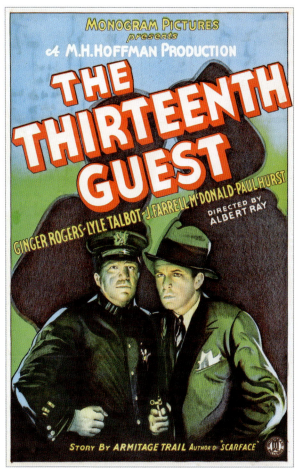

CREEPY CRIMES

Just like gangster movies, the "old dark house" thrillers of the 1920s extended their box-office success into the next decade, initially with a spate of remakes. That was all to the good, because many properties of proven appeal—such as *The Bat* and *The Cat and the Canary*—had originally been stage plays, which enabled scenario writers to transplant their dialogue and plot structure virtually intact to talkies. Roland West's *The Bat Whispers* (1931), a remake of his 1926 silent smash, was every bit as visually inventive, even down to the employment of a short-lived wide-screen process. Universal's *Cat and the Canary* retread, *The Cat Creeps* (1930), similarly benefited from the addition of sound. During the early '30s, it was fashionable to embellish otherwise conventional whodunits with horror-film trappings, especially prominent in *Murder by the Clock* (1931), *Dr. X* (1932), and *Mystery of the Wax Museum* (1933). Notice in these posters the prevalence of green—a color long considered to convey creepiness.

Sleuthing for

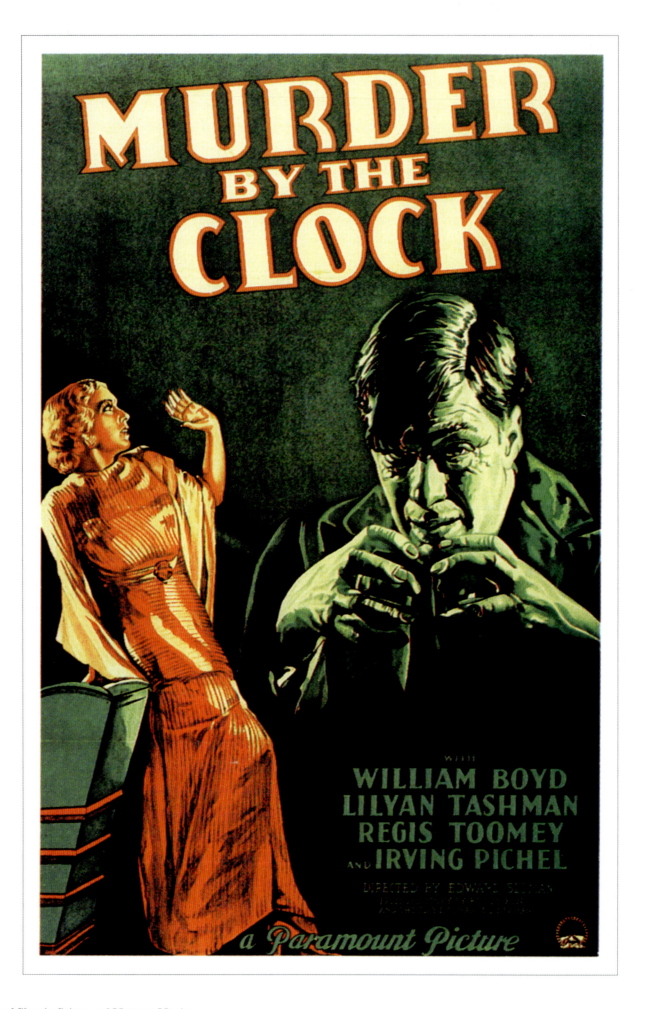

The Art of Classic Crime and Mystery Movies

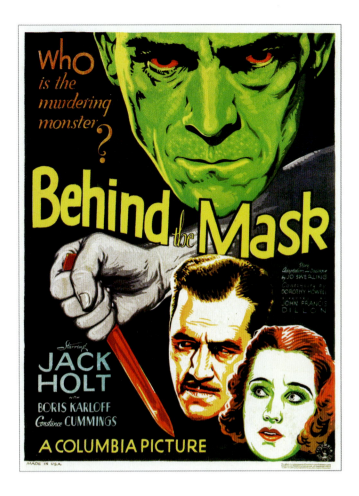

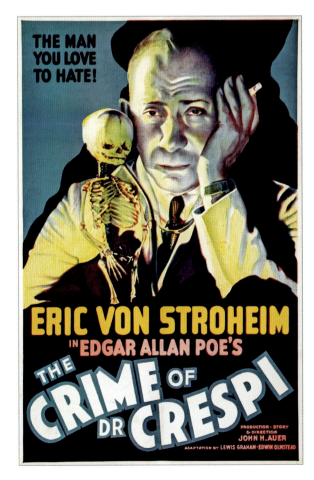

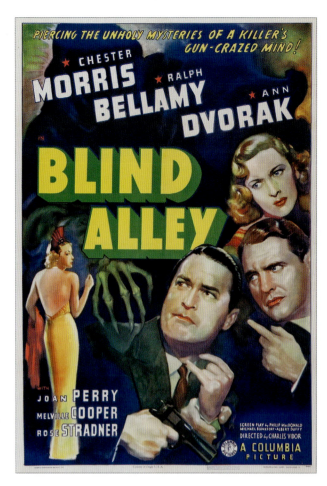

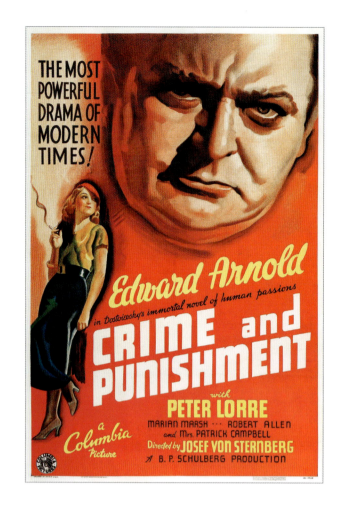

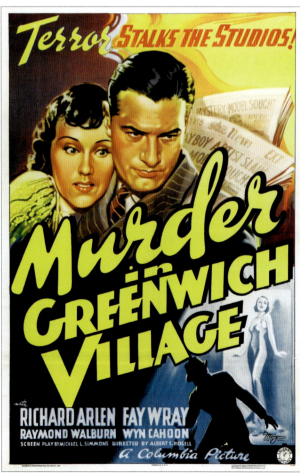

UNIVERSAL AND COLUMBIA: KINGS OF THE B MOVIE

Hollywood's two "mini-majors" shared characteristics that kept them from being taken as seriously as M-G-M, Fox, and the other big studios. The primary one was their lack of corporately owned theater circuits, which robbed them of ready venues in major markets. Big downtown picture palaces generated the most revenue, especially when exhibiting blockbuster movies with major stars. Universal and Columbia had excellent distribution networks, but their films played mostly in limited-capacity houses in small towns, rural hamlets, or suburban bedroom communities. Therefore, both studios concentrated on producing inexpensive, "bread-and-butter" movies tailored to less sophisticated audiences, which meant lots of mysteries—especially those with stereotypical plots and plenty of comic relief. Occasionally, these films boasted fairly well-known stars, but often they were cast with inexpensive contract players and shot on standing sets to boost profitability. Of the two, Columbia evinced a greater reliance on character-driven series, while Universal preferred mysteries of the stand-alone type. Both, it should be noted, turned out some of the best "B" whodunits in the market.

4

THE
MYSTERIOUS
ORIENT

ASIAN INFLUENCES ON CRIME CINEMA

Motion pictures with Asian villains begin to emerge during the medium's formative years, among the most notable being a 1915 feature film, *The Mission of Mr. Foo*, and a 1916 serial, *The Yellow Menace*. Many more will flash across movie screens during the 1910s and '20s. But it is a Chinese Hawaiian police detective named Charlie Chan, created by novelist Earl Derr Biggers, who breaks down anti-Asian stereotypes and becomes one of filmdom's most beloved characters, as interpreted by Swedish actor Warner Oland. There will be other celluloid sleuths that hail from the mysterious East, but none can duplicate Charlie's success . . .

In late 1924, journalist turned fiction writer Earl Derr Biggers, intending to capitalize on the surging popularity of whodunits, wrote a novel-length mystery and sold it to the *Saturday Evening Post*, at that time the premier fiction market in America. His story, *The House without a Key*, is set in Hawaii and has a strong romantic subplot. Almost a quarter of the yarn has already unfolded when Biggers introduces his sleuth, Charlie Chan, a detective with the Honolulu Police Department. Quiet and unobtrusive but extremely shrewd, Charlie eventually exposes the killer of Dan Winterslip, a wealthy islander with a questionable past.

Biggers, who had vacationed in Hawaii several years earlier, based Charlie on a real-life Honolulu police detective named Chang Apana, a local legend renowned for (among other things) apprehending an entire ring of drug smugglers armed only with a bullwhip. But the author imbued Chan with characteristics that Apana didn't possess, including a penchant for pithy aphorisms drawn most frequently from the sayings of Confucius.

A hardcover edition published by Bobbs Merrill in 1925 elicited glowing reviews and sold phenomenally well. Over the next six years, Biggers penned five more Chan novels, several of them bestsellers. In late 1926, the film distribution company Pathé released a ten-chapter serial based on *House Without a Key*; it was followed in 1928 by Universal's adaptation of the second Chan mystery, *The Chinese Parrot*, and the next year by Fox Film Corp.'s version of the third, *Behind That Curtain*. In the latter film, a ponderous early talkie, Chan is almost

ABOVE: *Thank You, Mr. Moto* (1937), the second and best in this abbreviated series, was unusually suspenseful while maintaining a fast pace. Eventually, Peter Lorre grew tired of the character, but here he delivers an energetic, engaging performance.

an afterthought, shoehorned into the plot with four-fifths of the tale already told. Fox had also licensed movie rights to the fourth and fifth novels and in 1931 produced *Charlie Chan Carries On*, with Swedish-born actor Warner Oland in the title role. Despite his ancestry, Oland had been playing Oriental characters—mostly villainous ones—on-screen since 1917. Most recently, he had appeared as Sax Rohmer's Dr. Fu Manchu in three early talkies for Paramount. Yet, he easily made the Chan character his own, effortlessly transitioning from malevolence to benevolence. Oland's Charlie was soft spoken and mild mannered, with a disarmingly avuncular quality.

The immediate success of *Charlie Chan Carries On*—inexpensively made by the cash-strapped studio, with modest expectations—persuaded Fox executives to mount a sequel while the first film was still in circulation. *The Black Camel* (also 1931) was produced on a larger scale and boasted extensive location shooting in Hawaii. A skillful adaptation of the similarly titled Biggers novel, it benefited from the presence in the cast of Bela Lugosi, who had recently scored big in Universal's *Dracula*.

ABOVE: Thomas Beck (*wearing Panama hat and white suit*) tends to an apparently wounded Peter Lorre during the taking of this scene from *Think Fast, Mr. Moto* (1937). That's director Norman Foster at left, sitting on the floor with his arms wrapped around his knees. With only a couple of exceptions, the Moto films were thrillers rather than straight whodunits.

A Luxurious Liner—
Light-hearted Tourists
but—A Murderer
is Aboard!

with
WARNER OLAND
JOHN GARRICK
MARGUERITE CHURCHILL
WARREN HYMER
MARJORIE WHITE

FOX
PICTURE

Further endearing Oland's Chan to moviegoers was the steady stream of aphorisms, some taken from Biggers's works but others devised by ace Fox screenwriters Philip Klein and Barry Conners. Film fans loved the character, encouraging the studio to launch a series of Charlie Chan mysteries, released at a rate of two per year. Curiously, Fox chose not to adapt Biggers's sixth and final Chan novel, *Keeper of the Keys*, instead commissioning Klein, Conners, and other contract writers to generate original stories.

Over the next six years, Fox—which in late 1935 merged with Darryl Zanuck's Twentieth Century Pictures to become Twentieth Century-Fox—cranked out fourteen additional Chan films. They were produced for roughly $200,000 each, making them glorified "B" pictures. They filled the bottom half of double bills in prestigious Fox-owned theaters but played as the top half or even as single feature in houses catering to small-town and rural audiences. The Chans were strictly formula pictures, revolving around murders committed all over the world (London, Paris, Shanghai, Egypt, Monte Carlo) and at unexpected locations (a circus, a racetrack, a Broadway nightclub, even the 1936 Olympic Games in Berlin). Invariably, a variegated group of suspects gather in a central location once Charlie has completed his investigation. He then systematically explains the reasoning behind his deductions before confronting the guilty party with a soft-spoken "You are murderer" (occasionally changed to "You are guilty man," presumably for variety's sake).

The ritualistic, predictable aspect of Fox's Chan pictures was ameliorated by the cleverness of Charlie's aphorisms, which were now being contributed by every writer on the lot (and referred to by them as "Chanograms"). Audiences eventually caught on to plot tricks designed to divert attention from the real murderer, who would almost always be revealed as the Least Likely Suspect. It didn't matter. They loved Charlie. To be more precise, they loved Warner Oland's Charlie.

Oland died suddenly in 1938 and was replaced (after thirty-four actors were screen-tested) by Sidney Toler, a veteran Broadway actor of Scottish ancestry. Toler settled into the role but never attained the same level of acceptance Oland had enjoyed. Although some of his early series entries were outstanding (1939's *Charlie Chan at Treasure Island* being clearly the best of the lot), he lacked that avuncular quality that made Oland such a warm, comforting presence. Ultimately, however, Toler made twenty-two Chan mysteries, half of them for low-rent Monogram Pictures, before his death in 1947.

In 1937, Twentieth Century-Fox launched a second series of "B" pictures with an Asian protagonist. Mainstream novelist John P. Marquand had written several novels (which, like the Chan yarns, were serialized in the *Saturday Evening Post* prior to book publication) about a Japanese government operative named I. A. Moto. These were not whodunits per se but adventure yarns in which mysterious murders were sometimes committed. The enigmatic Mr. Moto—described by Marquand as "a small man, delicate, almost fragile"—initially impressed Westerners as slow witted and eccentric, but as the stories progressed he was shown to be tough, dynamic, and ruthless as circumstances demanded.

ABOVE: *Charlie Chan Carries On* (1931), adapted from an Earl Derr Biggers novel of the same title, changed moviegoers' perception of Warner Oland, heretofore seen primarily in the role of villainous Orientals. Although considered a "lost" film today, it survives—sort of—in a Spanish-language version titled *Eran Trace* (*There Were Thirteen*), shot on the same sets with different actors.

Moto was portrayed on-screen by the diminutive German actor Peter Lorre, who very much looked the part after applications of subtle makeup. The films were extremely well done—among the very best of their budgetary class—but the character was dropped in 1939 when Japan's invasion of China and its increasing aggressiveness toward the West became too pronounced for Americans to ignore. Marquand revived and rehabilitated Moto in a 1957 novel, *Stopover: Tokyo*, the film version of which rather curiously omits the character.

A minor Charlie Chan simulacrum, private investigator James Lee Wong, appeared in numerous short stories written by Hugh Wiley for the magazines *Collier's* and *Blue Book* and was impersonated by Boris Karloff in a series of decidedly substandard whodunits produced by Monogram. The painfully cheap and dreary Mr. Wong films didn't last long—a blessing for all involved. ◯

ABOVE LEFT: Warner Oland, Sidney Blackmer (*with cane*), and various extras rehearse a shipboard sequence for *Charlie Chan at the Race Track* (1936). Oland's drinking problem forced directors to stage lengthy dialogue sequences during mornings, because after imbibing a liquid lunch—dry martinis in a thermos bottle—he would get drowsy and slur his lines.

ABOVE RIGHT: "Treasure Island," built to house the 1939–40 San Francisco World's Fair, is the scene of what most whodunit fans believe to be the best of Sidney Toler's Charlie Chan films. It's extremely well plotted, even if the murderer's identity becomes obvious before Chan makes his final deductions. Note the poster's use of tinted photographs in lieu of a painting.

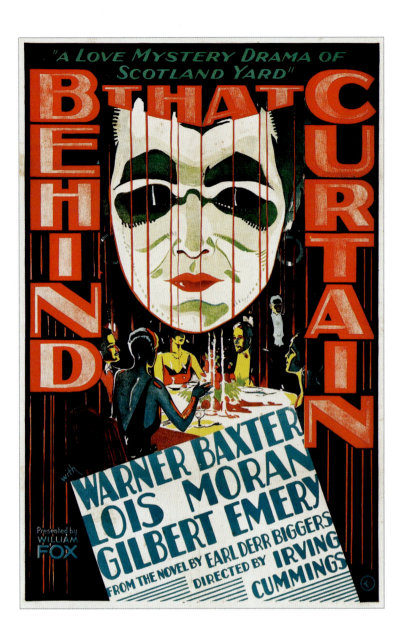

EARLY CHARLIE CHAN TALKIES

Fox Film Corp.'s *Behind That Curtain* (1929), based on Earl Derr Biggers's third Charlie Chan novel, made the Honolulu-based sleuth a supporting character indifferently played by E. L. Park. Two years later, Fox adapted the fifth yarn, *Charlie Chan Carries On*, giving the title role to Swedish actor Warner Oland, then just coming off a three-picture stint as Sax Rohmer's evil doctor Fu Manchu. Accustomed to playing heavies, Oland clearly relished the opportunity to make Charlie a warm, soft-spoken, but formidable detective. The film attained an unanticipated level of success, persuading Fox to launch a series of Chan pictures. Four more entries followed, all based on Biggers novels, before producer John Stone instructed screenwriters to devise new adventures for Charlie set in locales all around the world—London, Paris, Shanghai, Egypt, and so on. Audiences loved Oland, his never-ending supply of "Chanograms," and his rapport with actor Keye Luke, portraying Charlie's "Number One Son," Lee. Foreign-language versions proved equally popular, especially in Oland's native Sweden.

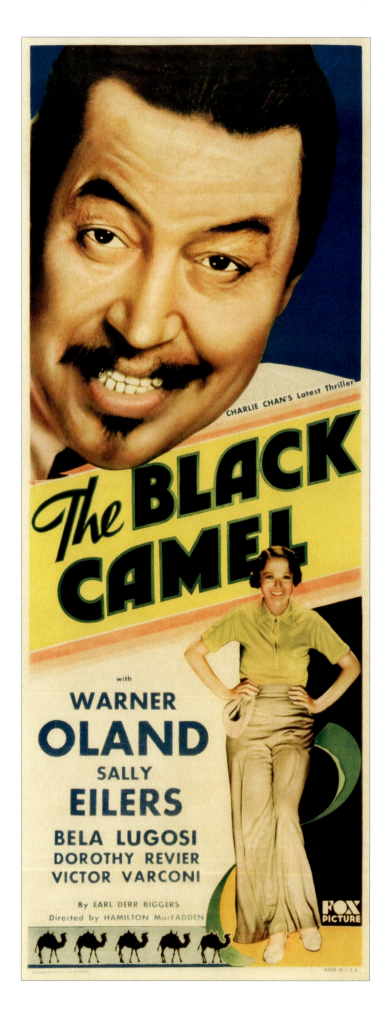

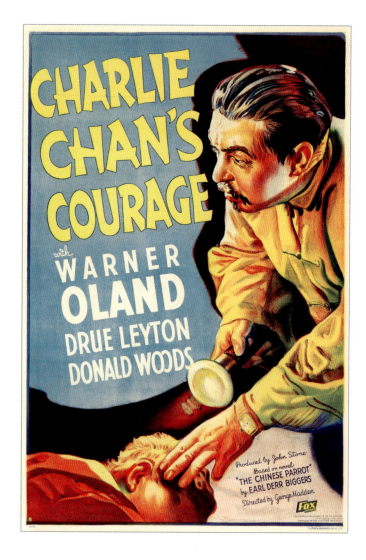

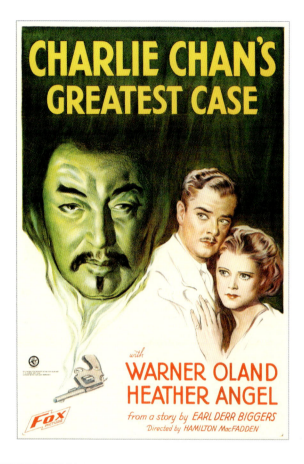

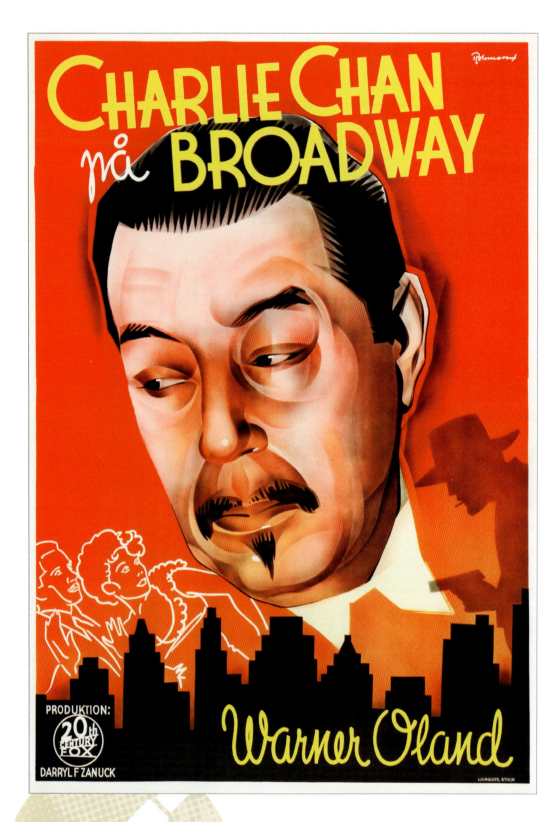

CHARLIE GETS A NEW EMPLOYER

The Charlie Chan series helped keep Fox above water during the early and mid-'30s. In 1935, it merged with Twentieth Century Pictures, an independent studio owned by Joseph Schenck and Darryl F. Zanuck. The latter was delegated to oversee the new corporate entity's output, and he elected to keep the Chan series going. Producer John Stone turned out entries like clockwork, maintaining full creative control as long as he brought them in on or under the modest budgets allotted to him. Warner Oland embraced the character so completely that he invariably spoke like Charlie—aphorisms and all—when appearing in public and granting interviews. The high-water mark was reached in 1937, with the release of *Charlie Chan at the Opera*, which teamed Oland with horror-movie icon Boris Karloff. The film's domestic and international posters gave equal prominence to both men.

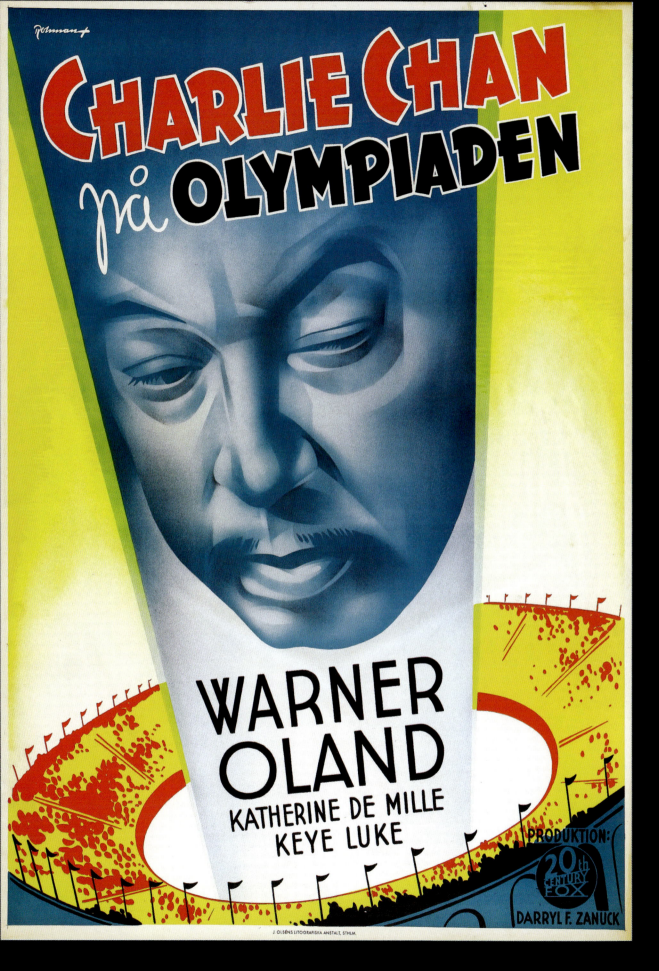

ENTER A NEW CHAN: SIDNEY TOLER

Warner Oland's death in 1938 panicked the executives at Fox, who were understandably loath to terminate a still-popular and profitable series. Reportedly more than thirty actors were tested for the part before character actor Sidney Toler was selected to fill Oland's shoes. Toler was reasonably effective as Charlie, but he fell short in emulating his predecessor's kindly disposition. Moreover, his interactions with "Number Two Son" Jimmy (Victor Sen Yung) lacked the warmth so clearly and sincerely conveyed between Oland and Keye Luke. Ever so gradually, the profit margins diminished, and the Chan budgets were reduced accordingly. Fox dropped the series in 1942, but Toler, by now typecast, licensed the character from Biggers's widow and persuaded Monogram Pictures, a shoestring studio, to keep it going. Toler's death in 1947 should have ended the Chan pictures, but the series stayed on life support for another two years, during which the title role was essayed by mediocre supporting player Roland Winters. During the Toler years, Chan poster imagery relied heavily on colored photographs of the star rather than painted portraits.

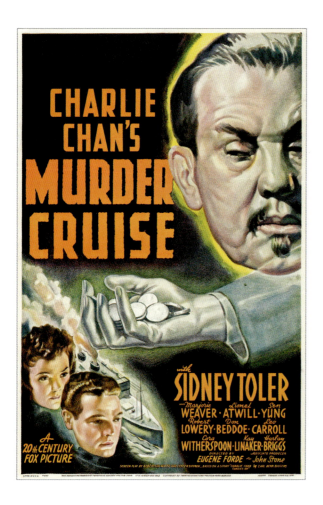

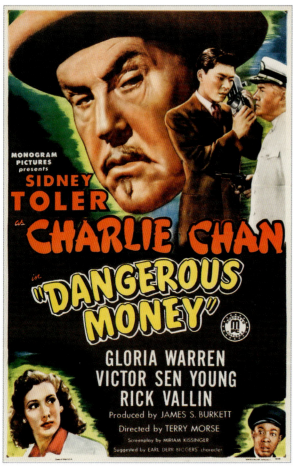

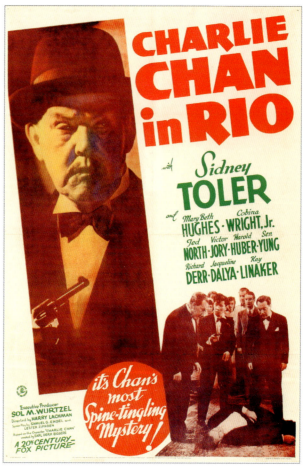

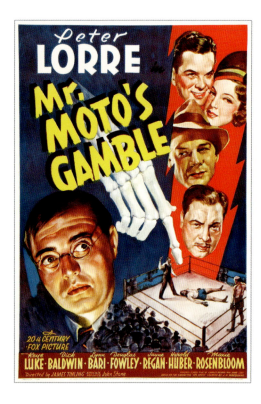

MISTERS MOTO AND WONG

The Charlie Chan series was bound to have imitations, and the first came from Twentieth Century-Fox itself. In 1935, author John P. Marquand had created an enigmatic Japanese government operative known as Mr. Moto at the behest of the *Saturday Evening Post*'s editor, who sorely missed Earl Derr Biggers's Chan novels. Several of Moto's adventures had been published by the time Fox came calling in 1937. In the apparent belief that it could make lightning strike twice in the same place, Fox assigned the series to writer/director Norman Foster. Diminutive German actor Peter Lorre, who was just beginning to make a name for himself in Hollywood, won the starring role and played it superbly in eight high-class B movies produced in two years. (A cheaply made 1965 revival starred Henry Silva as Moto but quickly disappeared from theaters.) Considerably less successful than the Moto thrillers was Monogram's 1938–40 series featuring Boris Karloff as Hugh Wiley's Chinese private detective James Lee Wong. Former "Number One Son" Keye Luke played a younger Wong in the final entry.

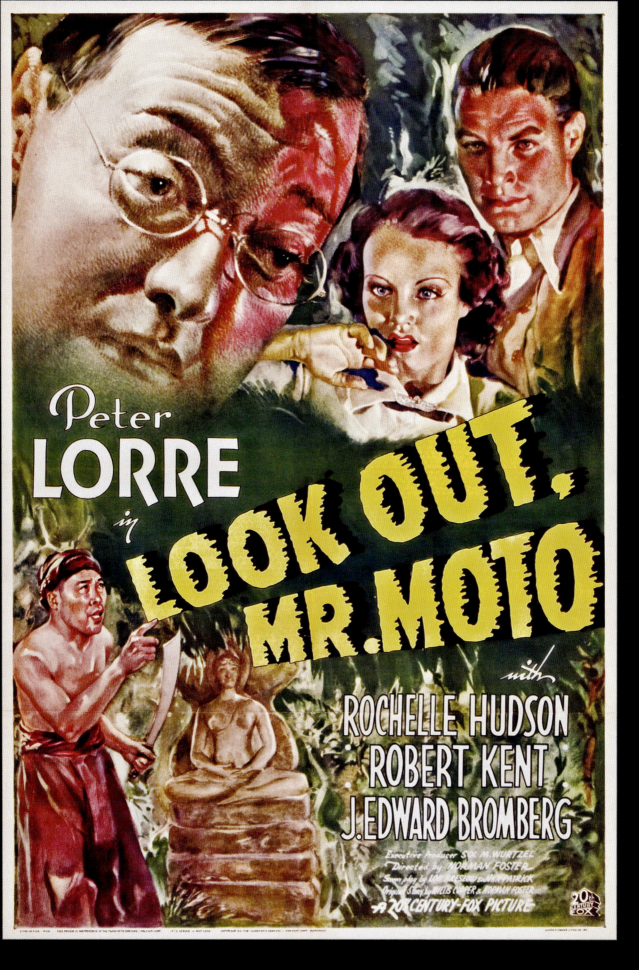

PETER LORRE

in

LOOK OUT, MR. MOTO

with

ROCHELLE HUDSON
ROBERT KENT
J. EDWARD BROMBERG

Executive Producer SOL M. WURTZEL
Directed by NORMAN FOSTER
Screen play by LOU BRESLOW and JOHN PATRICK
Original Story by WILLIS COOPER and NORMAN FOSTER
A 20th CENTURY-FOX PICTURE

20th
CENTURY
FOX

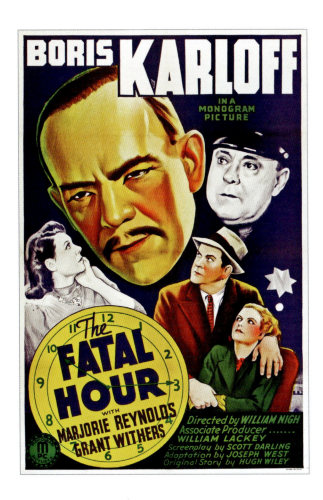

THE DEVIL DOCTOR

Introduced in a 1912 short story titled "The Zayat Kiss," Sax Rohmer's Dr. Fu Manchu was hardly the earliest exemplar of the "yellow peril" tradition in Edwardian-era popular fiction, but he was the one with the most staying power. Rohmer's brilliant, highly educated "devil doctor" appeared in fourteen books between 1914 and 1959. He first appeared on film in the person of Harry Agar Lyons, who essayed the role in two mid-'20s series of short subjects. Warner Oland played Fu Manchu in three early talkies for Paramount before heading to Fox in 1931 for the Charlie Chan films; Boris Karloff, in one of his early post-*Frankenstein* starring vehicles, gave a memorable interpretation of the character in *The Mask of Fu Manchu* (1932). Henry Brandon had the title role in a 1940 Republic serial, *Drums of Fu Manchu*, and British actor Christopher Lee cut an imposing figure as the star of a Fu Manchu quintet of '60s feature films made in various European countries by the peripatetic producer Harry Alan Towers.

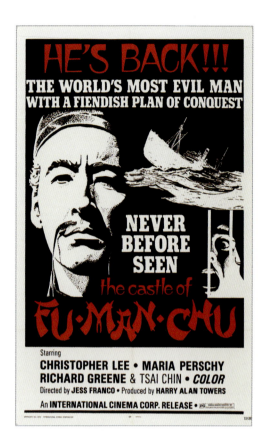

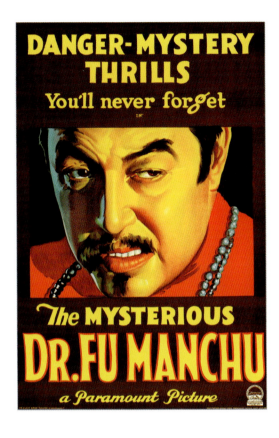

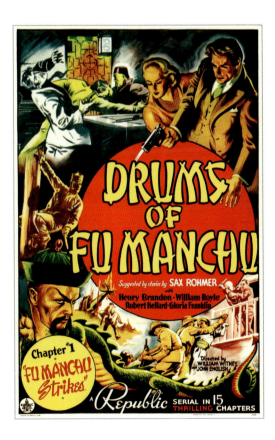

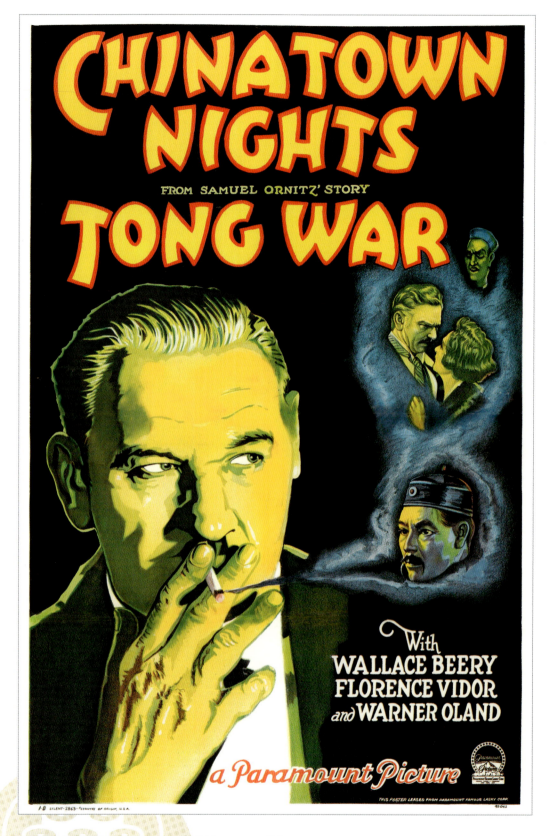

FROM OUT OF THE EAST

Motion pictures with Oriental themes, settings, and characters date to the beginning of the medium itself. All too frequently, Asian *dramatis personae* on film have been depicted with unfortunate stereotypes, for which we can blame the old traditions of popular fiction. Since the Boxer Rebellion, and even before, the Chinese have been portrayed as sinister, inscrutable, untrustworthy . . . always lurking in the shadows, knives or hatchets at the ready. Such characterizations persisted in films until the late 1930s, when the horrors of the Sino–Japanese War aroused American sympathies.

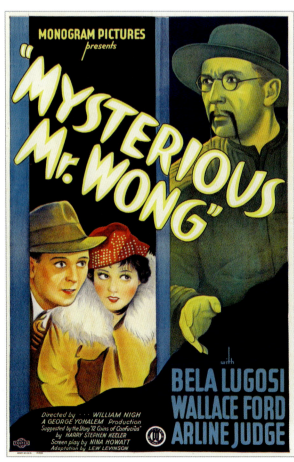

5

FAMOUS DETECTIVES OF FICTION

FROM PRINTED PAGE TO SILVER SCREEN

The wave of Hollywood whodunits that deluged America's movie theaters during the 1930s and '40s includes a sizable percentage of films adapted from mystery novels, which have improved in quality even as they have increased in number. Once considered the province of dime novels and pulp magazines, the "fair play" murder puzzle—in which writers present clues in such a way that observant readers can discern a killer's identity as the story's sleuth does— is now mainstream literature, with numerous examples of the form making bestseller lists and therefore becoming ripe for optioning by major and minor studios alike . . .

As previously noted, the simultaneous advent of talking pictures and the American public's fascination with fictional murder mysteries was nothing if not serendipitous. It didn't take long for the two forms of entertainment to become inextricably intertwined, and movie audiences were delighted to see their favorite printed-page detectives brought to life on the screens of their local movie theaters, be they luxurious downtown picture palaces or more modest small-town venues catering to less affluent, less sophisticated clienteles.

Then, as now, the Hollywood studios habitually underestimated their audiences. Classic "fair play" mystery novels demanded a level of intellectual engagement not required of most mainstream literature. Readers were neither assumed nor expected to possess the arcane knowledge their favorite sleuths brought to any table, but the best authors sprinkled their yarns with nuggets of information that, if mentally assayed with a modicum of imagination, often yielded paydirt— the solution to a baffling crime that whodunit devotees reached in sync with the detective.

Filmmakers rarely gave their audiences the same benefit of the doubt, making sure every intellectual problem was reduced to its lowest common denominator. In the movies, complex "locked room" murder puzzles (much beloved by hard-core fans of mystery novels) were frequently watered down in the belief that most picture patrons wouldn't be able to understand how murderers had arranged their seemingly impossible crimes. Screenwriters in

ABOVE: In the months immediately following Pearl Harbor and America's entry into World War II, most of the B-movie sleuths temporarily quit chasing ordinary murderers and instead went after the Nazi spies and saboteurs who had supposedly infiltrated the nation to disrupt the war effort. Ellery Queen exhibited unusual vigor in running these miscreants to earth.

many cases cut down a book's number of viable suspects from, say, seven or eight to three or four, in the belief that too many would simply confuse viewers. Such condescension wasn't unusual, although filmmakers did on occasion trust audiences to comprehend intricate schemes presented in granular detail. In *The Kennel Murder Case* (Warner Bros., 1933), scriptwriters Robert N. Lee and Peter Milne translated from the S. S. Van Dine novel a particularly clever means of exiting and resealing a locked room, using sewing thread and strategically placed needles. Director Michael Curtiz shot the sequence with Van Dine's Philo Vance staging a reconstruction of the feat while explaining it in detail.

Vance was the first character from mystery fiction's golden age to reach the screen, and at just the right time: his debut film, *The Canary Murder Case* (Paramount, 1929), went into production as a silent but, after a shutdown of several months, resumed shooting as a talkie. William Powell, up to that time best known as a heavy, altered the trajectory of his career by perfectly capturing the personality of Van Dine's suave, erudite detective. The early Philo Vance novels enjoyed tremendous success, but the character's pomposity and affectations, at first considered charmingly offbeat, eventually annoyed

ABOVE: William Gargan and Margaret Lindsay in *Enemy Agents Meet Ellery Queen* (1942), the last of seven Ellery Queen B mysteries produced by Columbia. Gargan, who replaced Ralph Bellamy in the title role, was a poor choice for the master detective, having spent most of his Hollywood career playing Irish roughnecks.

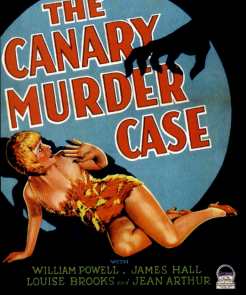

THE CANARY MURDER CASE

WITH
WILLIAM POWELL , JAMES HALL
LOUISE BROOKS and JEAN ARTHUR

readers. Nonetheless, of twelve novels in the series, ten were brought to the screen between 1929 and 1939.

Vance naturally inspired a number of imitators, his most insufferable qualities frequently being incorporated into their characterizations as well. *The Roman Hat Mystery* (1929) introduced readers to Ellery Queen, a New York–based mystery writer whose father, Richard Queen, is an irascible police inspector regularly tasked with solving bizarre murders. Ellery frequently aids his dad and invariably exposes the culprits. In his early cases, the young Queen is every bit as annoying and affected as Philo Vance, often addressing his father as "pater" and using such phrases as "I say, old thing."

In an effective marketing ploy, the Ellery Queen mysteries, while written in the third person, were credited to one Ellery Queen. In fact, authorial chores were divided among two cousins, Frederic Dannay and Manfred Lee, lifelong detective-story fans who worked in advertising and wrote *The Roman Hat Mystery* as a contest submission. Its acceptance by the Stokes publishing house kicked off a forty-year career that produced thirty novels, dozens of short stories and radio episodes, and a multitude of anthologies. Dannay and Lee were smart enough to purge Ellery of his Vance-like characteristics when the Van Dine novels lost favor with the reading public, and, beginning in 1935, they licensed the Queen novels and character rights to Hollywood. Among the most cleverly devised whodunits ever written, Ellery's cases were invariably streamlined and simplified for the movies. As played on film by Donald Cook, Eddie Quillan, Ralph Bellamy, and William Gargan, he was virtually unrecognizable from his printed-page counterpart. Still, the character was so well liked that his movies still satisfied whodunit fans eager to see their favorite on the big screen.

Fictional New York police commissioner Thatcher Colt, another gentleman sleuth cast in the Philo Vance mold (though, happily, lacking his inspiration's affectations), was the creation of journalist/playwright/editor Fulton Oursler, using the pen name Anthony Abbot. Colt is a fastidious dresser whose courtly demeanor and impeccable manners make him welcome in high society, even though the cases he works often force him to mingle with the lower classes. Brought to cinematic life in the formidable person of well-cast Adolphe Menjou, he appeared to good advantage in two stylish Columbia whodunits, *Night Club Lady* (1932) and *The Circus Queen Murder* (1933), but lacked the indefinable *something* that ensured acceptance by picture patrons.

Undeterred, Columbia licensed the film rights to the first two novels featuring another gentleman sleuth, Rex Stout's Nero Wolfe, a ponderously proportioned dilettante who enjoys beer and raises orchards at his Manhattan townhouse. *Meet Nero Wolfe* (1935, adapted from the character's initial whodunit, *Fer-de-Lance*) cast the distinguished actor Edward Arnold in the title role and adapted the yarn with reasonable fidelity but bungled in giving the role of Wolfe's capable sidekick, Archie Goodwin, to gravel-voiced comic actor Lionel Stander. The following year, studio execs compounded the error by replacing Arnold with the bilious Walter Connolly, who was totally unsuited for

the part. Unimpressed with Columbia's efforts, author Stout refused to option subsequent novels to Hollywood.

Erstwhile pulp fictioneer Erle Stanley Gardner, whose mysteries featuring lawyer-detective Perry Mason soared to the top of national bestseller lists within a couple of years of the character's introduction, fared little better when he excitedly leased the early Mason books to Warner Bros. The ensuing six movie adaptations, made between 1934 and 1937, were breezily entertaining but did such violence to Gardner's creation that he refused future entreaties from Hollywood until 1957, relinquishing story rights for television only after being assured he would be able to exert control over the way Mason and his aides were depicted (which he did, forcefully).

Other sleuths made the leap from printed page to silver screen with better results, but relatively few did so unscathed. Hollywood generally thought it could improve characters who had already and conclusively demonstrated their appeal in other mediums. ⬡

ABOVE LEFT: Director John Huston and his son Tony wait patiently while the crew sets up a shot on location in Ireland for *The List of Adrian Messenger* (1963). Twelve-year-old Tony had a small role in the film, as did his father. Based on a novel by Philip MacDonald, *Messenger* is a smart and skillfully executed mystery with a surprising solution.

ABOVE RIGHT: Edna Mae Oliver as spinster schoolteacher Hildegarde Withers seems to be flirting with James Gleason, playing police detective Oscar Piper, in *The Penguin Pool Murder* (1932), the first of a handful of Withers whodunits produced by RKO. Author Stuart Palmer actually knew Oliver and thought of her as he wrote Hildegarde's adventures.

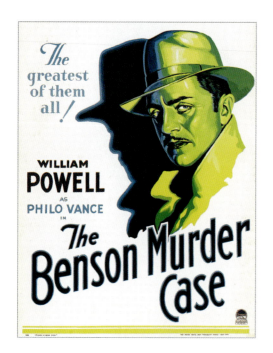

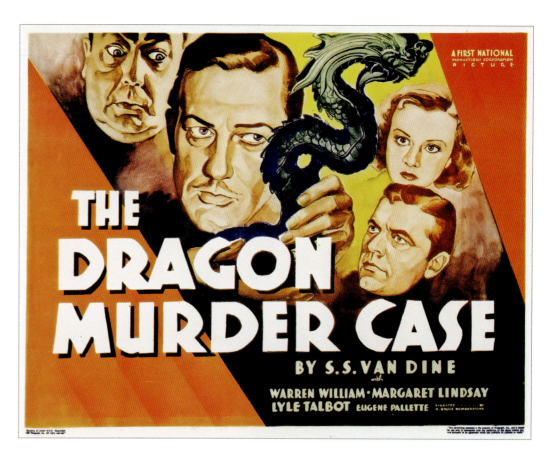

PHILO VANCE

The cerebral sleuth created in 1926 by S. S. Van Dine (real name: Willard Huntingdon Wright) helped usher in what aficionados call the golden age of American detective fiction. His early adventures dominated sales in the genre but also broke into the mainstream and were named in yearly bestseller lists alongside novels by such literary giants as Sinclair Lewis, Thornton Wilder, Booth Tarkinson, and John Galsworthy. It was inevitable that Hollywood would come calling, and though he was a raging snob, Van Dine happily took the huge sums of money offered for screen rights to Vance's exploits. William Powell was the first and best actor to play the erudite detective, a character he would come to loathe. None of his successors were right for the part, although Warren William came close. That might account, at least in part, for the failure of Philo Vance to attain the popularity enjoyed by, say, Charlie Chan or Sherlock Holmes.

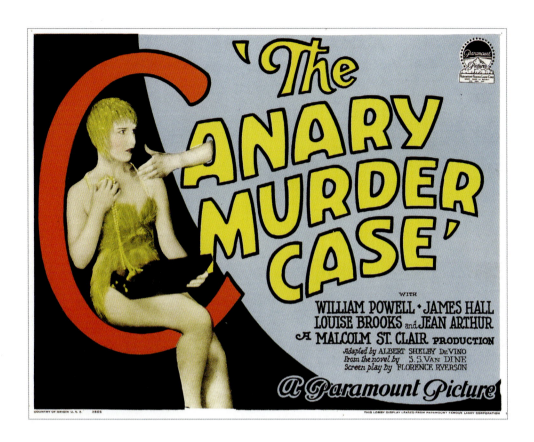

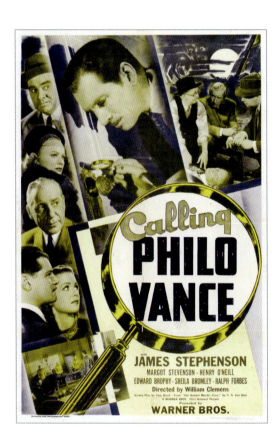

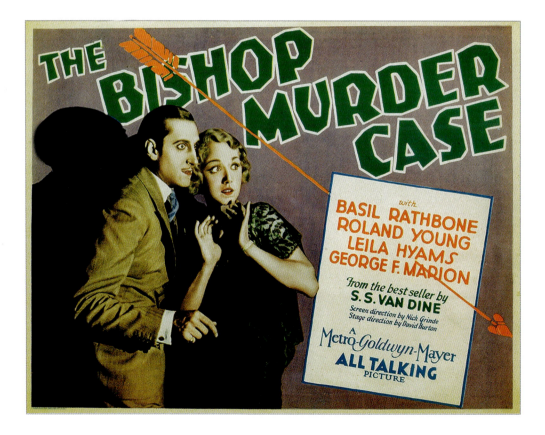

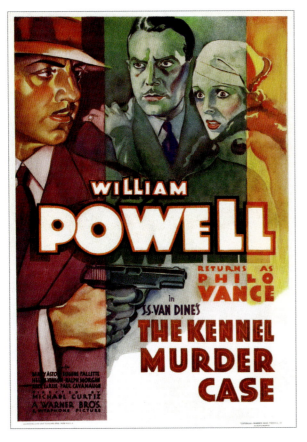

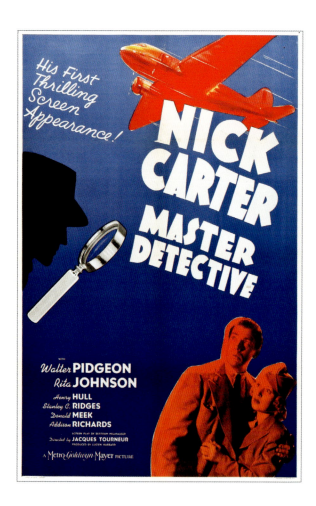

THE SOPHISTICATED SHAMUS

Philo Vance's success inspired a slew of imitations: well-educated, highly cultured, and intellectually gifted men, more often than not socially prominent New Yorkers. Ellery Queen was not only the name of one such sleuth but also the byline used by his marketing-savvy creators. The early Queen closely imitated Vance, but by the time Hollywood came calling, he had loosened up considerably. Still, the films never did justice to the novels from which they ostensibly were adapted. Faring somewhat better was Anthony Abbot's Thatcher Colt, New York's high-society police commissioner. Adolphe Menjou played Colt admirably well in two early '30s Columbia mysteries, and Sidney Blackmer did right by him in a 1942 PRC with Poverty Row production values. Rex Stout's beer-loving, orchard-growing Nero Wolfe was also optioned for two pictures by Columbia; *Meet Nero Wolfe* has an effective Edward Arnold in the title role and is pretty good, but the follow-up, *League of Frightened Men*, features a badly miscast Walter Connolly and bungles one of Stout's finest mysteries. Stolid Walter Pidgeon lent a little class to dime-novel detective Nick Carter, but not enough to keep his series from going beyond three so-so entries. Philip MacDonald's urbane investigator Anthony Gethryn was portrayed in *The List of Adrian Messenger*, a delightful 1963 romp.

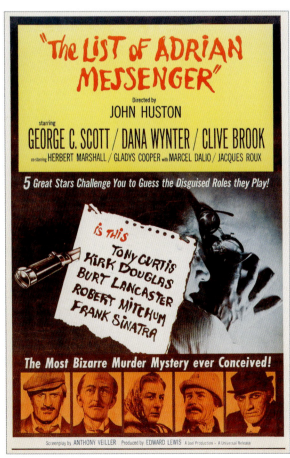

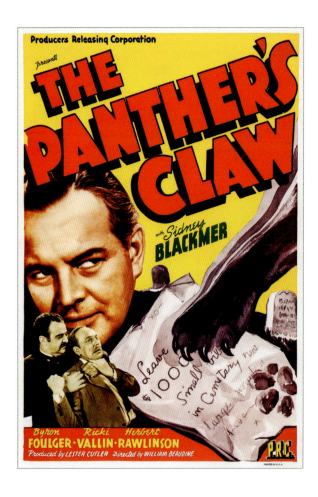

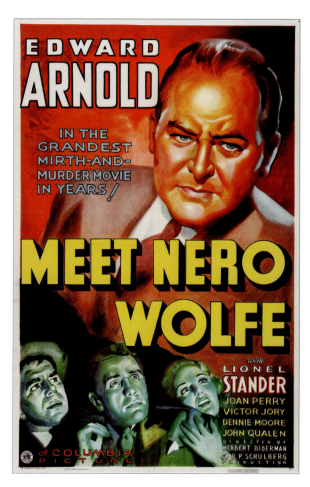

"An Extraordinary Film!

A rare unpredictable thriller worthy of special attention!" —REX REED, N.Y. Daily News

ORSON WELLES · MARLENE JOBERT · ANTHONY PERKINS · MICHEL PICCOLI

in Ellery Queen's **Ten Days' Wonder**

Produced by **André Génovès** · Adaption by **Paul Gegauff** · Screenplay by **Eugene Archer** and **Paul Gardner** · Based on the novel by **Ellery Queen** · Directed by **Claude Chabrol**

A Syn-Frank Enterprises, Inc. Presentation · Distributed by Levitt-Pickman Film Corporation · Technicolor®

PG PARENTAL GUIDANCE SUGGESTED
Some material may not be suitable for pre-teenagers

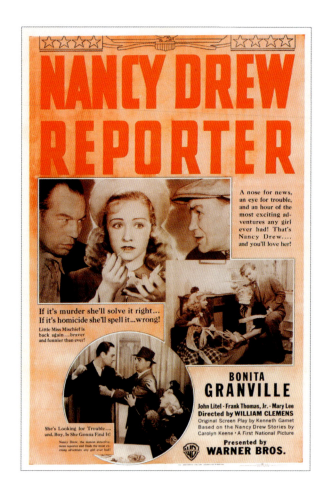

DISTAFF DETECTIVES

Crime-solving females in American mystery fiction date back to the spinster sleuth of Mary Roberts Rinehart's *The Circular Staircase* (published in 1908, filmed in 1915), but investigators of the fairer sex really began showing up their male counterparts in the 1930s. Stuart Palmer's schoolmarm shamus Hildegarde Withers made her striking debut in a 1931 novel, *The Penguin Pool Murder*, brought to movie screens the following year with matronly Edna Mae Oliver in the lead role. Palmer actually wrote the Withers mysteries with Oliver in mind, and she appeared in two more film adaptations before relinquishing the part to Helen Broderick and Zasu Pitts. Mignon G. Eberhart's matronly nurse Sarah Keate plied her trade in numerous whodunits, adapted by Warners and Twentieth Century-Fox with a bewildering array of actresses of varying ages: Helen Broderick (again), Jane Darwell, Marguerite Churchill, Kay Linaker, and Ann Sheridan. Warners also produced a short but satisfying series of four entries with former child star Bonita Granville as girl detective Nancy Drew.

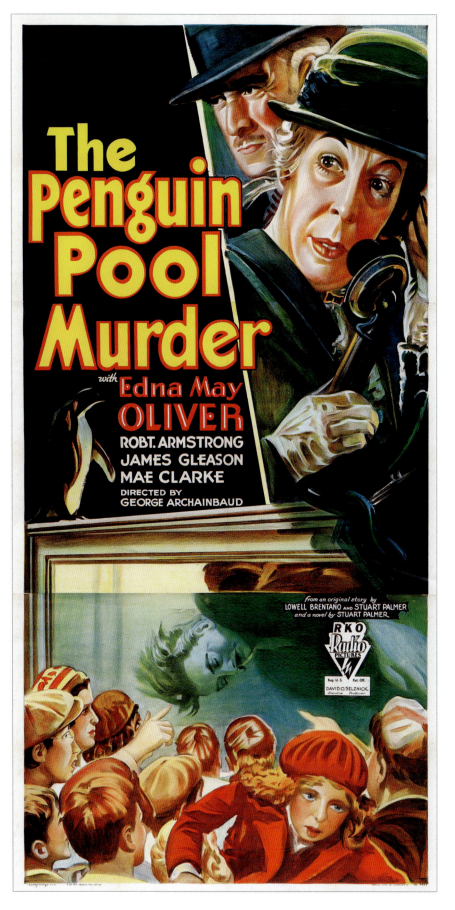

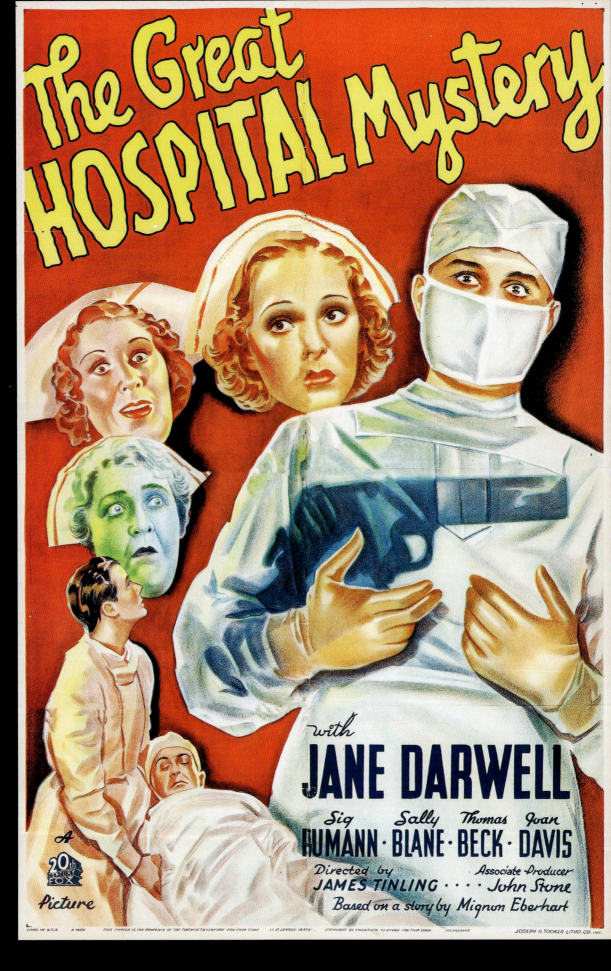

THE PATIENT in ROOM 18

PATRIC KNOWLES · ANN SHERIDAN

ROSELLA TOWNE · JEAN BENEDICT
ERIC STANLEY · JOHN RIDGELY
Directed by BOBBY CONNOLLY and CRANE WILBUR
A FIRST NATIONAL PICTURE Presented by WARNER BROS. Pictures Inc.

WHO WILL BE THE KILLERS NEXT VICTIM?

STARTLING! BAFFLING!

MYSTERY HOUSE

with
DICK PURCELL
ANN SHERIDAN
ANNE NAGEL
WILLIAM HOPPER

The Family Called it
ACCIDENT!
The Coroner called it
SUICIDE!!
The Police called it
MURDER!!!

THE NURSE'S SECRET

with
LEE PATRICK
REGIS TOOMEY
Directed by Noel M. Smith
Presented by
WARNER BROS.

FORTY NAUGHTY GIRLS

with
JAMES GLEASON
ZASU PITTS

DIRECTED BY EDWARD CLINE
PRODUCED BY WILLIAM SISTROM
SCREEN PLAY BY JOHN GREY

PRIVATE EYES AND CLEVER LAWYERS

Independent investigators, occasionally working outside the law and frequently at odds with police, were ubiquitous figures in fiction and film alike, especially during the '30s and '40s. Brett Halliday's (a.k.a. Davis Dresser) Michael Shayne rocketed to favor in 1939 and made his screen debut the following year. Lloyd Nolan took the role in a series for Twentieth Century-Fox; he didn't physically resemble Halliday's character but had the requisite insouciant attitude. Since Fox turned out Shayne movies faster than his author could write novels, the studio licensed mysteries written by other authors and replaced their detectives with Mike. (*Time to Kill*, for example, was based on Chandler's Philip Marlowe yarn *The High Window*.) Earlier, Warner Bros. had licensed Erle Stanley Gardner's novels featuring criminal lawyer Perry Mason. In his first ten or so exploits, Mason was as hard-boiled as any private eye and did a lot of his own investigating, but Warners made him an eccentric gourmand and put too much comedy in his films. Warren William played him first, followed by Ricardo Cortez and Donald Woods. Incensed, Gardner refused to license any further Mason yarns to Hollywood studios until the 1950s TV show, over which he exercised considerable control.

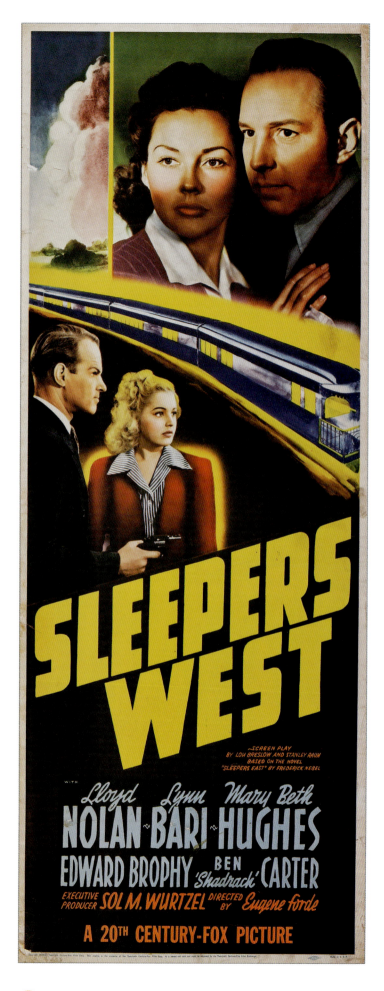

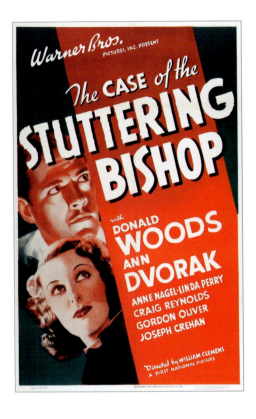

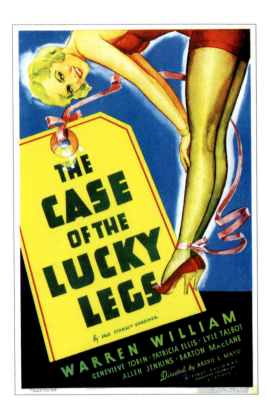

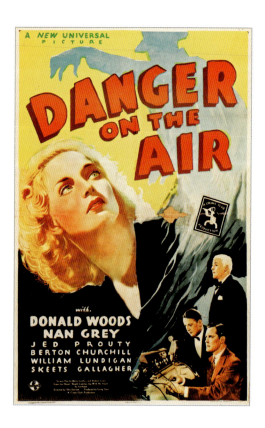

UNIVERSAL'S CRIME CLUB SERIES

In 1928, the publishing company Doubleday and Doran launched a subsidiary, the Crime Club, Inc., to specialize in crime fiction and sell books not only in stores but via subscription, with members receiving new releases by mail every month. In addition to importing a large number of mysteries that had been previously published in England, the Crime Club also became home to such popular characters as the Saint, Bulldog Drummond, and Dr. Fu Manchu—all of whom became movie regulars. But in 1937, Universal Pictures cut a deal with Doubleday and Doran to film adaptations of successful Crime Club titles featuring lesser-known characters. The pictures were strictly B grade in terms of star power and production mounting, but they were largely faithful to their sources. The trio of entries based on Jonathan Latimer's ribald Bill Crane mysteries—*The Westland Case*, *The Lady in the Morgue*, and *The Last Warning*—were especially good. The series lasted only two years, though, because theaters were flooded with whodunits featuring better-known detective characters. Four of the eight Crime Club movies were sold to Astor Pictures and reissued during the '40s.

6

ROGUES
AND
ADVENTURERS

FIGHTING CRIME THEIR OWN WAY

During the Depression and World War II years, filmgoers' hunger for crime and mystery films is practically insatiable. Orthodox murder mysteries are produced with considerable frequency, often boasting top stars and grade A production mounting. Less expensive B thrillers are far more numerous, especially those featuring popular series characters. Many of the protagonists of these films are reformed criminals or freelance adventurers who don't strictly adhere to the law while they pursue and apprehend evildoers. Nonetheless, movie patrons love them ...

H. C. "Sapper" McNeile's Bulldog Drummond had already appeared on-screen several times, in British-made silent movies, when, in 1929, Samuel Goldwyn produced an adaptation of a 1921 Drummond stage play written by McNeile and Gerald du Maurier. Not surprisingly titled *Bulldog Drummond*, it contained the first talking-picture performance by the debonair Ronald Colman, who bore no physical resemblance whatsoever to the character described in McNeile's novels. It didn't matter; Colman's devil-may-care demeanor struck just the right note. Goldwyn's film struck box-office gold but didn't inspire a series, though Colman was induced to reprise the role in *Bulldog Drummond Strikes Back*, a 1934 production of Darryl F. Zanuck's recently formed Twentieth Century Pictures, also starring Loretta Young and Warner Oland (the latter taking a brief respite from his Charlie Chan chores). A lighthearted and thoroughly enjoyable thriller, it erased forever the public perception of McNeile's hero as a brash, homely brawler more likely to use his fists than his wits.

Licensing the Drummond character from its author a year before he died, Paramount Pictures tested the waters with *Bulldog Drummond Escapes* (1937), starring up-and-coming British actor Ray Milland as the suave adventurer. Its box-office performance was something less than spectacular but good enough to launch a series of fast-moving B pictures, with twenty-four-year-old John Howard the latest to play the Bulldog. The first three entries feature obscure Paramount starlet Louise Campbell as Drummond's fiancée, Phyllis, and John Barrymore as Scotland Yard colonel Neilson, with Reginald Denny as comedic sidekick

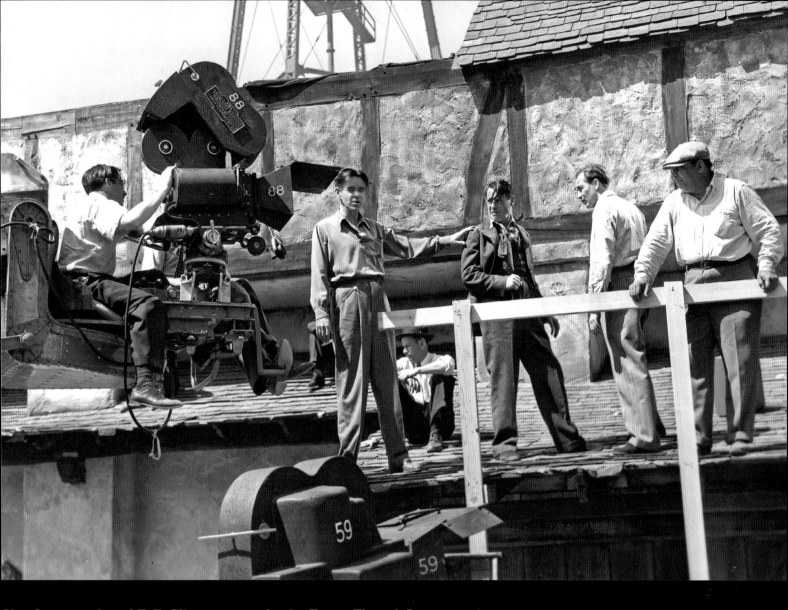

Algy Longworth and E. E. Clive as trusted valet Tenny. Though Barrymore's was strictly a supporting role, he received top billing and prominent placement in the poster art. But the former "Great Profile" had become a hopeless alcoholic and was released after three films, as was Campbell. H. B. Warner replaced Barrymore as Neilson, and Heather Angel assumed the role of Phyllis, which she had played in *Bulldog Drummond Escapes*. The series was terminated in 1939; periodic attempts to revive it were met with audience indifference. Rather amazingly, however, the Bulldog returned briefly during the Swinging Sixties in a baffling attempt to capitalize on the James Bond phenomenon. Finally, after two lackluster entries starring Richard Johnson as Drummond, *Deadlier Than the Male* (1967) and *Some Girls Do* (1969), the Bulldog was retired for good.

As a young man, Leslie Charteris worked in a tin mine, on a rubber plantation, and as a gold prospector. But he always wanted to be a writer and by the age of twenty had already penned—and sold—three novels. The third, *Meet the Tiger* (1928), introduced a daring young man named Simon Templar, nicknamed "The Saint" for his initials. Some considered Templar a soldier of fortune, but he preferred to think of himself as a modern Robin Hood, preying

ABOVE: Director James Hogan (*center*) rehearses a fight scene between Eduardo Ciannelli and John Howard in *Bulldog Drummond's Bride* (1939), the final entry in Paramount's popular series of Drummond adventures.

OPPOSITE: *Bulldog Drummond* (1929) was a highly acclaimed film of the early talkie days, taking the already burgeoning career of leading man Ronald Colman to a new level and making a star of inexperienced leading lady Joan Bennett. It also enhanced the reputation of production designer William Cameron Menzies, whose imaginative sets and lighting schemes were major contributing factors to the film's effectiveness.

on wealthy criminals and occasionally being hired as an avenging angel. Very popular in Britain, the Saint stories enjoyed a similar reception in the US during the 1930s. RKO took notice and in 1938 produced a thrifty adaptation of *The Saint in New York*, the author's bestselling book to date. Louis Hayward plays Templar as debonair but dangerous, coolly eliminating enemies sworn to kill him. Amazingly, this unassuming little B picture proved to be one of RKO's top moneymakers of the year, leading the studio to announce that it would feature the Saint in a series. British actor George Sanders, until now cast primarily as a smooth heavy, took the role from Hayward and made it his own in five extremely well-received pictures.

Charteris, who had lobbied for Cary Grant to play his character, insisted that the Saint films receive bigger budgets and better actors in supporting roles. He became so obstreperous that RKO severed ties with him in 1941. Rather than sacrifice a very profitable series, though, the studio purchased the movie rights to a similar character, Michael Arlen's Gay Lawrence, a.k.a. the Falcon, who was essentially just the Saint by another name. Sanders played this character exactly as he had Simon Templar, and producer Howard Benedict lavished the same care on the Falcon films as he had on the Saint series. Eventually tiring of the role, Sanders relinquished it after several entries to his actor sibling, Tom Conway, who had been introduced in—what else?—*The Falcon's Brother* (1942). Conway played Tom Lawrence in another ten films before RKO terminated the series in 1946. Posters turned out by the major studios' art departments during this period were generally first rate, but it should be noted that RKO's sheets for the Saint and Falcon films were exceptionally well designed and illustrated, with vivid colors, dramatic shading, and superb likenesses of the actors pictured.

ABOVE LEFT: *Enter Arsene Lupin* (1944) was a breezy little thriller that didn't take itself too seriously and defied tradition by having its likeably larcenous protagonist apprehended at the end. At that time, Universal Pictures was giving Hungarian émigré Charles Korvin a big buildup, but audiences stubbornly refused to accept him as a leading man.

ABOVE RIGHT: On the set of *Enter Arsene Lupin*, during a hastily convened birthday party, producer/director Ford Beebe (*holding scroll*), surrounded by crew members, presents Korvin (*in jacket*) with some phony proclamation dreamed up by Universal's publicity department.

During the 1930s and '40s, Harry Cohn's Columbia Pictures proved the most series crazy of the major studios (although Columbia, like Universal, was considered a "mini-major"). Without its own slate of major stars—such as those maintained by M-G-M, Paramount, Warner Bros., and Twentieth Century-Fox—Columbia relied for its financial well-being on loads of inexpensive B's, produced on an assembly-line basis, like so many automobiles, and shoveled into the marketplace as fast as they could be completed. Among its seemingly innumerable crime and mystery series, two particularly good ones feature heroes who have operated on the wrong side of the law for years before reforming. There are other similarities between Boston Blackie and Michael Lanyard, a.k.a. the Lone Wolf: Both have been on the straight and narrow for lengthy periods but are immediately suspected by local law enforcement when a major theft takes place in their jurisdictions. Both enjoy cordial relationships with the very police detectives who, time and again, leap to the conclusion that *they* are responsible for the latest outrage. Both have comedic sidekicks whose intelligence leaves a great deal to be desired but who compensate for it with boundless loyalty.

Boston Blackie, a former jewel thief and safecracker, was the protagonist of some two dozen short stories written between 1914 and 1920 by Jack Boyle, a former newspaper editor and opium addict who had turned to crime himself and served a stretch in San Quentin. Michael Lanyard, another master thief, appeared in eight novels penned by veteran fiction writer Louis Joseph Vance from 1914 to 1933. Both appeared in numerous silent films but never captured the imaginations of moviegoers until they were played by Chester Morris and Warren William, respectively, in Columbia potboilers short on production values but long on winning personalities and predictably breezy entertainment. ⬡

ABOVE LEFT: *The Lone Wolf Spy Hunt* (1939) marked the first appearance of Warren William as gentleman cracksman Michael Lanyard, although by this time he was well known to fans of mystery movies for having earlier portrayed private investigator Philo Vance and suave defense attorney Perry Mason.

ABOVE RIGHT: A publicity photo of Warren William and the adorable ingenue Ida Lupino, taken to promote *The Lone Wolf Spy Hunt*. Lupino gave a good account of herself but was overshadowed by Columbia's resident glamour girl, Rita Hayworth, who would soon become the studio's top box-office attraction.

BULLDOG DRUMMOND

Author H. C. McNeile initially described his creation as possessing "that cheerful sort of ugliness which inspires immediate confidence in its owner." On occasion, he also exhibited characteristics that are not usually associated with heroic characters in crime stories—arrogance, petulance, and a short temper. But Hugh Drummond's portrayers in cinema were almost exactly the opposite of their printed-page counterpart. Ronald Colman, who played the Bulldog in two early talkies, was not only handsome but also amazingly ebullient, even in the face of danger. Since Colman's Drummond films were enormous critical and commercial successes, subsequent actors cast in the role tried to emulate him to at least some degree. Ray Milland came closest, his suave manner and English accent being major assets. John Howard, just twenty-three when he signed to star in Paramount's series, didn't attempt to speak with an accent, but his boyish exuberance played well with audiences. Walter Pidgeon was too stolid for the part; Ron Randell was colorless. In the '60s, Richard Johnson twice essayed the role, which had been altered to make Bulldog like James Bond—a serious miscalculation that resulted in two flops.

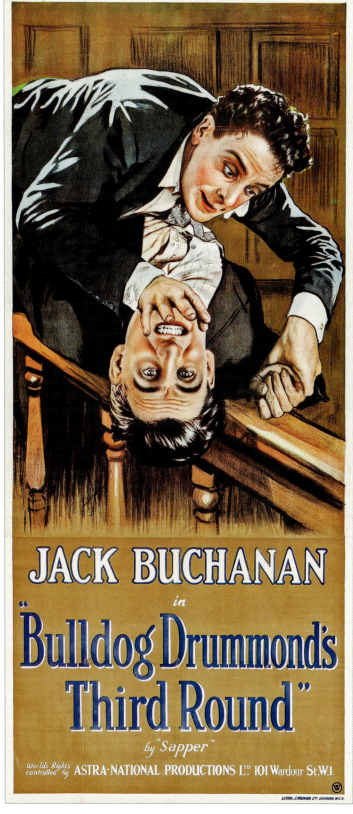

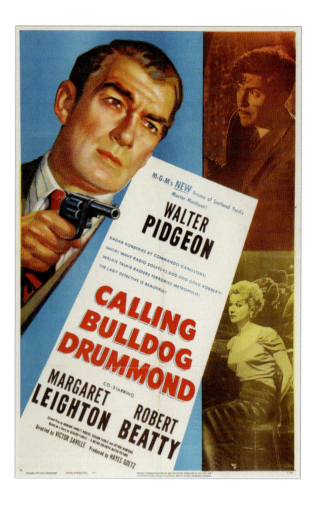

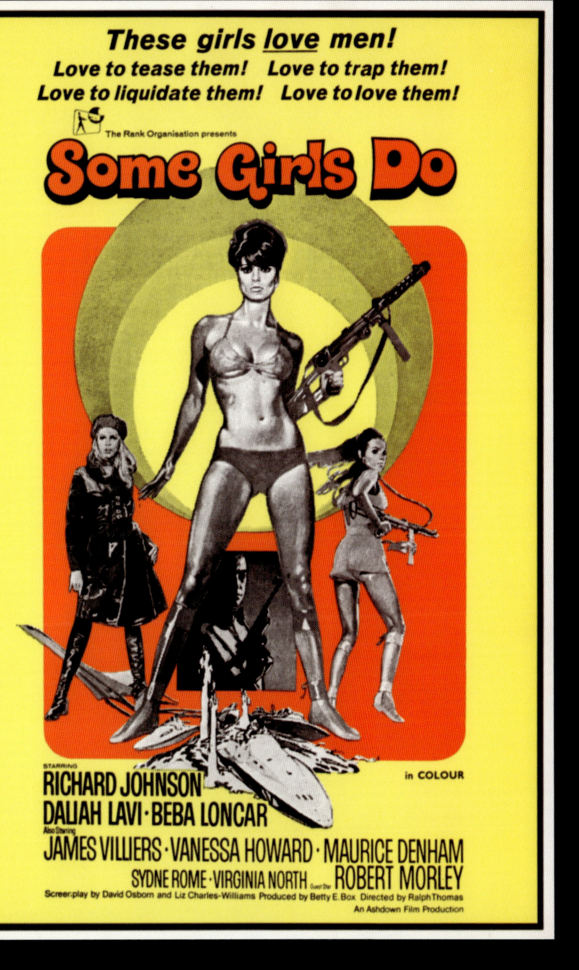

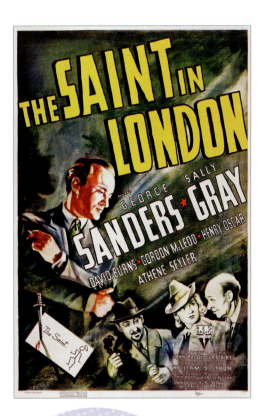

THE SAINT

The "modern Robin Hood," created by Leslie Charteris at the tender age of twenty, was a natural for motion pictures, which stressed the character's love of dangerous adventure. His first film, *The Saint in New York* (1938), established Simon Templar as an avenging angel for hire. Louis Hayward displayed cold-blooded professionalism and a sardonic manner that delighted picture patrons, but he was unwilling to appear in follow-up films. Fellow Brit George Sanders assumed the role with *The Saint Strikes Back* (1939). The series ended after six entries when Charteris—who felt that Cary Grant should have been cast as Templar, and complained bitterly about the films—annoyed RKO executives to such an extent that they refused to continue it. Two British-made Saint films, released in North America by RKO and Republic Pictures, respectively, blundered by casting the reed-thin, flop-eared Hugh Sinclair in the lead role. Charteris was much happier when Roger Moore became the Saint for a British-made TV series during the '60s. A few episodes of the series were cobbled together for theatrical release as *Vendetta for the Saint*.

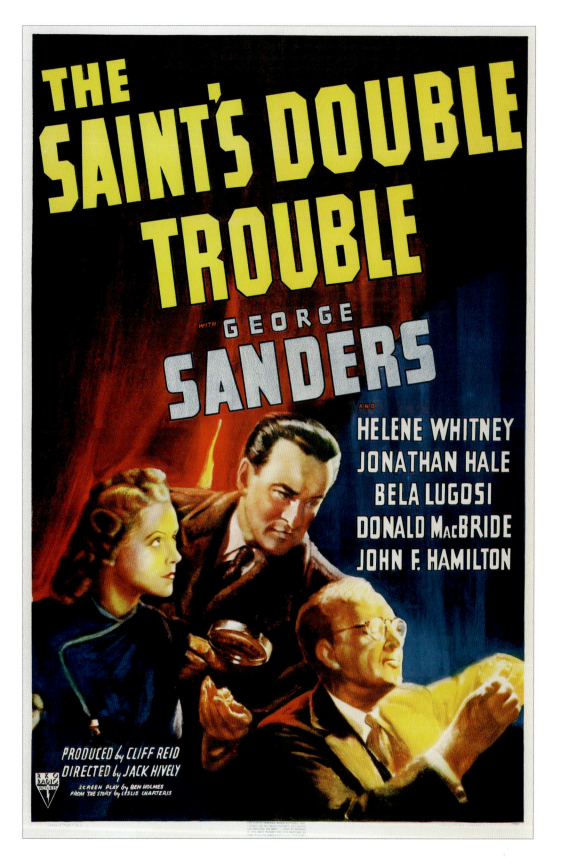

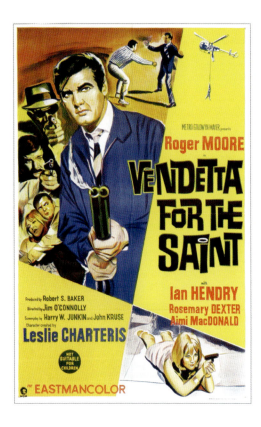

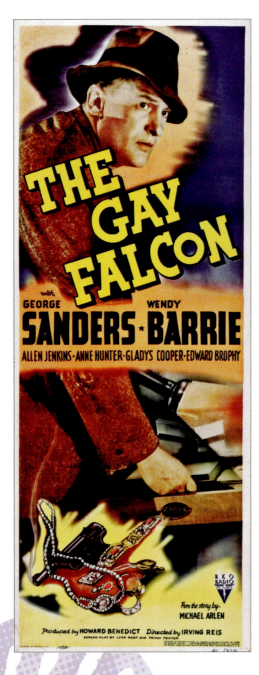

THE FALCON

By 1941, RKO had had a bellyful of Leslie Charteris but was reluctant to terminate a popular series of B thrillers. The solution: license screen rights to a little-known fictional character and make him over in the Saint's image and likeness. George Sanders was retained to play Gay Lawrence, alias the Falcon, just as he had the Saint. Sanders grew bored with both the scripts and his characterization, so in another inspired touch born out of necessity, RKO decided to replace him with his real-life brother, Tom Conway, who would play the Falcon's brother, Tom Lawrence. The younger sibling's characterization was not markedly different, and if anything Conway was more energetic than Sanders. He enjoyed support from comic-relief sidekicks played by Allen Jenkins, Don Barclay, and Ed Brophy. Despite their threadbare production values, the Falcon films built and maintained a surprisingly loyal fan base before fizzling out in 1947. A subsequent attempt to revive the character in the person of real-life magician John Calvert resulted in three mediocre movies that lost money.

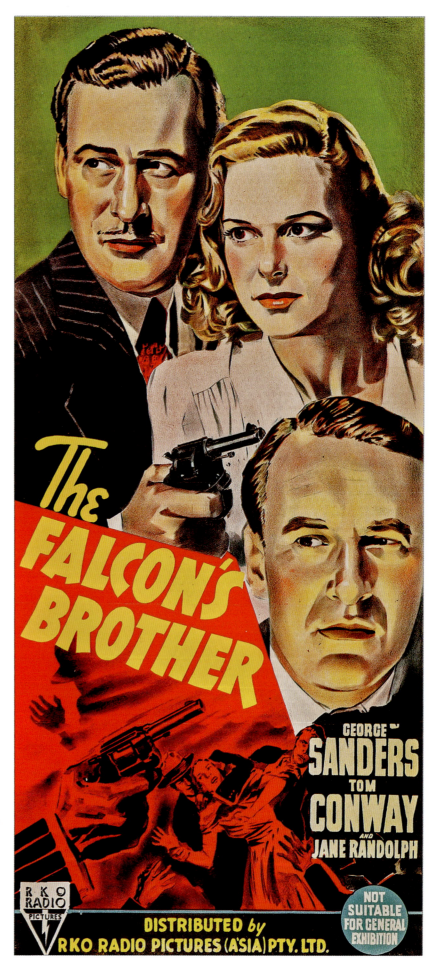

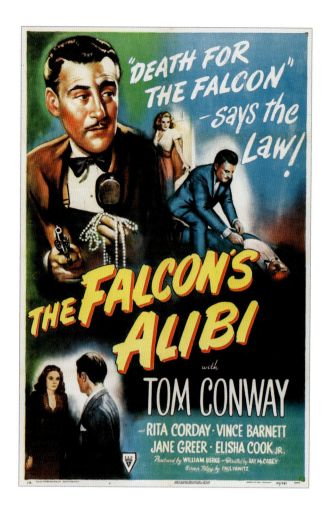

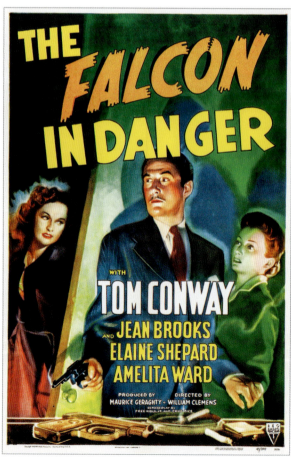

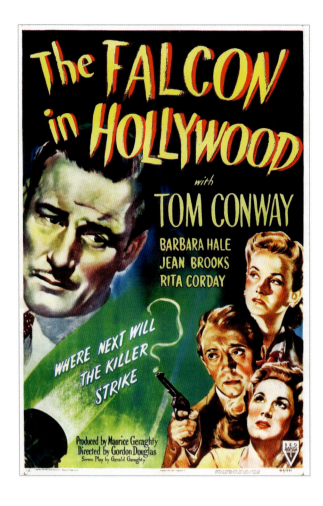

THE LONE WOLF

Unlike such adventurers as Bulldog Drummond, the Saint, and the Falcon, Michael Lanyard—a former thief whose penchant for working sans partners or assistants earned him the "Lone Wolf" sobriquet—had a criminal record. Lanyard fully reforms over the course of events described in Louis Joseph Vance's *The Lone Wolf* (1914), but the character's film appearances nearly always have him being accused of a crime and having to prove his innocence by apprehending the real culprit. Handsome stage actor Bert Lytell made his screen debut as Lanyard in *The Lone Wolf*, a 1917 adaptation of Vance's novel, and reprised the role numerous times throughout the silent era. Melvyn Douglas starred in *The Lone Wolf Returns* (1935), and a wildly miscast Francis Lederer portrayed the reformed crook in *The Lone Wolf in Paris* (1938), but it is early talkie star Warren William who's best remembered in the part. Another matinee idol, nicknamed "the poor man's John Barrymore" for his chiseled features, William played Lanyard in nine Columbia B pictures made between 1939 and 1943. He brought a sense of fun to the character, and he wasn't averse to self-deprecating gags.

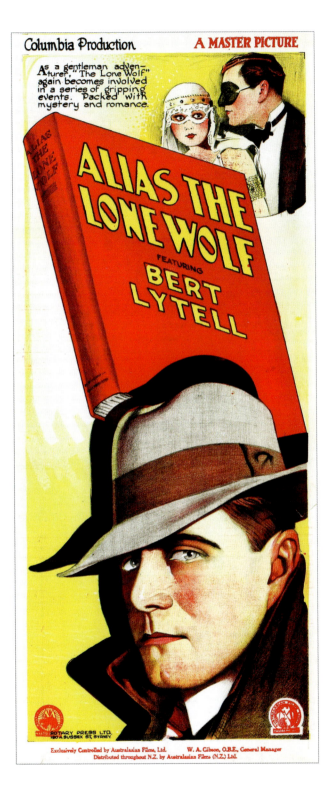

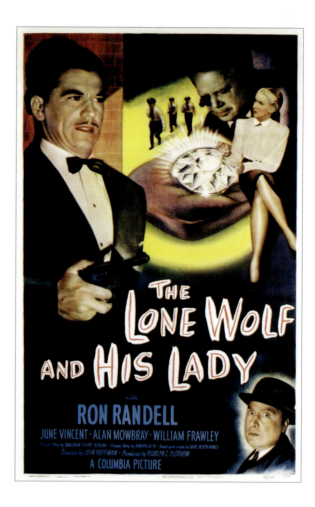

BOSTON BLACKIE

Another reformed thief—a master safecracker, specifically—with a prison record, Boston Blackie had an interesting genesis. His creator was Jack Boyle, a former journalist and newspaper editor who turned to crime to support his opium habit. Captured, convicted, and imprisoned in San Quentin, Boyle wrote Blackie's adventures from his jail cell. On-screen, the character was played by Bert Lytell, Lionel Barrymore, William Russell, and Raymond Glenn during the silent era. Chester Morris, another stage and vaudeville actor who migrated to Hollywood when talkies became the rage, took the role in 1941 and basically reinvented it. His Blackie wasn't as somber as Boyle's; Morris affected a breezy, fast-talking manner, and he rarely seemed to take the character's predicaments seriously. Morris was a talented amateur magician, so Blackie was too. While on the run from the police (which happens in every one of Columbia's fourteen series entries made between 1941 and 1949), Blackie frequently resorts to intricate disguises, enabling Morris to use a variety of accents and dialects. Clearly, the actor was having fun, which rubbed off on moviegoers.

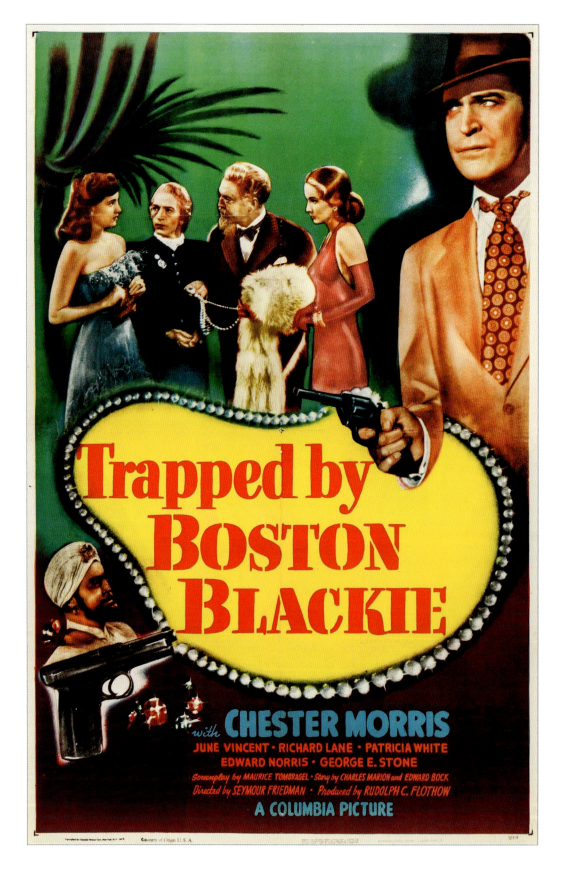

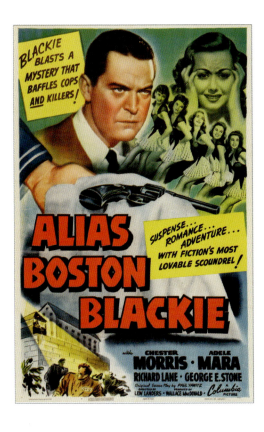

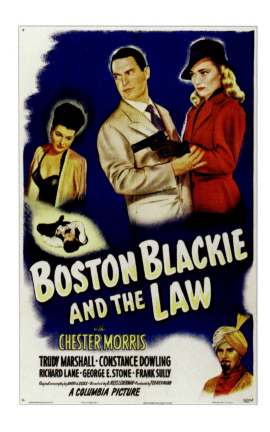

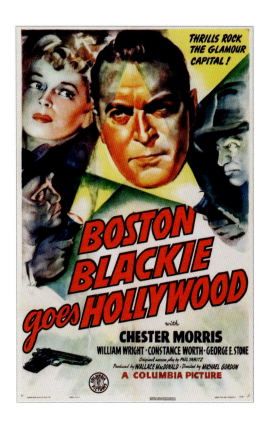

GENTLEMEN CRACKSMEN

The Lone Wolf and Boston Blackie had forsaken crime by the time their authors began chronicling their later exploits. Other professional thieves of fiction include Maurice Leblanc's Arsène Lupin, E. W. Hornung's Raffles, and the granddaddy of them all, O. Henry's Jimmy Valentine. The latter, introduced in the 1903 short story "A Retrieved Reformation," was immortalized in a 1910 stage play, *Alias Jimmy Valentine*, which was adapted for motion pictures three times during the silent era alone. He came out of retirement, so to speak, in two Republic B movies, *The Return of Jimmy Valentine* (1936) and *The Affairs of Jimmy Valentine* (1942). Raffles, too, was a frequent presence in picture palaces, his portrayers including John Barrymore (1917) and House Peters (1925) in silents, and Ronald Colman (1930) and David Niven (1939) in talkies. Barrymore also essayed the role of Lupin in 1932; Melvyn Douglas (1935) and Charles Korvin (1944) followed him. Whether retired, reformed, or still plying their trade, the gentlemen cracksmen were invariably courteous, chivalrous, and—most importantly—one step ahead of the police.

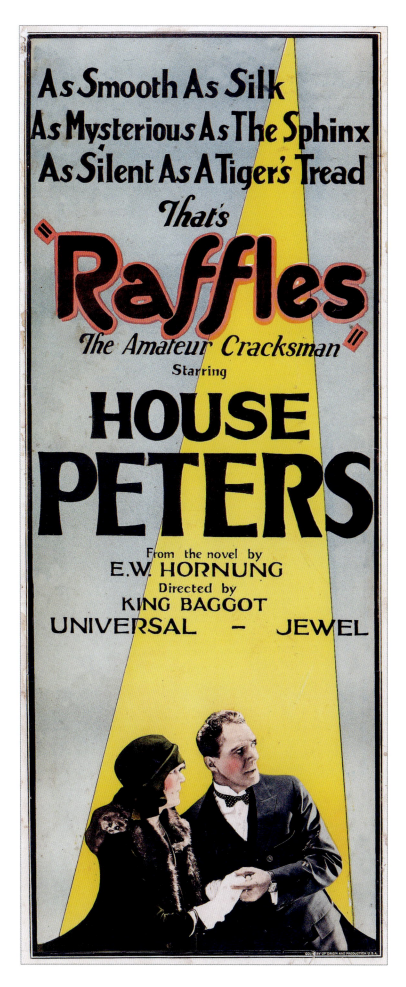

ADAPTED FRO
SCATT

PRIVATE EYES, MURDEROUS MOBSTERS, AND MORE

ABOVE: When Warner Bros. took a third crack at *The Maltese Falcon* (1941), it was considered a gamble, being the tyro directorial effort of screenwriter John Huston and the second starring vehicle for Humphrey Bogart. The studio's art department didn't even bother using a newly photographed image of Bogie for this poster, which shows him as "Mad Dog" Earle from the just-released *High Sierra*.

The demand for crime and mystery films remains constant throughout Hollywood's golden age, forcing studios to come up with numerous variations on the same basic themes, lest audiences tire of homogeneous product. Theater patrons crave uniformity only to the extent that they can count on being entertained for an hour or so; otherwise, they're perfectly happy with exposure to different approaches. They demand only that criminals be brought to justice by a story's end—where, how, and by whom is left to the filmmakers, and even the occasional lampooning of familiar detective-movie tropes is welcomed . . .

The "hard-boiled" detective, a character type popularized by pulp-fiction magazines during Prohibition and the early Depression years, often operates outside the law and administers rough justice to miscreants beyond the system's reach. He is half investigator and half vigilante, destined to prowl what crime-fiction writer Raymond Chandler called "these mean streets"—the shadowy thoroughfares of crime-ridden cities. Often, he is the only means of righting wrongs ignored by crooked cops and corrupt politicians, though this is a burden he would just as soon not have to shoulder.

The apotheosis of the hard-boiled detective novel was reached in 1930 with Dashiell Hammett's *The Maltese Falcon*, which introduced San Francisco–based shamus Sam Spade. Warner Bros. optioned the property almost immediately after its publication and cast silent-era star Ricardo Cortez as Spade. The eponymous film adaptation went into release in 1931 and was moderately successful despite the miscasting of Cortez in the lead. Hammett's yarn was remade five years later as *Satan Met a Lady*. The plot remained more or less intact, but all the character names were changed and the film played for laughs. Warren William portrayed the detective (not quite as tough as Spade) and Bette Davis took the femme fatale role—with the greatest of reluctance, we might add. The film flopped—deservedly so.

John Huston had been screenwriting for a full decade when he began lobbying his employers at Warner Bros. to let him direct a film. He was finally granted

the opportunity with several caveats: he would have to choose a property the studio already owned, use a contract player instead of an expensive star in the lead, and hold costs down to the level of an expensive B picture. Huston picked *The Maltese Falcon* for his directorial debut and cast Humphrey Bogart as Sam Spade. (He had previously written the script for Bogie's best film to date, *High Sierra*.) Then Huston did something *really* shocking: rather than try to "improve" the story, as was Hollywood's wont, he adhered faithfully to Hammett's novel, using most of the pulp scribe's original dialogue.

Warner Bros. didn't have big expectations for the second remake of a property it had owned for more than ten years. The original poster design features a photo of Bogart from *High Sierra*, in the hope that moviegoers would remember that film and take a chance on *Falcon*. But the picture was a surprise success, eliciting rapturous reviews, exceeding box-office expectations, and scoring three Oscar nominations (including Best Picture).

ABOVE: Director Howard Hawks rehearses cast members on the set of *The Big Sleep* (1946), adapted from Raymond Chandler's first Philip Marlowe novel. *Left to right:* Hawks, Sonia Darrin, an unidentified script girl, Lauren Bacall, Humphrey Bogart, and Louis Jean Heydt. Chandler's plot was so complicated that Hawks and screenwriter Leigh Brackett phoned the author during production to find out who killed a minor character. Chandler replied that he didn't know either.

ABOVE: Director Edward Dmytryk (*seated at left*) coaches Dick Powell and Claire Trevor on the playing of a difficult scene from *Murder My Sweet* (1944), RKO's second adaptation of Raymond Chandler's Philip Marlowe mystery *Farewell My Lovely*—previously brought to the screen, sans Marlowe, as *The Falcon Takes Over*.

The impact of *Maltese Falcon* on subsequent mysteries featuring hard-boiled private eyes is virtually incalculable. Movie buffs can see it in countless films made since, right up to *Chinatown* (1974)—in which, coincidentally, Huston had a substantial supporting role. An equally tough Hammett novel, *The Glass Key*, was brought to the screen twice, in 1935 and 1942, with exemplary results.

Next to Sam Spade, pulp fiction's most influential hard-boiled private dick was Raymond Chandler's Philip Marlowe. Marlowe's first "official" appearance takes place in Chandler's debut novel, *The Big Sleep*, but that yarn was cannibalized from several shorter tales originally published in the classic pulp magazine *Black Mask*. He first reached the nation's movie theaters disguised (or perhaps we should say camouflaged) as the Falcon, a B-movie detective played by George Sanders, in *The Falcon Takes Over* (1942), which uses the plot of Chandler's second book, *Farewell My Lovely*, substituting the more familiar character for Philip Marlowe. Two years later, the novel was properly adapted and released as *Murder My Sweet*, which surprisingly but effectively cast former movie-musical crooner Dick Powell as Marlowe. Humphrey Bogart himself took a crack at the part in a 1946 adaptation of *The Big Sleep*. There would be several other movie Marlowes, including—most improbably— Elliott Gould.

Spade, Marlowe, and Mickey Spillane's Mike Hammer came to personify the hard-boiled detective, but a dozen or more imitators would follow until the subgenre finally petered out in the '70s.

Another crowd-pleasing innovation introduced in a Dashiell Hammett mystery novel was *The Thin Man*'s sleuthing spouses, Nick and Nora Charles. Hammett conceived them as idealized versions of himself and longtime lover Lillian Hellman, but they materialized on screen in the considerably more charming persons of William Powell and Myrna Loy. They played Nick and Nora in six comedic mysteries made between 1934 and 1947, but the first, taken directly from Hammett's novel, was by far the best. The Powell–Loy chemistry carried the rest, but, as mysteries, the last several series entries were feeble, to say the least. Nonetheless, the craze for married detectives continued throughout the 1930s and '40s.

The Thin Man and its progeny placed nearly as great an emphasis on humor as on homicide, but they remained character-driven. A secondary school of mirthful mysteries was star-driven, with comedy the predominant element. Beginning in the Depression years and continuing through World War II and even into the early '50s, the biggest comedy teams and most of the solo humorists in film took turns spoofing the genre. Abbott and Costello, Laurel and Hardy, Bergen and McCarthy, Martin and Lewis, the Ritz Brothers, Bob Hope, Jack Oakie, Milton Berle, and Red Skeleton were among those funnymen who poked fun at movie mysteries to good effect. The posters for these films frequently employed caricature and cartoonish illustrations, rather than the straight portrait renderings common to dramatic subjects. They also occasionally pictured the stars with Holmesian accouterments, such as deerstalker caps and magnifying glasses, just to ensure that passersby glancing at the posters outside theaters had no illusion as to the films' intentions.

Another character-driven trend that favored the comedic focused on female crime solvers more or less forced by circumstances into detective work. The most entertaining of these was demon reporter Torchy Blane, played by fast-talking Glenda Farrell in a series of B mysteries produced by Warner Bros., which devoted more celluloid to "sob sisters" than any other studio in town. Torchy had the edge on her rival news hawks by virtue of her relationship with police lieutenant Steve McBride (played by perennial movie heavy Barton MacLane, in a pleasant change of pace). There were others, but she was the best by far. ✪

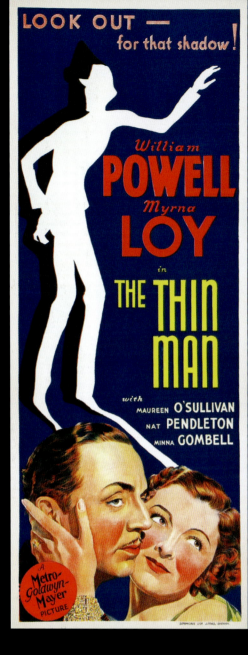

ABOVE: Posters for *The Thin Man* (1934) invariably used a slender silhouette that most moviegoers believed was that of Powell's character Nick Charles, rather than Edward Ellis's Clyde Wynant, the scientist whose mysterious disappearance undergirds the film's plot. But just like Boris Karloff, who became associated with the name Frankenstein even though he famously played Frankenstein's monster, William Powell had to get used to being called the Thin Man.

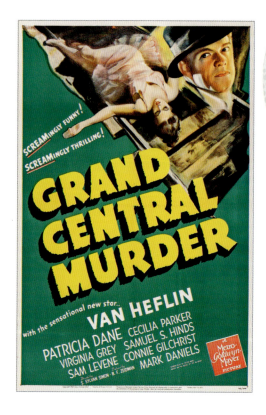

THE HARD-BOILED DICKS

"Hard-boiled" detectives—those whose approaches to crime solving rely more on physical force than deductive reasoning—were originally found in the pages of *Black Mask*, an influential pulp magazine of the 1920s and '30s. The first was Carroll John Daly's Race Williams, who described himself as "a halfway house between the cops and the crooks." Race was not the sort to analyze cigar ash or footprints in soggy earth; he learns things by roughing up suspects and often administers justice with a well-placed bullet. Daly was the grandfather of a genre whose most famous exponents include Dashiell Hammett, Raymond Chandler, and Mickey Spillane. Their hard-boiled private eyes—Sam Spade, Philip Marlowe, and Mike Hammer, respectively—were destined for the movies, being colorful characters to begin with. Their two-fisted, rat-a-tat exploits made for exciting films, some of them real classics: *The Maltese Falcon*, *Murder My Sweet*, and *Kiss Me Deadly*, to name a few. Unfortunately, poor old Race Williams never made it to the screen.

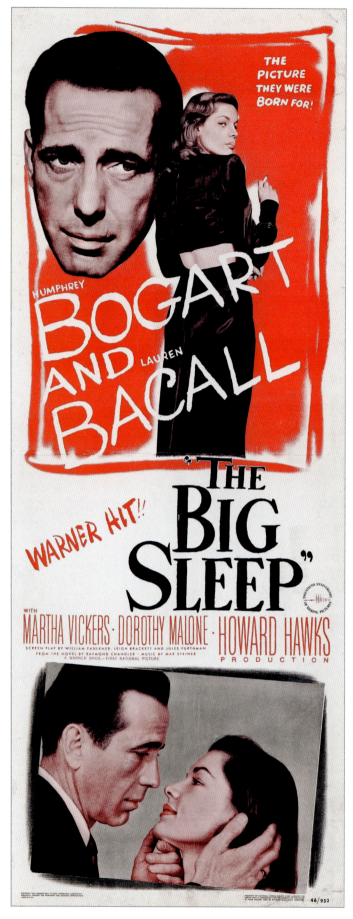

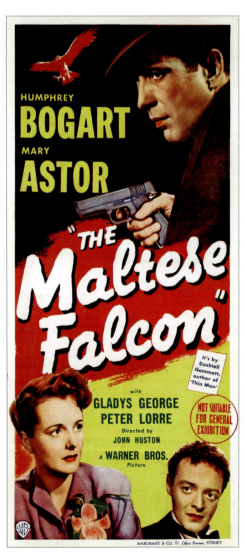

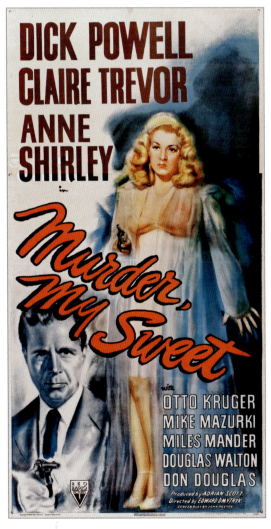

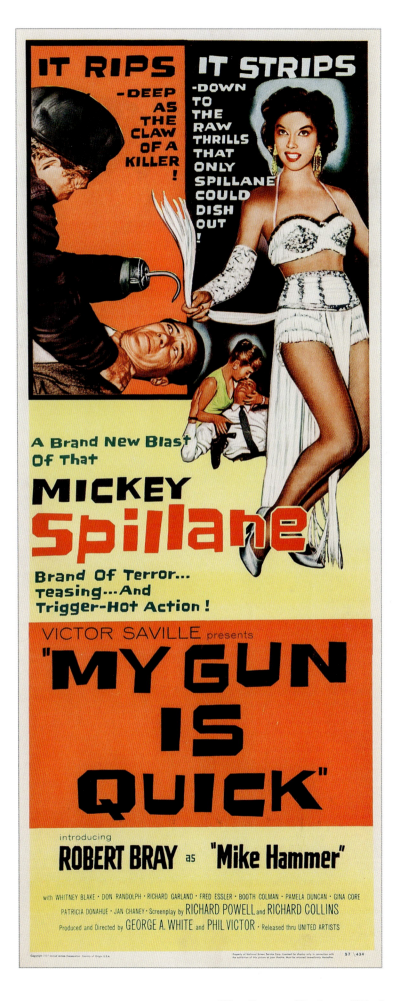

SLEUTHING SPOUSES

Although Dashiell Hammett has acquired literary fame and pop-culture immortality for his hard-boiled classics *The Maltese Falcon* and *The Glass Key*, his bestselling novel on its original release was *The Thin Man*, a less tough and fairly lighthearted tale featuring husband-and-wife detectives Nick and Nora Charles. M-G-M's 1934 film version, starring William Powell and Myrna Loy, became one of the year's top-grossing movies and inspired a series of follow-ups (five sequels over the next thirteen years) and a raft of imitators. Rare-book dealers Joel and Garda Sloane appeared in a trio of mysteries beginning with *Fast Company* (1938) but were played by a different couple in each, preventing audiences from becoming fully invested in the characters. Dorothy L. Sayers's Lord Peter Wimsey and his new bride cavort in *Haunted Honeymoon* (1940), and Craig Rice's Jake and Helene Justis romp through *Having Wonderful Crime* (1945). There were other sleuthing spouses in film, but none had the appeal or longevity of Hammett's Nick and Nora.

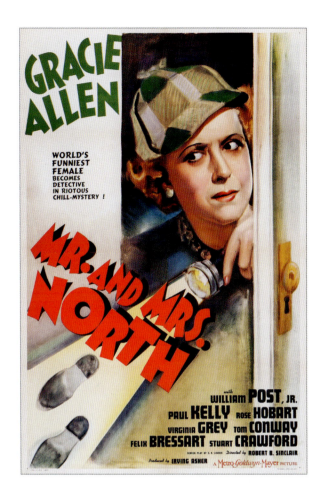

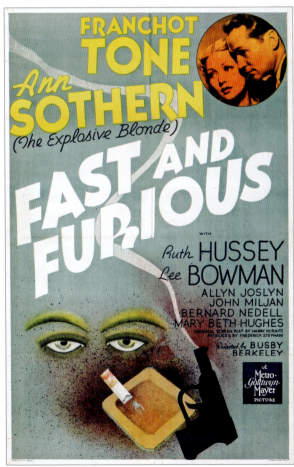

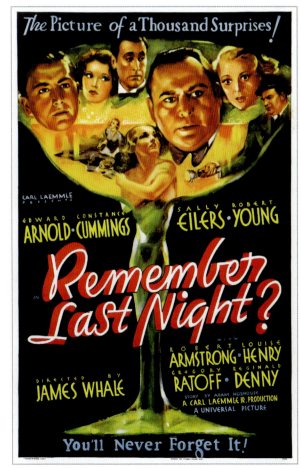

WILLIAM POWELL
Myrna LOY
THE FIRST THIN MAN PICTURE IN 2 YEARS-
AND IT'S A HONEY!
SHADOW OF THE THIN MAN
WITH
Barry NELSON Donna REED Sam LEVENE
Alan BAXTER Henry O'NEILL Dickie HALL
Directed by MAJ. W. S. VAN DYKE II Produced by HUNT STROMBERG
SCREEN PLAY BY IRVING BRECHER AND HARRY KURNITZ
A Metro-Goldwyn-Mayer PICTURE

MURDER AND MIRTH REDUX

During Hollywood's golden age, there never was a time that studios couldn't make money on whodunits liberally sprinkled with comedy, and by the mid-1930s it was common for individual comics and comedy teams to star in out-and-out farces that poked fun at genre conventions and treated bullet-riddled bodies as little more than props to help generate laughs. The immediate pre-WWII years saw such venerable properties as *The Cat and the Canary*, *The Ghost Breakers*, *The Gorilla*, and *Whistling in the Dark*—all filmed previously more than once—dusted off and retooled for the studios' current favorite funnymen. Owing to the industry's cyclical nature, comedy-mystery movies faded from popularity after too many were released in too short a period of time, but there were periodic exceptions, among them the Dean Martin / Jerry Lewis *Scared Stiff* (1953), yet another remake of *Ghost Breakers*; *The Old Dark House* (1959), reviving Universal's 1932 chiller-diller; and *A Shot in the Dark* (1964), into which was shoehorned Peter Sellers's *Pink Panther* character, Inspector Clouseau.

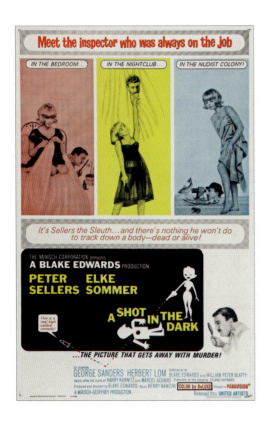

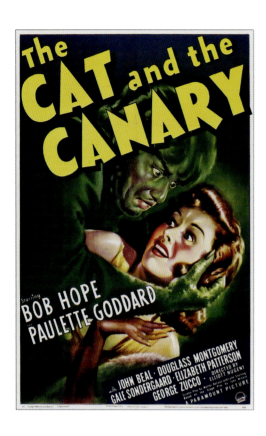

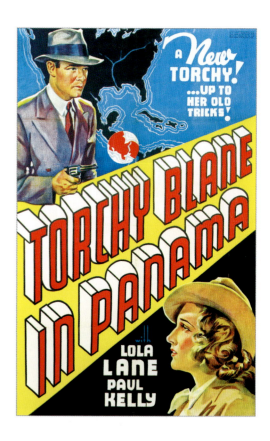

THOSE DIZZY DETECTING DAMES

Distaff detectives were already well established in film when Warner Bros. in early 1937 released a modest little B picture built around a big city "sob sister" (a female newspaper reporter), Torchy Blane. She competes for scoops with more experienced newspapermen but has an advantage in her boyfriend, police lieutenant Steve McBride, who claims to be impartial but usually finds ways to tip off Torchy to new developments in high-profile cases. Interestingly, *Smart Blonde*'s script, by Kenneth Gamet and Don Ryan, was an extremely faithful adaptation of a *Black Mask* pulp story—except that in the print version, the demon reporter is a man named Kennedy. Audiences liked the byplay between costars Glenda Farrell and Barton MacLane, and a series ensued. Similarly breezy attempts to replicate the Torchy Blane formula included *The Adventures of Jane Arden* (1939) and *Detective Kitty O'Day* (1944), neither of which gained much traction at the nation's box offices. *Nine Girls* (also 1944) was an offbeat variation whose dizzy detectives are sorority sisters investigating the murder of one of their own.

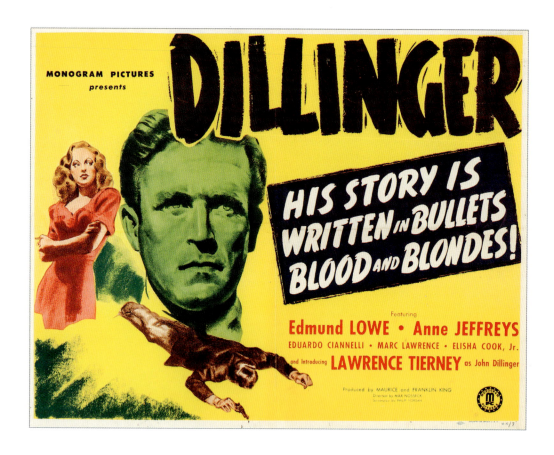

MORE GANGSTERS AND G-MEN

The mid-'30s Production Code crackdown on gangster pictures—and the concomitant elevation of government law-enforcement men as protagonists—temporarily ended the cycle ushered in during the late '20s, but there always existed a demand for the species. The Code's administrators allowed periodic exceptions to their ban as long as malefactors were brought to justice at the film's end—by imprisonment, by execution, or by a G-man's well-placed bullet. The old clichés were dispensed with, and the likes of *Dead End* (1937), *The Roaring Twenties* (1939), and *High Sierra* (1941) boasted well-crafted scripts with strong characterization. During the World War II years, there were several "biopics" of real-life gangsters such as John Dillinger and Roger Touhy. After *White Heat* (1949), the subgenre was thought to have exhausted itself, but the late '50s saw a brief resurgence in highly fictionalized biographies of real-life mobsters such as Al Capone, Legs Diamond, and Baby Face Nelson. One such film, *The Scarface Mob* (1959), served as the pilot for Desilu's hit TV series *The Untouchables*.

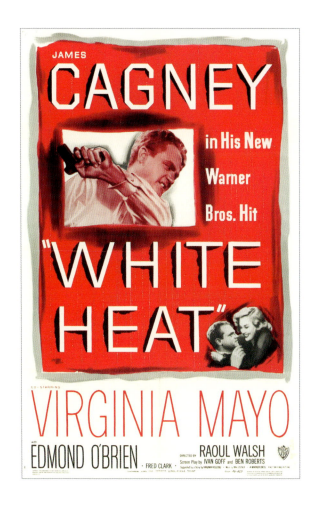

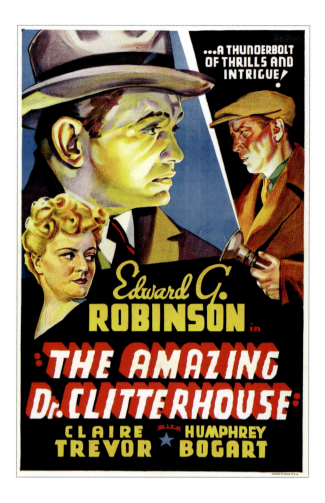

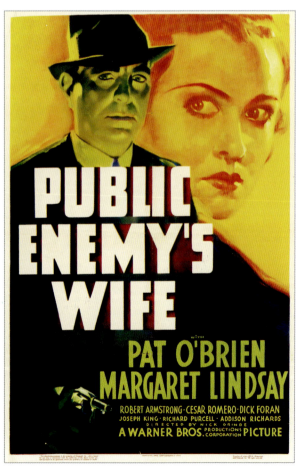

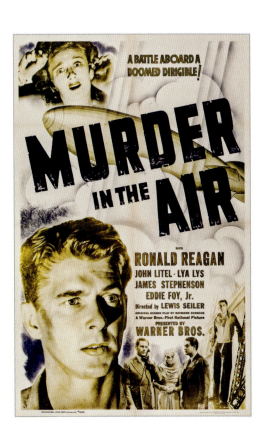

8

CRIME BUSTERS FROM OTHER MEDIA

PHANTOMS, SHADOWS, AND WHISTLERS

Mainstream mystery novels aren't the only source materials for detective movies. The demand is such that Hollywood licenses properties from other media, including radio programs, comic books, newspaper strips, and pulp magazines. For the most part, these crime busters are either private investigators or costumed vigilantes, all of whom have built-in followings making them attractive to filmmakers intent on capturing the lion's share of youthful audiences. Their exploits are largely the stuff of B movies and serials, exhibited primarily at Saturday matinees . . .

Today, dramatic radio is a seldom-attempted novelty in the United States, but it was a staple of commercial broadcasting as far back as the 1920s, being especially popular during the Great Depression, when a lack of disposable income kept millions of families home. There were three distinct types of narrative radio series: the so-called soap operas, geared to female audiences and aired during the morning and early afternoon hours, while kids were at school; mid-to-late-afternoon adventure serials, targeted to youngsters; and more serious dramas, aimed at adults. The latter two types provided Hollywood with numerous candidates for motion pictures, as stand-alone feature films and both series and serials alike. Mystery-oriented radio programs were especially popular during the 1930s and '40s, some designed for family consumption and others intended solely for adults—and adults with strong stomachs at that.

Radio's all-time champion crime buster was created in 1930, as the narrator of *Detective Story Hour*, broadcast on Thursday evenings over New York–based WABC, then the flagship station of the CBS network. The series dramatized short stories published in *Detective Story Magazine*, a weekly Street and Smith pulp. The Shadow, as he called himself, claimed to know what evil lurked in the hearts of men, and after hearing his sepulchral tones and spine-chilling laughter, listeners weren't about to dispute him.

The series was intended to promote *Detective Story Magazine*, but when the broadcast's fans visited their newsstands and asked for "that Shadow detective magazine," Street and Smith decided to launch a pulp devoted to the character's

ABOVE: *Dick Tracy* (1937), the first of four serials starring Ralph Byrd as Chester Gould's famous comic-strip detective, boasted some of the nicest posters ever turned out by the art department at Republic Pictures. This one uses three design elements: a close-up portrait of Byrd, a hand-colored photo showing a scene from chapter 3, and a trio of Gould-drawn panels from the strip.

own exploits, made up out of whole cloth by fictioneer Walter B. Gibson, writing as Maxwell Grant. *The Shadow Magazine* quickly became the bestselling periodical of its type, and by 1937 the character was starring in his own radio adventures, rather than narrating those of other sleuths. The pulp Shadow wore a black hat and cape, which helped him melt into darkness when occasions demanded. The radio Shadow, in an inspired gimmick perfect for that medium, possessed the hypnotic power to cloud men's minds so that they could not see him.

Hollywood saw potential in the Shadow right away. Universal optioned the character rights in early 1931 and made a series of twenty-minute featurettes that kept him in narrator mode, periodically interrupting other people's stories to warn them of danger ahead. The Universal short subjects were poorly made and failed to make a dent at the nation's box offices. Six years later, the cloaked crime fighter appeared in his first feature film. Both *The Shadow Strikes* (1937) and its sequel, *International Crime* (1938), somewhat bafflingly kept him off-screen but for a couple of brief glimpses, puzzling and disappointing devotees

ABOVE: Actress Ann Richards visits director William Castle (*left*) and star Warner Baxter on the set of *The Crime Doctor's Man Hunt* (1946). While under contract to Columbia, Castle served his directorial apprenticeship cranking out B pictures featuring the Whistler, the Crime Doctor, and Boston Blackie. He later graduated to bigger-budgeted movies, but he never lost his enthusiasm for thrillers.

of his pulp and radio adventures. A 1940 Columbia serial, tilted heavily toward juvenile audiences, fared somewhat better thanks to an effective star turn by Victor Jory, who until then had been usually cast in villainous roles. Further attempts at bringing the Shadow to cinematic life were progressively weak.

Filmmakers had better luck with a not-dissimilar character. *The Whistler* was broadcast weekly on West Coast stations affiliated with the CBS network from 1942 onward, its narrator both eponymous and anonymous. His signature was a thirteen-note tune whistled over the sound of footsteps at the beginning and end of each episode. Every story was self-contained and usually revolved around the acts of people seduced by the prospect of committing some crime and escaping without drawing suspicion to themselves. They are invariably tripped up, often by overlooking a trivial detail. The final scene nearly always ends with a twist, its irony pointed out by the Whistler himself, who otherwise appears in the story as a sort of Greek chorus.

Within months, *The Whistler* had established itself as one of the top crime programs. Harry Cohn's Columbia Pictures, already filling up theaters with a handful of B-grade crime and mystery series, snapped up the movie rights and entrusted the property to producer Rudy Flothow, a specialist in such screen fare. The first entry, titled *The Whistler* and scripted by former crime-pulp writer Eric Taylor, was directed by up-and-coming William Castle. It starred Richard Dix, a popular leading man of the silent and early talkie eras, as a depressed, recently widowed industrialist who, lacking the courage to commit suicide, hires a hit man through a third party.

The Whistler got mixed reviews but was a surprise hit. Columbia continued the series, sticking close to the radio show's format. Most of the later installments improved on the first; Castle directed several, and Dix starred, playing various characters, in all but the last. Posters showed the Whistler wearing a broad-brimmed black hat and long black coat, giving him an uncanny resemblance to the Shadow.

Another airwave avenger of crime, the Green Hornet, burst onto the serial screen in 1940, courtesy of Universal Pictures. By day, he was crusading newspaper publisher Britt Reid, who editorialized against gangsters and crooked politicians. By night, aided by his faithful Japanese (later Filipino) valet Kato, he donned a hornet-decorated face mask and wielded a soundless gun that emitted a harmless but instantly soporific gas. His episodic exploits were generally faithful to those dramatized on the radio program.

Totally forgotten now but a real sensation in its day was a series titled *I Love a Mystery*, which enjoyed phenomenal popularity in runs on both NBC and CBS between 1939 and 1944. The mystery lovers were Jack Packard, Doc Long, and Reggie York, erstwhile soldiers of fortune who formed a Hollywood-based detective agency and routinely tackled cases in bizarre settings with supernatural trappings. A brief series of three Columbia films should have been more profitable, but after a promising opener, it slumped due to weak scripts and pedestrian direction.

ABOVE: Columbia's B pictures based on the radio series *The Whistler* were unusually well done for films in their budgetary class, and directors such as William Castle and D. Ross Lederman deserve a great deal of credit for their imaginative work. But the series also benefited from the licensing of excellent stories; this entry was based on the haunting "All at Once, No Alice" by pulp fiction's master of suspense, Cornell Woolrich.

Other well-received programs such as *Gang Busters* and *The Crime Doctor* made it to the screen, but radio wasn't the only medium to supply Hollywood with supersleuths. During the late '30s, two-fisted cops such as Dick Tracy, Red Barry, and Pat O'Hara migrated to the movies from their four-colored homes in the comic sections of newspapers, and their long-underwear brethren from comic books—Batman, Captain America, and the Masked Marvel—weren't far behind. Heroes from the lurid pulp magazines were generally bypassed by the studios, but a noteworthy exception was the Spider, Master of Men, whose 1938 chapter-play debut was so bloodthirsty—with the hero gunning down a dozen crooks in the first two episodes alone—that the industry's self-censorial Production Code Administration urged its producer to reedit subsequent installments to make the avenging arachnid seem less lethal. ✪

BELOW: Kane Richmond (*left*), Dorothea Kent, and George Chandler share a laugh between scenes for *Behind the Mask* (1946), the second of three Shadow mysteries produced by Monogram Pictures. Richmond's Shadow was a hybrid of the character's pulp-fiction and radio-drama incarnations, drawing on both but not satisfying fans of either. The short-lived series should have focused on one version or another.

DICK TRACY

Created in 1931 by cartoonist Chester Gould as a direct response to the Prohibition-era glorification of gangsters as folk heroes fighting the Establishment, plainclothes police detective Dick Tracy initially fought organized-crime kingpins and their minions. The Tracy comic strip was read daily by millions, and Republic Pictures optioned the character in late 1936 for use in a serial. The chapter play was an enormous success, and Republic made three sequels (1938, 1939, and 1941). At the time, serial posters were produced in two formats: one with a full-sheet painted image and another with a generic piece of art framing a boxed space into which was placed a photograph. The first style was used to promote opening episodes, while multiple versions of the second were prepared for subsequent chapters; previously, the studios had commissioned individual paintings for twelve or more separate posters. These serials made a star of the little-known Ralph Byrd, who reprised the role in the last two of four RKO feature films released between 1945 and 1947.

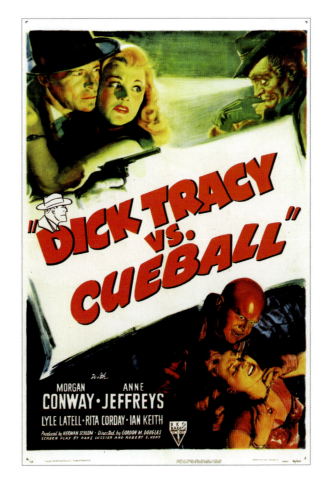

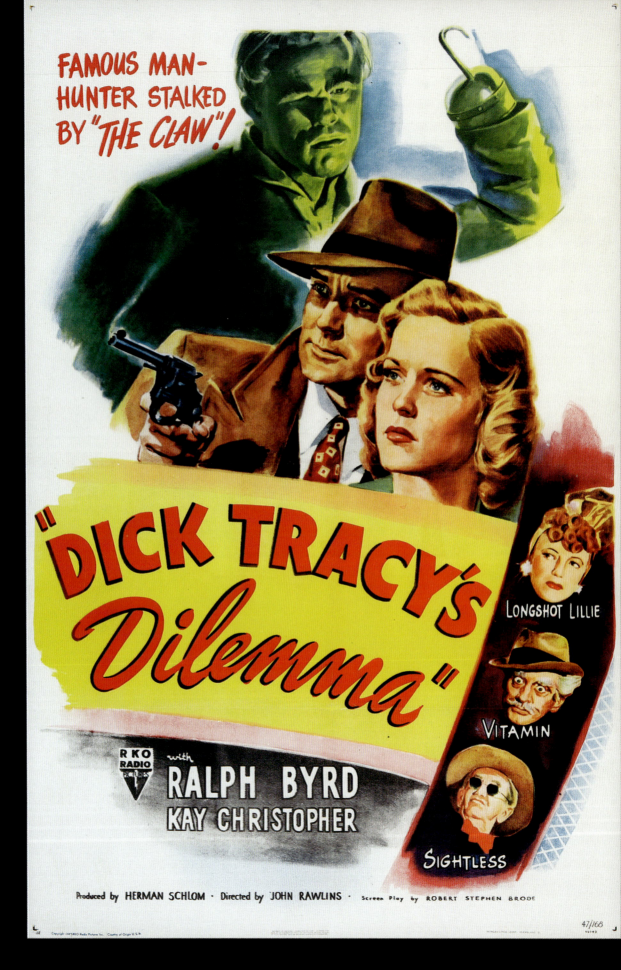

FAMOUS MAN-HUNTER STALKED BY "THE CLAW"!

"DICK TRACY'S Dilemma"

LONGSHOT LILLIE

VITAMIN

SIGHTLESS

RKO RADIO PICTURES

with RALPH BYRD

KAY CHRISTOPHER

Produced by HERMAN SCHLOM · Directed by JOHN RAWLINS · Screen Play by ROBERT STEPHEN BRODE

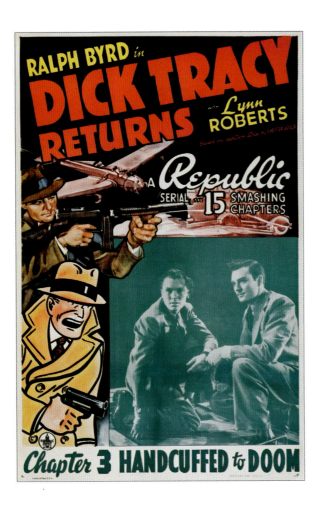

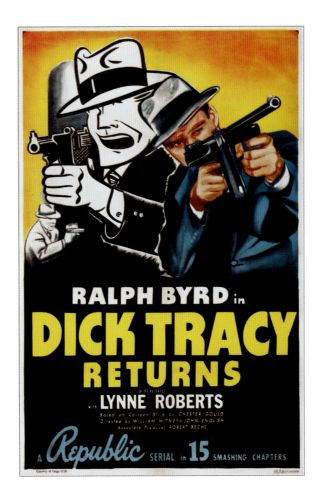

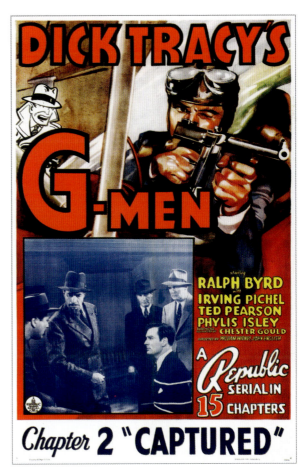

FROM RADIO, PART 1

The radio series *The Whistler* was among the best written of its type, and Columbia's B series maintained a high level of quality in its scripts. Although silent star Richard Dix features in all but the final installment, he plays different characters in each one—sympathetic in some, unsympathetic in others. But even his good guys have a haunted quality about them, and the stories tend to be downbeat. The atmospheric poster art stresses Dix, with the Whistler himself lingering in corners or backgrounds. Another popular airwaves drama aimed at adults was *Inner Sanctum*, ostensibly based on a mystery imprint of book publisher Simon and Schuster. Universal licensed the show's title, and most of the stories unfolded like radio shows, with narration supposedly emanating from the thoughts of their leading man, Lon Chaney Jr.—who, like Dix in the Whistler films, portrays different characters in each installment. Interestingly, all the *Inner Sanctum* posters bear the trademarked logo used on Simon and Schuster's mysteries, but not a single one of those novels was adapted for the series.

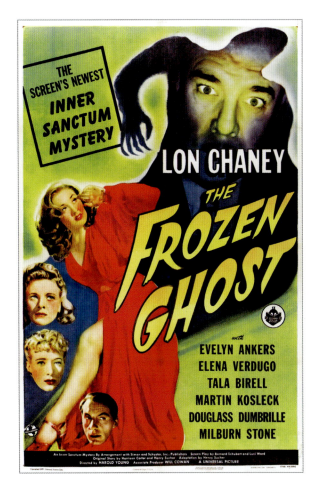

Romance on his lips . . . murder on his mind!

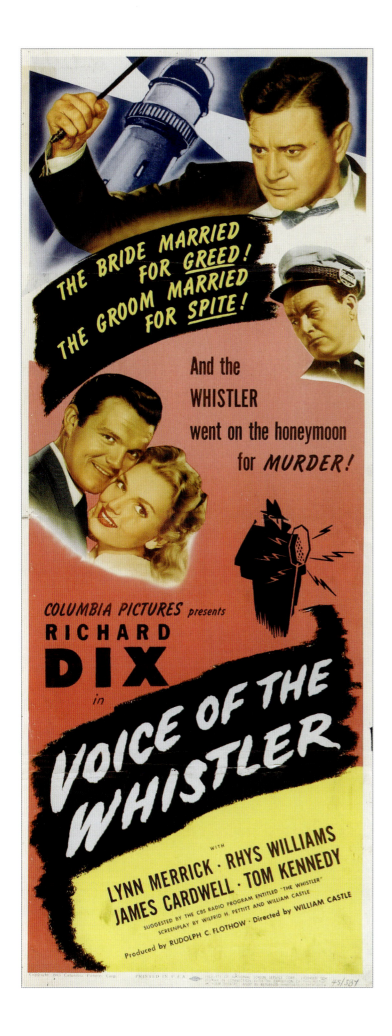

THE BRIDE MARRIED FOR GREED!
THE GROOM MARRIED FOR SPITE!

And the WHISTLER went on the honeymoon for MURDER!

COLUMBIA PICTURES presents

RICHARD DIX

in

VOICE OF THE WHISTLER

WITH
LYNN MERRICK · RHYS WILLIAMS
JAMES CARDWELL · TOM KENNEDY

SUGGESTED BY THE CBS RADIO PROGRAM ENTITLED "THE WHISTLER"
SCREENPLAY BY WILFRID H. PETTITT AND WILLIAM CASTLE

Produced by RUDOLPH C. FLOTHOW · Directed by WILLIAM CASTLE

THE SCREEN'S
Newest!
Weirdest!
Shocker!

The MISSING HEAD

Formerly "STRANGE CONFESSION"

starring

LON CHANEY
BRENDA JOYCE
J. CARROL NAISH
LLOYD BRIDGES

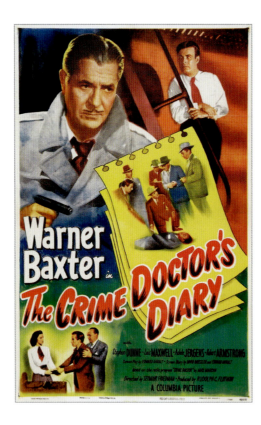

FROM RADIO, PART 2

Columbia's corporate appetite for B-grade mysteries seemed almost insatiable in the 1940s, with Ellery Queen, Boston Blackie, the Lone Wolf, and the Whistler all appearing in films bearing the famous "torch lady" trademark. Dramatic radio provided the sources for two further series launched by Harry Cohn's studio during the war years. *The Crime Doctor* had an interesting premise: a former crook gets amnesia, studies medicine, and eventually becomes a psychiatrist specializing in the criminal mind. On film, he was played by Warner Baxter—who, like *The Whistler*'s Richard Dix, had been a popular leading man in the 1920s. The series, interesting but never too exciting, lasted six years. Columbia's version of the sensational *I Love a Mystery* began promisingly but lost steam with the second entry and was terminated after the third. *The Green Hornet*, one of the best kiddie-oriented radio thrillers, buzzed his way through two Universal serials during 1940–1941 but never got a feature-film tryout, while the three *Mr. District Attorney* films from Republic bear little resemblance to their eponymous ether-wave inspiration.

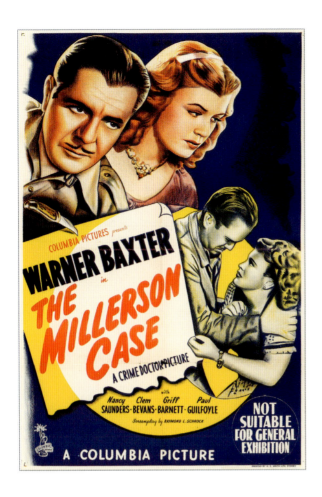

THE SHADOW

The utter failure of Hollywood to make even one wholly satisfactory motion picture about a character that achieved phenomenal success in multiple mediums—books, radio, and comics—remains incomprehensible. True, the radio Shadow was somewhat different from the pulp-fiction Shadow, and the comic-strip Shadow was an uneasy fusion of the other two. But in one medium or another, he was beloved by tens of millions of Americans during a quarter century of active adventuring. Filmmakers bungled multiple attempts to bring the character to cinematic life, beginning with two dreary Poverty Row feature films released by Grand National in 1937–1938. A Columbia serial produced two years later boasted an effective Shadow in Victor Jory but was too silly for words. Ditto the three 1946 Monogram features starring Kane Richmond, sabotaged by witless scripts and bargain-basement production values. An unsold hour-long TV pilot, released theatrically as both *Invisible Avenger* (1958) and *Bourbon Street Shadows* (1959), was embarrassingly awful. Oddly enough, the 1933 British mystery titled *The Shadow* has nothing to do with the American character but comes remarkably close to capturing the essence of his appeal.

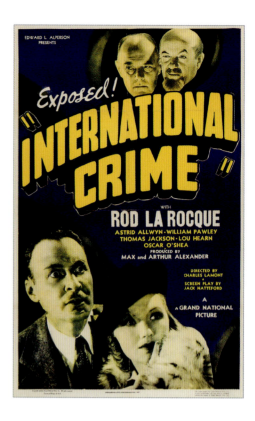

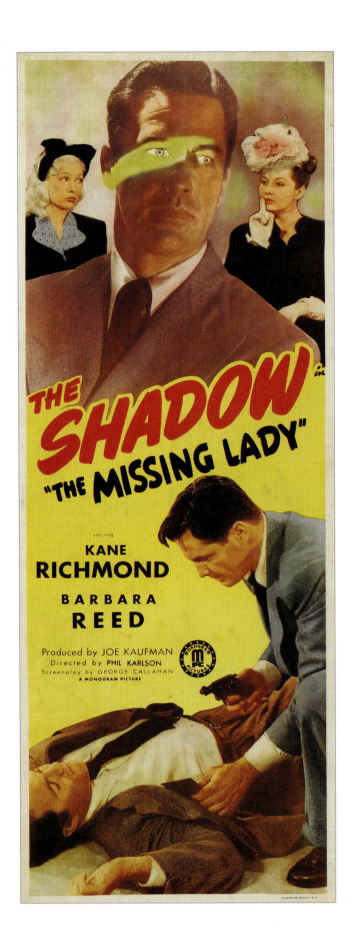

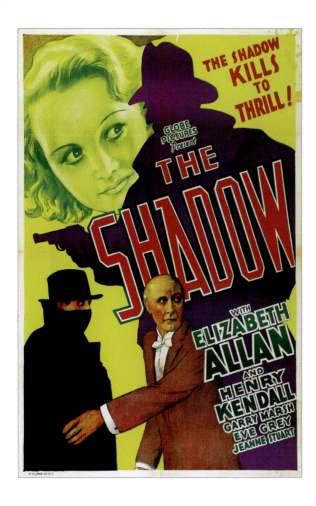

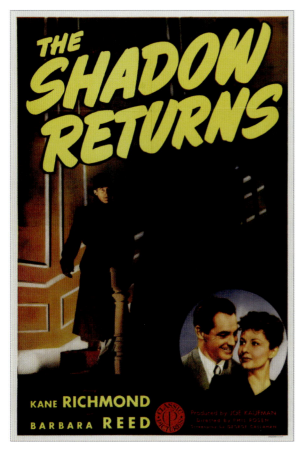

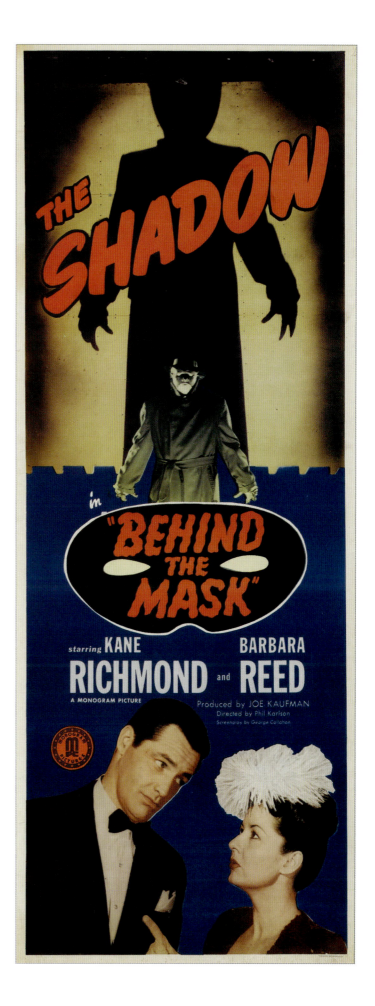

FROM COMICS AND PULPS

So many American youths followed newspaper comics that it's remarkable no Hollywood studio optioned the crime-oriented strips prior to 1935, when Universal licensed a slew of popular characters from the King Features Syndicate. Eventually, they all reached the screen as serials, the best of which were *Radio Patrol* (1937), *Secret Agent X-9* (1937 and 1945), and *Red Barry* (1938). With built-in audiences numbering in the millions, it is no surprise that these chapter plays did extraordinarily well. A few years later, with comic books flooding the nation's newsstands, Hollywood again took notice and licensed a further batch of masked, long-underwear "superheroes," including Batman, Captain America, Captain Midnight, and the Masked Marvel. They too wound up in serials—the posters for which virtually exploded with large, colorful renderings of these boldly costumed crime fighters. The Spider, another masked vigilante, was recruited from the pulps; one of those millionaire playboys who prefers grotesque costumes and disguises to dressing gowns and evening clothes, he generally shot evildoers to pieces in the pages of his magazine but adopted nonlethal tactics for a 1941 serial.

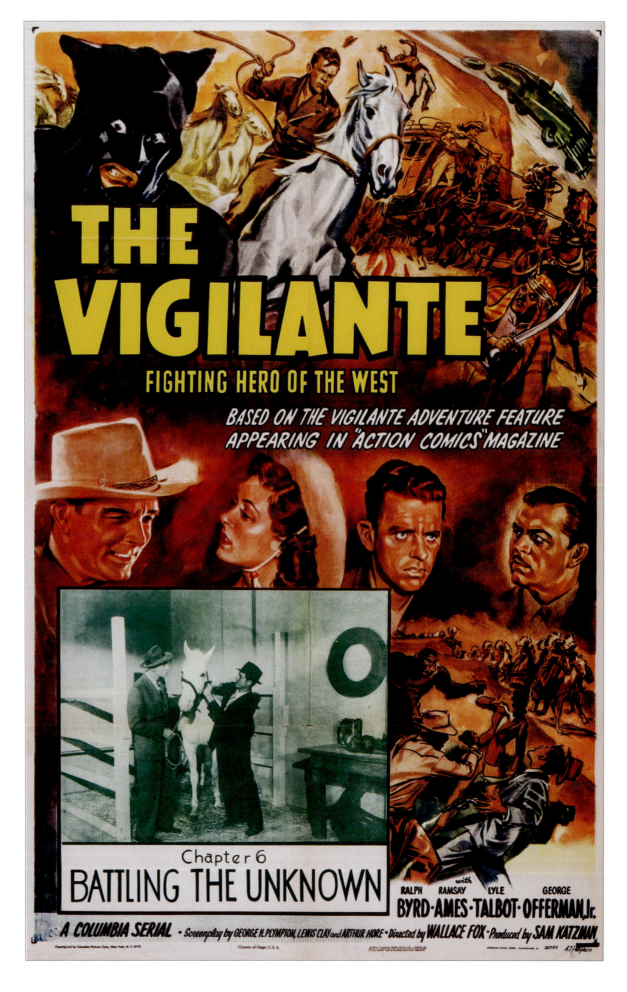

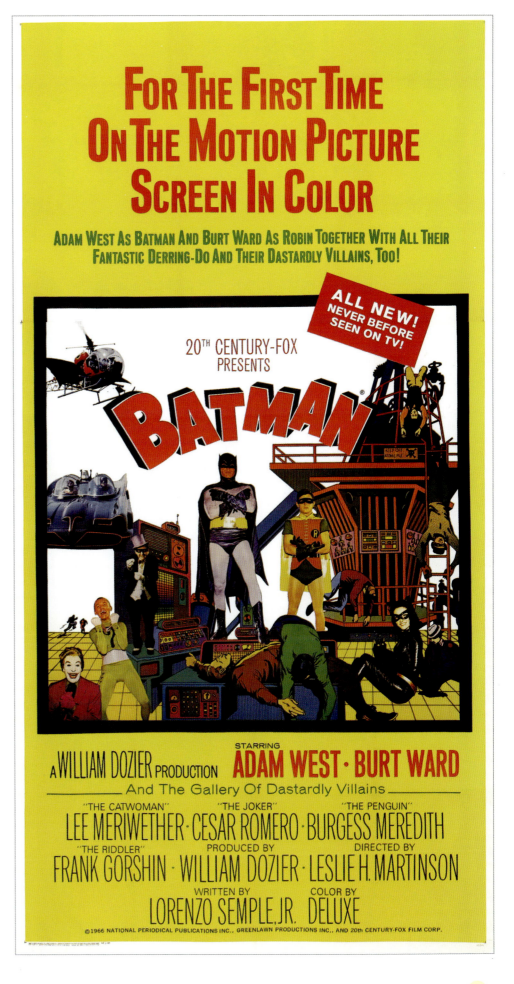

9

MASTERS
OF
SUSPENSE

ALFRED HITCHCOCK AND CORNELL WOOLRICH

O f the many creative people who have lent their talents to the making of crime and mystery movies, a few stand out for both the quality and quantity of their contributions to the genre. The "thriller," specifically, owes much of its enduring popularity to the work of two brilliant and towering figures in pop-culture history: director Alfred Hitchcock and writer Cornell Woolrich. During lengthy and extraordinarily productive careers, they turn out numerous classics in their respective fields of endeavor, easily warranting the exalted status they still enjoy among devotees of criminous cinema . . .

Widely regarded as one of the most influential filmmakers in motion-picture history, Alfred Hitchcock directed more than fifty feature films between 1925 and 1976—a half-century-long career that produced an unusually high percentage of exceptional works. Born in England, he was a good student with a particular interest in geography. For a time, he wanted to be an engineer; he learned everything he could about mechanics, electricity, and practical sciences, while also taking classes in painting and art history. The death of his father in 1914 forced Hitchcock to take a job as a clerk for a telegraph company. During World War I, he served on the home front as a cadet in the Royal Engineers. With the conflict's end, he devoted himself to more creative pursuits, writing short stories and editing a trade journal, in addition to resuming his art studies.

A devoted film fan, Hitchcock eagerly submitted samples of his drawings to Paramount's British studio in London and secured a job designing title cards. The ambitious artist dabbled in other areas of production, working in various capacities on at least two dozen films before being assigned by producer Michael Balcon to direct *The Pleasure Garden* (1925), a drama about the tumultuous personal lives of two London chorus girls. It flopped, but Hitchcock's work impressed Balcon, and it did not go unnoticed by other members of Britain's film industry.

The already rotund young director found his true métier in *The Lodger* (1927), a thriller built around the search for a Jack the Ripper–style murderer of young women in London. Both a critical and commercial smash, it cemented his reputation as an unusually thoughtful and inventive filmmaker.

ABOVE: *Black Angel* (1946), adapted from Cornell Woolrich's 1943 novel of the same title, was a suspenseful noir produced and directed by Roy William Neill, a crime film specialist and most recently the steward of Universal's Sherlock Holmes series. Woolrich's yarn harked back to his earlier *Phantom Lady*, which was also brought to the screen. Both films revolve around a loyal woman trying to clear her man from a murder charge.

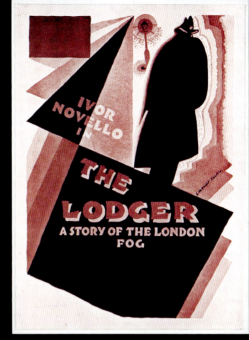

The transition from silent to sound presented Hitchcock with the same technical challenges that bedeviled (and in some cases defeated) his contemporaries. He found ways to make sound work to his advantage, especially in another thriller, *Blackmail* (1929). Although "Hitch" directed movies in several genres, he always returned to stories involving crime and criminals. But he never embraced dialogue-heavy whodunits; even though early-talkie audiences were infatuated with the endless interrogations endemic to the "fair play" murder mystery, Hitchcock thought them uncinematic and emotionless, preferring stories that depicted suspenseful pursuits of people or objects coveted for unknown reasons by villains seeming to possess unlimited resources and infinite patience.

ABOVE LEFT: A decidedly cherubic Hitchcock, pictured shortly after he arrived in America. While his British movies include several bona fide classics, the director soon outgrew his native country's film industry and needed the superior technical facilities offered by Hollywood studios to fully realize his vision. With almost unlimited resources at his command, he created some of the finest suspense pictures ever to go before a camera.

ABOVE RIGHT: *The Lodger* (1926) was the film that inextricably linked Alfred Hitchcock to crime, mystery, and suspense. The extent of its unanticipated success changed the trajectory of Hitch's career, although his finest achievements were still years in the future.

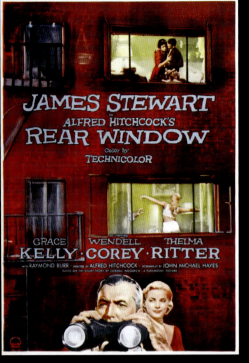

The Art of Classic Crime and Mystery Movies

Although Scotland Yard inspectors and other law-enforcement officials occasionally played important parts in Hitchcock thrillers, the director exhibited a fondness for protagonists who were ordinary men and women unexpectedly precipitated into suspenseful and dangerous situations by a quirk in fate. His 1935 breakthrough film, *The 39 Steps*, cast well-regarded actor Robert Donat in one such role. Framed for murder, Donat's Richard Hannay has the added burden of possessing a secret, the import of which is unknown to him. His pursuit by both the police and secret agents drives Hannay to extreme measures, making him the type of protagonist to which Hitchcock would return again and again.

Having secured American distribution for a string of British-made hits—including *The Man Who Knew Too Much*, *The 39 Steps*, *Young and Innocent*, and *The Lady Vanishes*—Hitchcock was bound to be noticed in Hollywood, and indeed he was. None other than legendary independent producer David O. Selznick offered him a four-year contract in 1938. Realizing he had accomplished all that was possible in Britain—whose film industry was not as highly developed as America's—Hitchcock accepted. His very first Hollywood picture, *Rebecca* (a romantic melodrama with a strong mystery element), earned him an Oscar nomination for Best Director, the first of five he would ultimately receive.

Hitchcock's subsequent accomplishments are too numerous—and frankly too well documented—to warrant detailed coverage here, but we must mention *Rear Window* (1954), another classic thriller, starring James Stewart as a wheelchair-bound photographer who, out of boredom, spies on neighbors from the window in his Manhattan apartment and sees what might be a husband's murder of his wife.

Ranking high on any list of Hitchcock's best films, *Rear Window* was based on the 1942 short story "It Had to Be Murder," written by one Cornell Woolrich for the pulp magazine *Dime Detective*. The sickly, perpetually self-doubting product of a broken family, Cornell George Hopley Woolrich took up fictioneering while matriculating at New York's Columbia University during the Roaring Twenties. His early works were Jazz Age novels comparable to those of F. Scott Fitzgerald, and one of them got him a brief contract as a Hollywood scenario writer. But he failed at both screenwriting and marriage, having wed the daughter of a former studio mogul. Disheartened, he moved back to New York, where he lived with his mother in a cheap hotel near Harlem.

Woolrich resumed the writing of fiction, but now he confined himself to crime stories for the detective pulps. Incapable of the intellectual rigor necessary to the fashioning of complex whodunits, he stuck to yarns about ordinary people trapped in desperate situations and often framed for crimes they did not commit. In 1940, he sold a novel to Simon and Schuster, and *The Bride Wore Black* restored luster to a somewhat tarnished career. Over the next decade, he produced a dozen more, many of them adapted for the screen, published both in his own name and under the pseudonyms William Irish and George Hopley. He also continued grinding out short stories and novelettes for the pulps, in constant fear that what he considered his meager talent would eventually peter

out, ruining his chance of selling novels to major publishers and leaving only the less demanding markets open to him.

Woolrich underestimated himself and the appeal of his dark fiction, with its despairing protagonists struggling to survive in a hostile universe arrayed with enemies both seen and unseen. Most of his novels and dozens of his shorter works were brought to cinematic life during his lifetime, especially when film noir became fashionable in the 1940s. He died alone in 1968. A handwritten note found among his papers offered as good an explanation as any for what he wrote and why: "I was only trying to cheat death. I was only trying to surmount for a little while the darkness that all my life I surely knew was going to come rolling in someday and obliterate me."

He never knew it, but Cornell Woolrich accomplished his mission. His suspenseful stories, and the motion pictures adapted from them, have outlived him—have surmounted the darkness. ◇

ABOVE: Alfred Hitchcock (*center, pointing*) explains the mechanics of a tracking shot to cast members working on his *Shadow of a Doubt* (1943), the exteriors for which were filmed in Santa Rosa, California. Hitchcock loved the idea of an idyllic American small town playing host to a homicidal maniac, and he considered *Shadow* his favorite movie.

HITCHCOCK: THE EARLY YEARS

One of the cinema's most brilliant careers began unassumingly in Britain, a country whose film industry significantly lagged behind America's during the 1920s. Initially, Alfred Hitchcock's contribution to movies was limited to the designing of illustrated title cards for silent pictures, but he soon graduated to other jobs in filmmaking and ultimately, having learned the business from the ground up, to directing. Although he worked in numerous genres, he found his true métier to be the crime thriller, attracting considerable attention for his handling of *The Lodger* (1926). He adapted easily to the demands of talking pictures but shunned orthodox whodunits, as popular then in the UK as they were in the States. Out-and-out thrillers, heavily weighted with gripping suspense, were more to his liking, and nobody did them better. It was evident that Hitch deserved the lion's share of credit for such masterpieces as *The 39 Steps* (1935) and *The Lady Vanishes* (1938), although posters for his British films don't give his name the prominence it deserved. Even on the one-sheet for his first American film, *Rebecca* (1939), he shares credit with producer David O. Selznick.

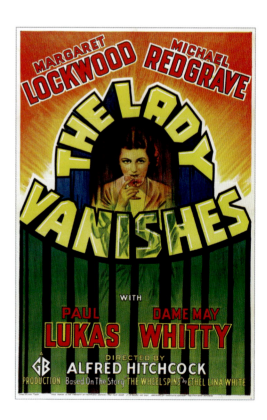

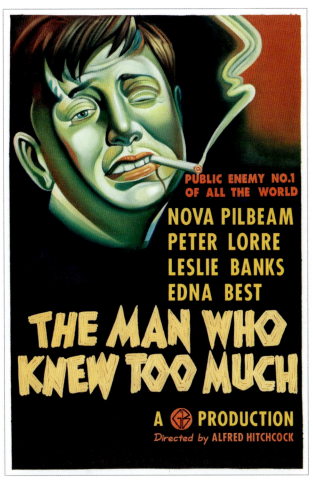

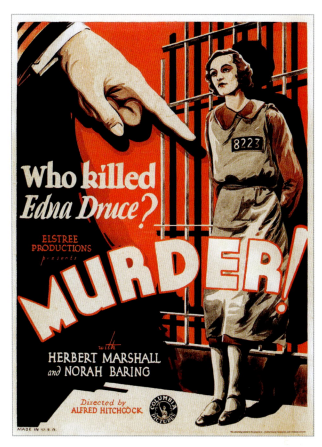

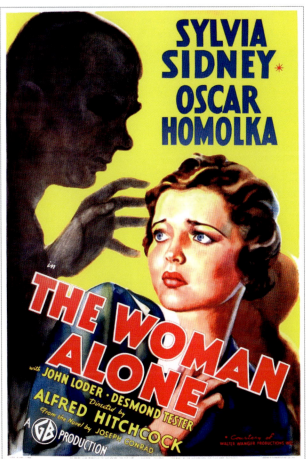

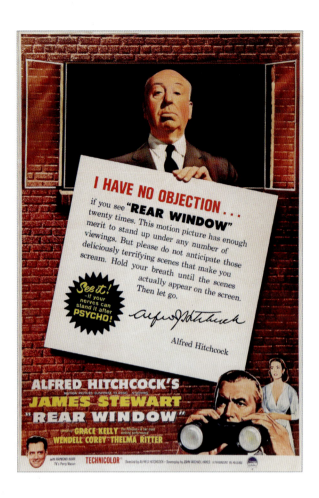

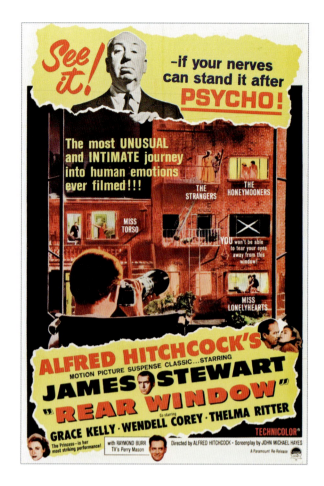

HITCHCOCK CONQUERS HOLLYWOOD

It didn't take long for the portly British director to establish himself in America's film capital as a major talent, and as early as 1940 he was getting over-the-title billing on posters for his films ("Alfred Hitchcock's production of *Foreign Correspondent*"). Hitchcock flourished in Tinseltown, having access to increased funding and the industry's most talented technicians. Within just a few years of his arrival in Hollywood, he had racked up a number of impressive hits, including *Suspicion* (1941), *Saboteur* (1942), and *Shadow of a Doubt* (1943). His mid-'40s output continued to enjoy box-office success and strengthened the Hitchcock "brand," even if the films weren't quite as innovative as those released earlier in the decade. But after five years of turning out conventionally entertaining dramas, he began experimenting again, notably with *Rope* (1948), an "inverted" mystery story (meaning audiences knew the killers' identities right away) apparently shot in one continuous take. In the '50s, Hitchcock embraced such technological advances as 3–D, widescreen, and stereophonic sound, closing out the decade with two of his best-remembered films, *Vertigo* (1958) and *North by Northwest* (1959).

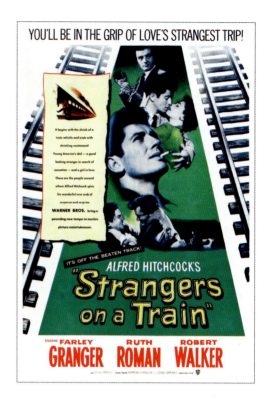

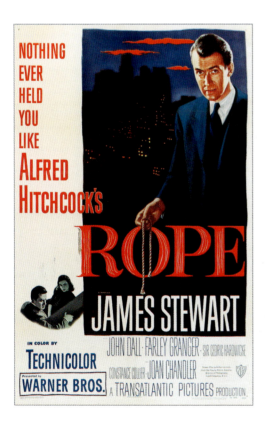

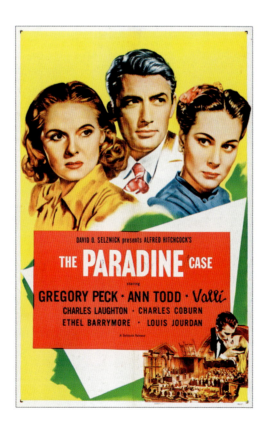

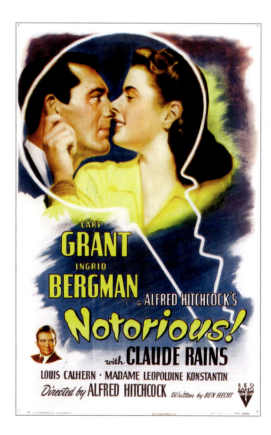

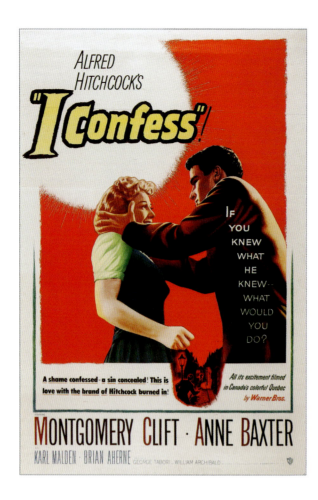

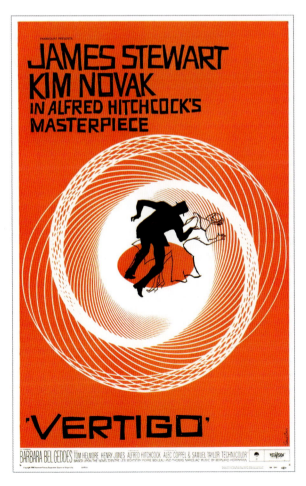

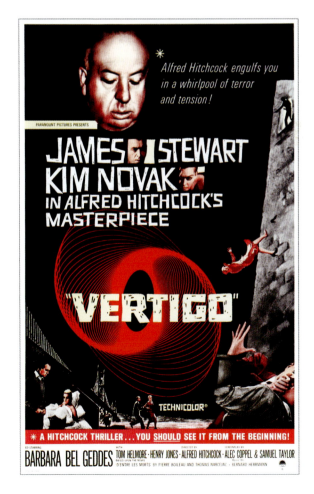

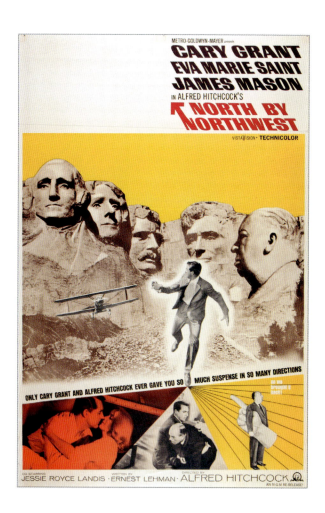

HITCHCOCK: THE LATER YEARS

Although his name and reputation were already well known to film fans by 1955, an eponymous TV program, *The Alfred Hitchcock Hour*, made his face and figure instantly recognizable to a sizable chunk of the population. He appeared on camera at least twice per episode, delivering sardonically humorous asides in his patented deadpan manner. Marketing departments in the major Hollywood studios took notice and began adding photos of Hitch to poster art. This ploy was a major asset to the advertising and promotional campaign for *Psycho* (1960), the director's last truly innovative thriller, and obviously helped sell his subsequent films as well. But Hitchcock was getting old and running out of ideas. His later films, such as *Torn Curtain* (1966), *Topaz* (1969), and *Family Plot* (1976), show a lack of inspiration and a bottom to Hitch's bag of directorial tricks. But the Master's touch is still evident in *Frenzy* (1972), a serial-killer thriller shot in his native England. Perhaps tellingly, the posters for that film have his name as large as the title.

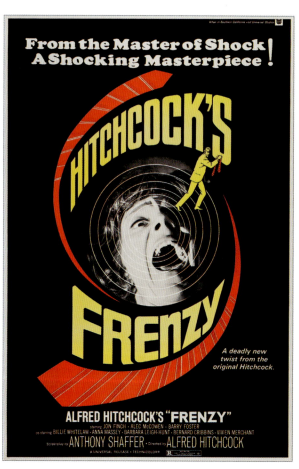

From the
devious mind of
Alfred Hitchcock,
a diabolically
entertaining
motion picture.

There's no body   in the family plot.

ALFRED HITCHCOCK'S

FAMILY PLOT

You must
see it twice!

starring KAREN BLACK · BRUCE DERN · BARBARA HARRIS · WILLIAM DEVANE
Music by JOHN WILLIAMS   Screenplay by ERNEST LEHMAN   From the novel "THE RAINBIRD PATTERN" by VICTOR CANNING
PG PARENTAL GUIDANCE SUGGESTED
SOME MATERIAL MAY NOT BE SUITABLE FOR PRE-TEENAGERS   Directed by ALFRED HITCHCOCK   A UNIVERSAL PICTURE TECHNICOLOR®

76/94

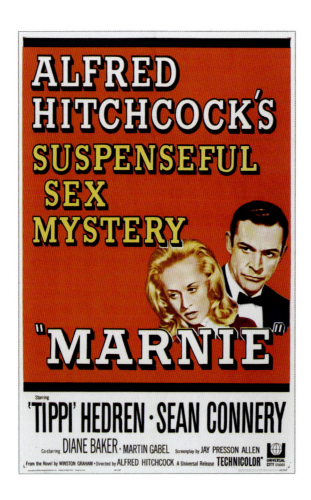

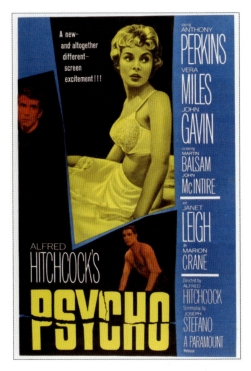

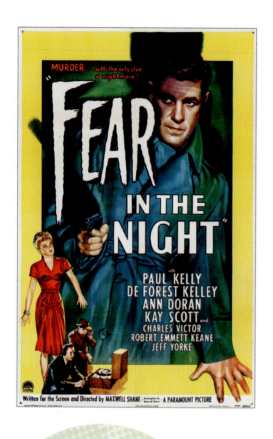

CORNELL WOOLRICH

Alfred Hitchcock's career intersected with that of pulp fictioneer Cornell Woolrich—known as "the Dark Prince of Noir"—just once: the director's 1954 classic *Rear Window* was adapted from one of Woolrich's suspenseful short stories, "It Had to Be Murder." But there were other, more tangential connections. For example, Hitchcock's longtime collaborator Joan Harrison produced *Phantom Lady* (1944), arguably the finest translation from print to celluloid of any work by Woolrich (who wrote the novel as William Irish). A legendarily haunted man, Cornell frequently wrote in the first person, as men or women—he was equally skilled at telling stories from both male and female viewpoints—accidentally plunged into desperate situations. The author's works posit the existence of a capricious, malevolent Fate, against whose machinations normal people are helpless. The doom-laden perspective that characterizes his fiction made Woolrich the patron saint of noir directors, and his chilling works were the basis of such outstanding specimens of the subgenre as *Street of Chance* (1942), *The Leopard Man* (1943), *Black Angel* (1946), and *Night Has a Thousand Eyes* (1948).

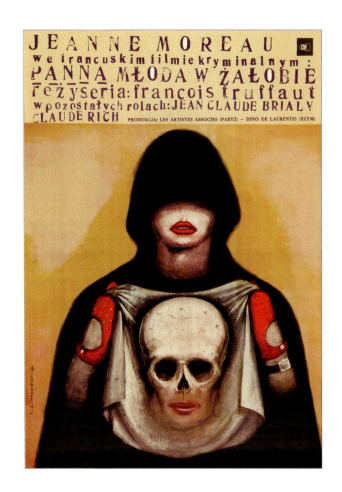

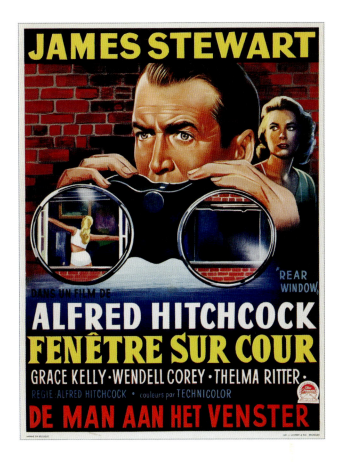

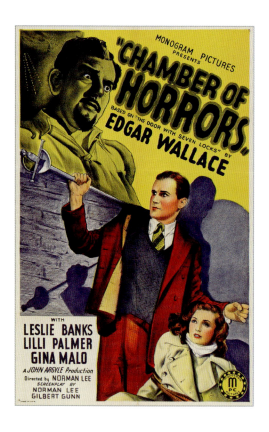

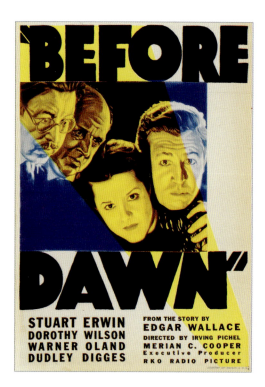

EDGAR WALLACE

A kindred spirit of both Hitchcock and Woolrich, the great British writer Edgar Wallace specialized in tales of crime and mystery during a career that spanned several decades. An illegitimate child born into poverty, he left school at the age of twelve and supported himself thereafter. A one-time war correspondent, he began his fiction career in 1904 with the self-published *Four Just Men*. Ultimately, Wallace penned 957 short stories, 170 novels, and 18 stage plays, in addition to historical nonfiction and numerous film scripts. For a time, one in every four books sold in England was an Edgar Wallace thriller, while combined sales of his works are said to surpass fifty million copies. Since 1916, more than two hundred films and TV programs—some of them international productions dubbed in multiple languages—have been adapted from his fiction. Like both Hitchcock and Woolrich, Wallace eschewed the orthodox whodunit as a vehicle of expression; he wrote rapidly, and it's said he lacked the patience to construct intricate murder puzzles, but his crime stories were uniquely engaging and formed the basis for many vastly entertaining films.

10

THE EMERGENCE OF FILM NOIR

During the 1940s, crime films begin to take on appearances and characteristics that represent an evolution in the national zeitgeist. Their psyches deeply affected by the traumas of war and fear arising from the potential of nuclear annihilation, movie patrons increasingly embrace a type of screen entertainment that shuns the breezy escapism and unsophisticated propaganda of previous years. As the decade progresses, a new type of crime drama evolves—bleak, cynical, unsettling, occasionally nightmarish. Eventually, it will become known as "film noir" . . .

For several decades, Hollywood filmmakers provided movie audiences with crime and mystery pictures cut to a well-defined, predictable pattern. Whodunits involved the discovery and apprehension of murderers by detectives who were either members of law enforcement, talented dilettantes amused by the challenge, or private investigators motivated primarily, if not solely, by the prospect of large fees to be paid by their clients. Occasionally, the sleuths had a personal stake in a case's outcome, but for the most part, they kept in mind the larger goal of maintaining order by bringing criminals to justice. The lines between the good guys and the bad guys were clearly drawn. Murder mysteries had a puzzle component, making the characterization of possible suspects less important than the clues they left behind. Collecting the clues and mentally fitting them into their proper places was far more important to picture patrons than the psychological underpinnings of a culprit's actions. If they managed to guess a killer's identity before the detective character, so much the better.

But every now and then came a crime film with a different agenda. An early such example was *The Stranger on the Third Floor*, a 1940 RKO B movie that's animated by the search for a murderer but otherwise not reliant on whodunit tropes. Peter Lorre stars as a boardinghouse inhabitant suspected of murder by a fellow tenant and young newspaper reporter (John McGuire). Combining elements from orthodox detective, gangster, and horror films, *Stranger* boasts a unique visual style, at various times drawing equally from surrealism and expressionism. This approach, suggested by director Boris Ingster but brilliantly

ABOVE: Musical star Alice Faye, who had been under contract to Fox since 1934, returned to her home studio in 1945 after a yearlong break following the birth of her second child. Realizing she couldn't sustain her popularity indefinitely with frothy tune fests, she took a gamble by lobbying for a dramatic role in *Fallen Angel*, a noir thriller that proved quite challenging for her.

executed by cinematographer Nicholas Musuraca, culminates in a disorienting sequence in which the reporter dreams that he is arrested, tried, convicted, and about to be executed for Lorre's murder of a neighboring tenant. Musuraca's camerawork throughout suggested what would become one of noir's tenets: there exists in the shadows a separate world . . . one of fear, paranoia, and unknown terrors.

There was nothing new about using cinematography to enhance mood, but this new type of movie utilized such tricks as low-key lighting, bizarre camera angles, and unbalanced compositions to set itself apart from typical crime and mystery movies. Moreover, the emphasis on visual trademarks was matched by thematic preoccupations that gradually emerged during the war years and immediately thereafter. Blatant eroticism in film narratives was expressly forbidden by the Production Code, but in trying to appeal to mature, worldly viewers, filmmakers

ABOVE: *Fallen Angel* director Otto Preminger goes over some dialogue with his female star, Alice Faye (*right*), and supporting player Anne Revere. Faye felt she had done some fine acting in the film and was heartbroken to learn that some of her best scenes wound up on the cutting-room floor when studio head Darryl F. Zanuck ordered that *Angel* be reedited to beef up the part of its secondary female lead, Linda Darnell. After attending a preview screening, she quit Fox and the movie business as well.

developed ways of suggesting rather than explicitly showing illicit sexuality. This was the more effective way to go because it forced audiences to use their imaginations and conjure up scenes that might have been even more steamy than the directors would have pictured.

Conventional crime films generally featured heroines of unquestioned virtue. They might be distressed damsels implicated in murder, or heiresses being stalked by would-be killers intent on claiming their fortunes, or innocent victims of complicated swindles. More often than not, they are last seen clinching with their male champions at film's end, apparently headed for the altar. But a different sort of leading lady began appearing with regularity during the 1940s.

There was nothing new about the cinematic femme fatale, a scheming woman who manipulates the men in her life and often ruins them before coming to a bad end herself. Her type dates back to early silent movies and the tempting "vamps" played by pioneering sex symbol Theda Bara in the 1910s. But the '40s femme fatale was more deadly and more aggressive. If she couldn't convince some poor sap to kill the guy making her life miserable, she was perfectly capable of doing it herself and framing the sucker. Shrewd, seductive, blonde (usually), and beautiful, she was played by Barbara Stanwyck in *Double Indemnity* (1944), Claire Trevor in *Murder My Sweet* (1944), and Lana Turner in *The Postman Always Rings Twice* (1946), to name just a few.

By the time Turner had persuaded John Garfield to help bump off her husband in *Postman*, French film critic Nino Frank had coined the term *film noir* (literally "black film," but colloquially "dark film") to describe the new breed of Hollywood crime movies. He referred not only to the look of such motion pictures—frequently set at night and photographically pregnant with shadows and silhouettes—but also to the moral tone of their stories. Their cinematic influences were multiple: the aforementioned German expressionism, the just-emerging Italian neorealism, and French poetic realism. Thematically, the form owed a lot to the relentlessly hard-boiled fiction found regularly in the pages of *Black Mask* and competing pulp magazines, as well as crime novels by such masters as Dashiell Hammett, Raymond Chandler, James M. Cain, and Horace McCoy.

Noir protagonists—practically all of them victimized by bad luck, which they attribute to the malevolent goddesses of Fate—are a variegated lot: sleazy private eyes, victims of circumstance, down-at-heel grifters, and ordinary citizens either tricked or manipulated (by a femme fatale) into committing a crime or taking the fall for it. Sometimes they are able to extricate themselves from dire predicaments, but they come to sad ends with equal frequency. Postwar cynicism and a pervasive feeling that the world had spiraled out of control undergird many a film noir.

The form's zenith, at least during its formative years, is generally agreed to have been reached with *Out of the Past* (1947, RKO), starring Robert Mitchum as an archetypal private eye—down to his wide-brim fedora, rumpled trench coat, and cigarette dangling from the corner of his mouth—seduced by racketeer's mistress Jane Greer into double-crossing her lover, Kirk Douglas. Based on a novel by Daniel Mainwaring, who collaborated on the script with James M. Cain and Frank Fenton, *Out of the Past* was directed by Jacques Tourneur, whose vision for the film was perfectly realized by the superb cinematography of Nicholas Musuraca. Often imitated (and remade in 1984 as *Against All Odds*), this nearly flawless example of the form perhaps best represents what film critic Blake Lucas identified as one of noir's central conceits: "The destruction of a basically good man by a morally ambiguous woman he loves."

By the late '40s, noir had established primacy over other types of crime movies, absorbing the characteristics of murder mysteries and gangster films and synthesizing them into a wholly satisfying amalgamation. The following decade would see a continuance of this evolution. ○

BELOW: Joan Bennett and director Fritz Lang, between scenes on *Scarlet Street* (1945). Lang, Bennett, and producer Walter Wanger shared ownership of an independent company named Diana Productions, which released its output through Universal. Their first two productions, *The Woman in the Window* (1944) and *Scarlet Street* (1945), were both critically and commercially successful. The third, *Secret beyond the Door* (1947), found Lang and Bennett squabbling incessantly during filming; it was the flop that ended the partnership.

FORMATIVE NOIR

World War II had the unexpected and ironically salutary effect of ending the decade-long Great Depression (thanks to massive government spending), but the accompanying fear, sorrow, and horror fundamentally altered the national zeitgeist. America had always prided itself on its optimism and can-do spirit, but even as her people labored valiantly in the war effort, a sense of dread quite understandably seeped into the collective consciousness. This perhaps begins to explain how film noir—bleak and unsettling—could make the grade as entertainment for moviegoers who, paradoxically, often craved escape from the grim reality of those years. Noir's characteristics not having fully coalesced during wartime, it's no surprise that the poster art for these films lacked any specificity of style. But in such samples as *Hot Spot* (the working title for what was released as *I Wake Up Screaming*), one can detect certain similarities: the use of shadowy lighting on faces, the depiction of characters as anxious or fearful, and the deployment of black, green, and purple in color schemes.

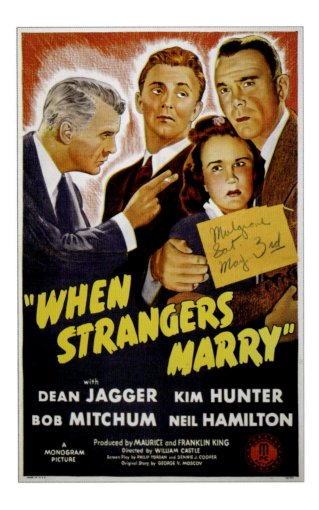

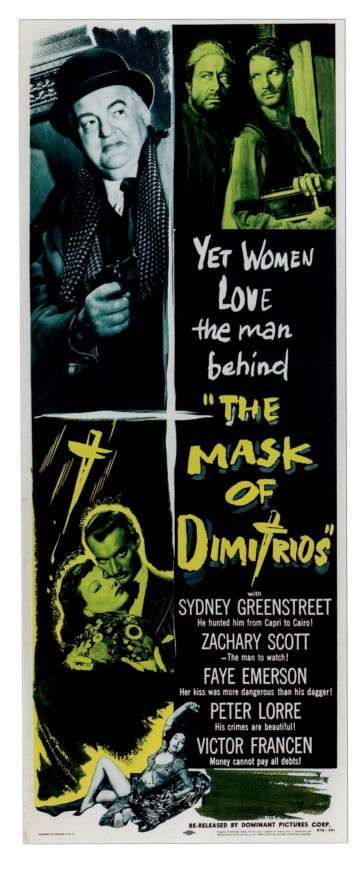

EARLY FEMMES FATALES

One of noir cinema's hallmarks—some call it the subgenre's defining characteristic—was the Bad Woman, a scheming, manipulative female who consciously uses her sex appeal to compel obedience from hapless, captivated males who know the difference between right and wrong but are powerless to resist her charms. The definitive example of this character type appeared fairly early in the noir cycle: Phyllis Dietrichson, the beautiful blonde temptress of *Double Indemnity* (1944), played by Barbara Stanwyck. Her personality traits would be detected in such notable future femmes fatales as Lana Turner in *The Postman Always Rings Twice* (1946), Jane Greer in *Out of the Past* (1947), and Rita Hayworth in *The Lady from Shanghai* (1948). There would be minor variations, among them Ann Savage's character in *Detour* (1946)—equal parts shrew and seductress—but, for the most part, Phyllis Dietrichson set the template. Occasionally, the femme fatale's feelings for her illicit lover were sincere, but even that rarely prevented her from making a sucker out of him.

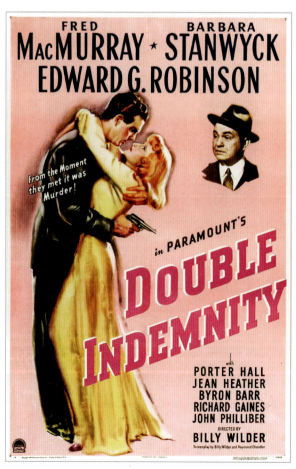

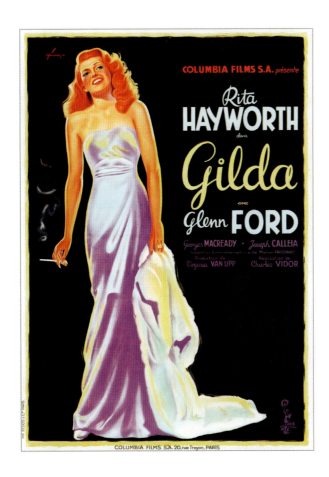

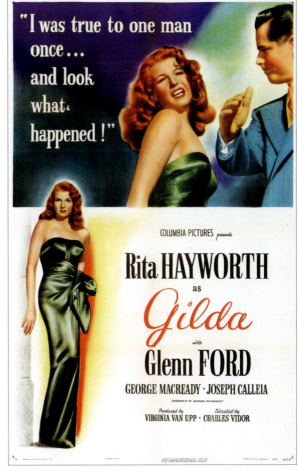

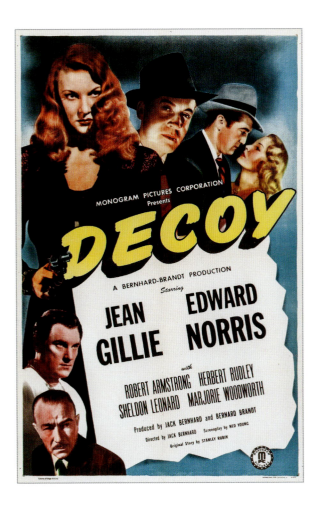

MONOGRAM PICTURES CORPORATION
Presents

DECOY

A BERNHARD-BRANDT PRODUCTION
Starring

JEAN GILLIE **EDWARD NORRIS**

with

ROBERT ARMSTRONG · HERBERT RUDLEY
SHELDON LEONARD · MARJORIE WOODWORTH

Produced by JACK BERNHARD and BERNARD BRANDT
Directed by JACK BERNHARD Screenplay by NED YOUNG
Original Story by STANLEY RUBIN

Their Love was a Flame that Destroyed!

M·G·M presents

LANA TURNER

JOHN GARFIELD

THE **Postman Always Rings Twice**

CECIL KELLAWAY
HUME CRONYN · LEON AMES
AUDREY TOTTER · ALAN REED

SCREEN PLAY BY HARRY RUSKIN AND NIVEN BUSCH
BASED ON THE NOVEL BY JAMES M. CAIN
DIRECTED BY TAY GARNETT
PRODUCED BY CAREY WILSON
A METRO-GOLDWYN-MAYER PICTURE

EDWARD G. ROBINSON
JOAN BENNETT
JAN DURYEA
REGIA: FRITZ LANG

la Strada Scarlatta

edizioni CUSSINO
UN FILM "UNIVERSAL"

He went searching for love... but Fate forced a DETOUR to Revelry... Violence... Mystery!

DETOUR

TOM **NEAL** · ANN **SAVAGE** · CLAUDIA **DRAKE**
Edmund MacDONALD · Tim RYAN · Esther HOWARD · Roger CLARK
A P.R.C. Production · Associate Producer Martin Mooney
Directed by Edgar G. Ulmer · Screen Play and Original Story Martin Goldsmith

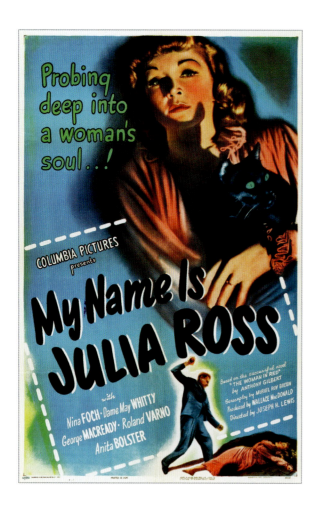

PEAK NOIR

In 1946, French critic Nino Frank coined the phrase *film noir* (literally meaning *black film*, but figuratively *dark film*) to describe American crime films with bleak, cynical, even nightmarish themes, incidents, and characters. At the time, Hollywood professionals didn't acknowledge the term—most probably had never heard it—but noir stylization had come to dominate crime and mystery films, and it didn't just apply to their content. Such cinematographers as John Alton and Nicholas Musuraca spent years experimenting with the interplay of light and shadow for the purposes of establishing mood. The classical Hollywood studio method of "high key" photography (bright, fully illuminated sets, lit from above) somehow didn't seem adequate for stories peopled with morally ambiguous characters and set in dingy, predominantly urban locales. Low-key lighting, off-kilter angles, and unbalanced frame compositions—along with the use of heavy shadows—came to typify noir cinematography and enhance these films' unwholesome atmosphere during the mid- and late '40s, when "dark film" finally came of age.

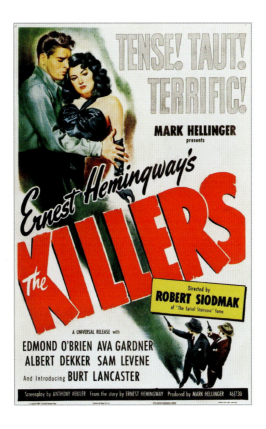

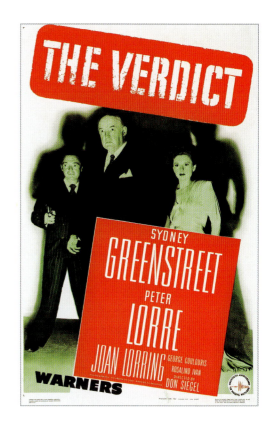

The Art of Classic Crime and Mystery Movies

COPS, G-MEN, AND PRIVATE EYES

Noir films were fundamentally different from earlier crime, mystery, and detective movies. They matured during the immediate postwar period—and, if only for stylistic reasons, they reflected reality more closely than the rather emotionally sterile whodunits and caper films of previous years. It was no accident that the Saints, Falcons, Charlie Chans, Sherlock Holmes, and Boston Blackies had either migrated to television or disappeared from movie theaters completely by 1949. Thanks to noir—not to mention the recent horrors and privations of war, and the looming threats posed by atomic energy and the Soviet Union—picture patrons had become accustomed to sterner stuff. Consequently, the super-detectives, roguish adventurers, and thick-headed cops were replaced by recognizably authentic law-enforcement professionals who solve crimes by dogged investigation rather than intuitive deduction, follow routine, and respect their department's chain of command. They also use force only when necessary, thus lending a real dramatic impact to their physical encounters. It's no accident that many crime films of the late '40s—among them 1948's *Naked City*, *Call Northside 777*, and *He Walked by Night*, to name just a few—were staged and shot in a semidocumentary style.

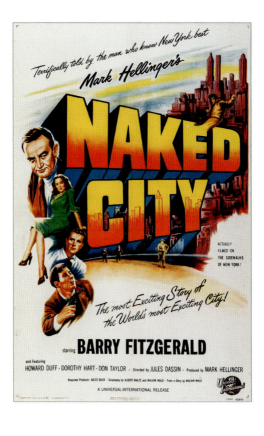

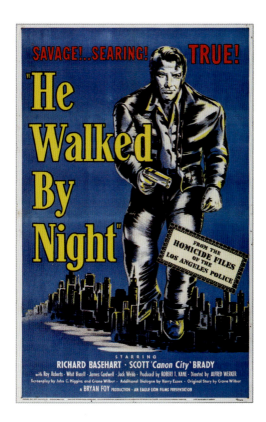

ASSORTED SAPS AND SUCKERS

You couldn't necessarily tell from the posters—unless their catch lines gave it away—but a plurality of late 1940s noir offerings revolve around protagonists drawn, either deliberately or accidentally, into desperate situations from which extrication is unlikely. Often, a Bad Woman is responsible, but just as frequently the poor dope has no one but himself to blame. And, on occasion, he is the unwilling pawn in a game he never agreed to play. The reason varies from film to film; in *Ride the Pink Horse* (1947), for example, a cynical veteran played by Robert Montgomery tries to blackmail the mobster who killed his best friend, only to find himself "on the spot." The same year's *Dark Passage* stars Humphrey Bogart as a convicted wife-killer who escapes from prison to prove his innocence, while in *The Big Clock* (1948), Ray Milland plays a magazine editor blamed for a murder actually committed by his publisher. Noir films don't always have happy endings, so viewers couldn't count on beleaguered protagonists surviving to the fadeout.

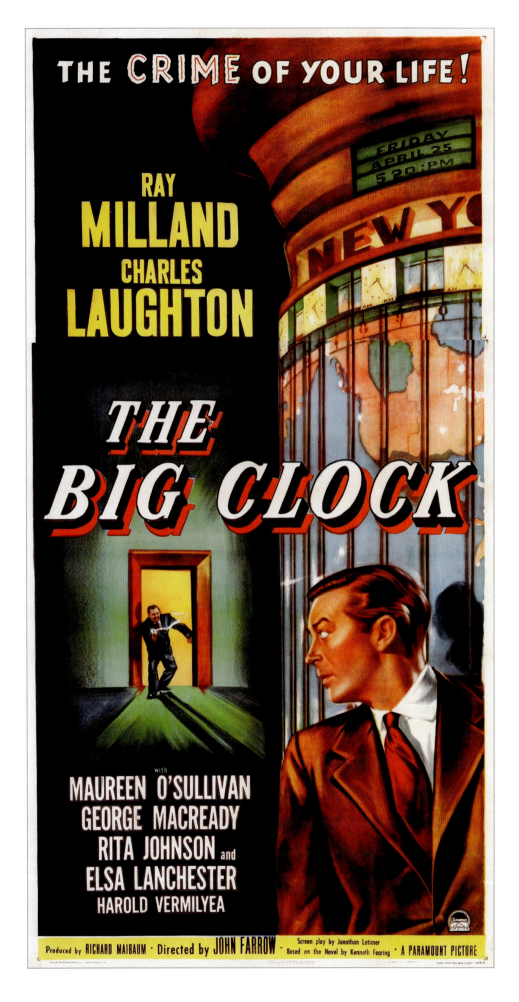

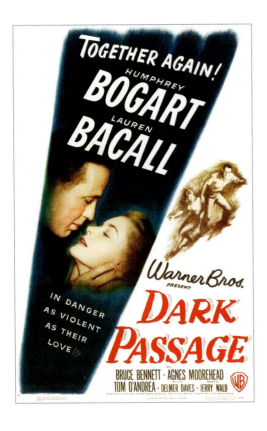

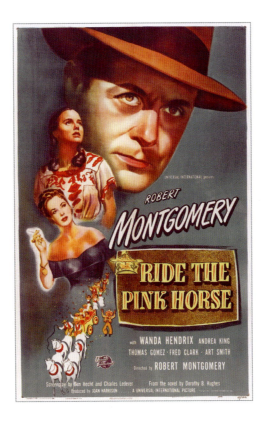

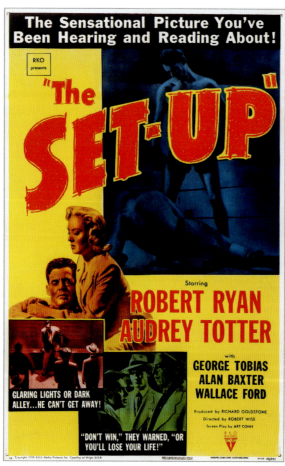

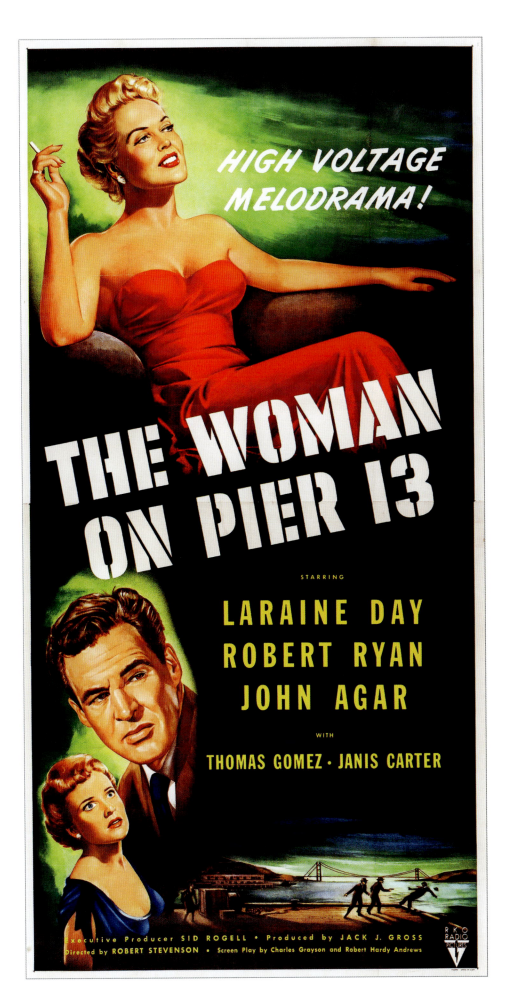

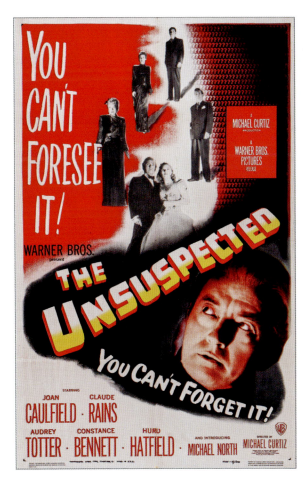

11

TOUGH
TIMES,
TOUGH
CITIES

The 1950s bring dramatic, wrenching changes to the motion-picture industry. A long-simmering antitrust case brought against Hollywood's major studios by the federal government—and taken all the way to the Supreme Court—has resulted in consent decrees forcing the divestiture of their theater chains, affecting the way that films are sold to exhibitors. Additionally, movie attendance suffers as a steadily increasing percentage of American families purchase television sets and stay home to watch old movies free of charge. Crime and mystery remain popular with moviegoers, but only by continuing to evolve in tone, style, and attitude . . .

The 1950s began with Hollywood in turmoil, thanks to divestiture, rising production costs, and, especially, competition from television. Commercial TV had been around since the late '30s, although World War II slowed its development as a viable alternative to theatergoing. At first, only the wealthy could afford sets, and programming was extremely scattershot in nature. By the late '40s, prices had declined, and the monitors were within the financial reach of middle- and working-class families. Early on, many executives saw video programming as an extension to radio and envisioned broadcasting hours of live shows each day. When this proved impractical, station owners started purchasing old films to help fill the number of daily programming hours they had guaranteed when applying for their licenses.

Independent theater owners—now extremely powerful, thanks to divestiture—warned the big studios against making their film libraries available to TV stations, arguing that it would encourage consumers to stay home even more than was already the case. Entrepreneurial distributors stepped into the breach, snapping up broadcast rights to Depression-era movies made on Poverty Row, many of which were low-budget thrillers and whodunits. Independent producers filmed half-hour programs based on characters from radio and the pulps, among them *Dick Tracy*, *Front Page Detective*, *Craig Kennedy, Criminologist*, *Casey, Crime Photographer*, and especially *Dragnet*, the new medium's first major cop series.

ABOVE: Director Joseph H. Lewis, a graduate of the cutting room, apprenticed by making B westerns on minuscule budgets and six-day schedules in the late '30s and early '40s. He applied the many lessons learned during that period to the (slightly) bigger pictures he directed in later years. The noir touchstone *Gun Crazy* (1950), today considered one of his best films, is famous for its lengthy one-take bank robbery scene. Originally scheduled to consume three to five days, using many camera setups, it was lensed in a single day when the cost-conscious Lewis decided he could film the entire sequence—some seventeen script pages long—in one continuous shot.

The early TV series—crude, cheaply produced, and not even as well written as B movies—attracted more viewers than they probably deserved, but Hollywood still had the edge. Theatrical films of the '50s boasted newly developed technological advances such as 3–D images and stereophonic sound, plus Cinemascope and other widescreen formats. Technicolor, which previously and primarily graced wartime escapist fare (big-budget musicals and large-scale swashbucklers, mostly), was employed more frequently on dramatic pictures with contemporary settings, although it should be noted that noir filmmakers preferred to work in black and white because it better reflected the form's thematic and visual preoccupations.

Divestiture went a long way toward killing off the B movie: without having to program double features in their prestige theaters to compete with smaller venues with cheaper admission prices, the studios turned out fewer but more

ABOVE: Janet Leigh forcefully makes her point during a discussion with Orson Welles and Charlton Heston during a break in the production of *Touch of Evil* (1958). Note the sling around her left arm: Leigh broke it just before filming commenced and wore a cast during much of the shooting schedule, but ingenious costuming and clever camera angles disguised that fact most of the time. Leigh permitted the cast to be removed when absolutely necessary, then reapplied following completion of a scene.

expensive A movies with top stars. Moviegoers gradually weaned themselves off the double bills, especially because the early TV series trafficked in that sort of clichéd formulaic material. The majors didn't stop producing low-budget films altogether, but the market dried up for series fare such as the Charlie Chans, Crime Doctors, and Boston Blackies. (Charlie and Blackie both migrated to TV series, once their feature-film series were terminated.)

Crime films of the '50s were, if anything, tougher and grittier than their predecessors. For one thing, audiences hardened by wartime pressures, traumas, and tragedies were more receptive to stories, characters, and settings that more closely depicted real life. Whodunits of the Charlie Chan type were passé; moviegoers no longer found it credible that murder suspects could be herded into a room like sheep and made to calmly stand by while a detective tediously summarized recent events, one of them expecting any second to be revealed as a killer.

No, the day of the super-sleuth was over. Even that pompous elitist, Philo Vance, had been reborn a few years ago as a wisecracking, hard-boiled private eye, only to be kicked to the curb—figuratively speaking—by picture patrons weary of the type. Nick and Nora Charles, whose breezy outings had epitomized the Depression-era yearning for escapist entertainment, had stuck around long enough to become anachronisms.

Private eyes like Sam Spade, Philip Marlowe, and Michael Shayne had lost favor too. Police detectives replaced them as protagonists, running down gangsters and homicidal maniacs by the book, adhering to procedure and doggedly following clues. They bungled their assignments on occasion, just like law-enforcement agents in real life. But more often than not they got their men (and, sometimes, women) by virtue of their plodding professionalism.

Once forbidden by the Production Code from spotlighting crooked or patently unfit cops, the studios now built entire movies around them. *Detective Story*, based on a Broadway stage drama that ran for nearly eighteen months and won playwright Sidney Kingsley a coveted Edgar Award from the Mystery Writers of America, was brought to the screen brilliantly by producer/director William Wyler. The movie version stars Kirk Douglas as a self-righteous, sadistic cop whose rigid moral code demands he mete out harsh punishment to lawbreakers. By the film's end, he has become a pathetic figure, able to seek redemption only at the moment of his death.

Pathological police detectives were relatively rare during this period; audiences were far more likely to see thrillers built around corrupt cops. These included movies like *Pushover*, *Rogue Cop* (both 1954), and especially *Touch of Evil* (1958), the last great film made by Orson Welles, who wrote and directed this adaptation of a pulp novel and took the plum role of border-town police detective Hank Quinlan. Having grown to Falstaffian proportions, Welles also insisted on wearing makeup that rendered Quinlan a grotesque, repulsive figure, which made him easier to dislike. Deliberately shot in black and white, *Touch of Evil* boasts all the classic visual trademarks of film noir, in addition to the form's thematic hallmarks. Many believe it to be the last great noir.

Another type of crime film popular during the '50s was the exposé—a dramatization of real-life events involving systemic lawbreaking in major towns or cities. There was *Kansas City Confidential* (1952), *The Miami Story* (1954), *New York Confidential* (1955), *New Orleans After Dark* (1958), and so on. Perhaps the best of the bunch was *The Phenix City Story* (1955), a "torn from the headlines" thriller about a thoroughly corrupt Alabama town near the Army's Fort Benning. A "sin town" that offered vice of every type imaginable to servicemen as well as locals, Phenix City was run by crooks who went so far as to assassinate a newly elected state attorney general who had been voted into office on a reform ticket. Director Phil Karlson shot the entire film on location, even coaxing some of the town's residents to appear in it.

By decade's end, the Production Code Administration had been hollowed out. Crime movies of the '50s had broken new ground, mostly in response to competition from television programming. But the '60s and '70s had more surprises in store. ⬙

ABOVE: Ida Lupino was keen on working behind as well as in front of a movie camera, and she had already directed several films when she costarred with Robert Ryan in *On Dangerous Ground* (1951), a noir helmed by Nicholas Ray. When Ray suddenly fell ill during principal photography, producer John Houseman allowed Lupino to direct for several days, though she received no screen credit for filling in.

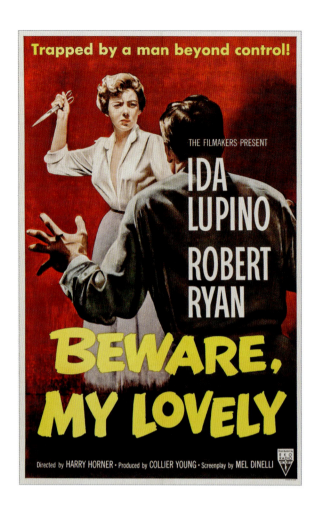

THE CRAZY AND THE DESPERATE

The 1950s saw a continuation of a trend that had begun in the postwar '40s: films built around murderous psychopaths. Long gone were criminal masterminds such as Professor Moriarty or Dr. Fu Manchu. Instead, moviegoers were treated to increased numbers of mentally or emotionally disturbed outcasts who express their disaffection by killing people. In some cases, their victims are chosen at random; in others, they are people the perpetrators believe have wronged them in some way. The usual motives—greed, jealousy, revenge—either don't exist or are camouflaged by the murderer's deep psychological problems. The job of portraying these usually complex characters usually fell to fine character actors such as William Talman (*The Hitch-hiker*), Arthur Franz (*The Sniper*), and Stephen McNally, but the popular leading men of the day also essayed such roles on occasion, notably Robert Mitchum (*The Night of the Hunter*) and Robert Wagner (*A Kiss before Dying*). Perhaps the finest characterization of this type was contributed by Humphrey Bogart, playing an alcoholic writer whose violent rages make him a murder suspect in 1950's *In a Lonely Place*.

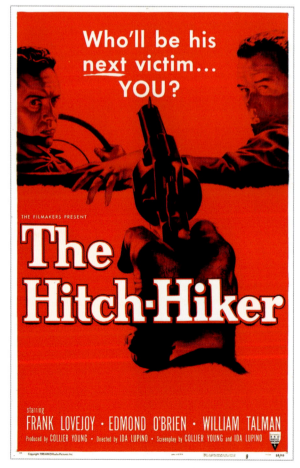

WATCH OUT !!

soon you will
see the screen
EXCITEMENT
of the year !

PANIC
IN THE STREETS

RICHARD WIDMARK · PAUL DOUGLAS

BARBARA BEL GEDDES

WALTER (JACK) PALANCE · ZERO
MOSTEL · DAN RISS · ALEXIS MINOTIS
GUY THOMAJAN · TOMMY COOK

Directed by ELIA KAZAN

Produced by SOL C. SIEGEL

Screen Play by RICHARD MURPHY · Adaptation by DANIEL FUCHS · From a Story by EDNA and EDWARD ANHALT

20th CENTURY-FOX

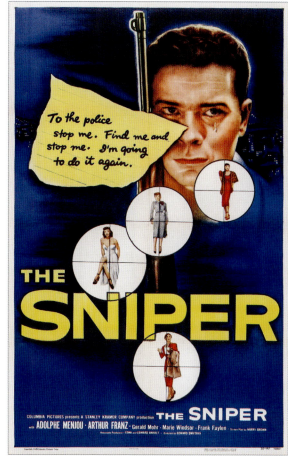

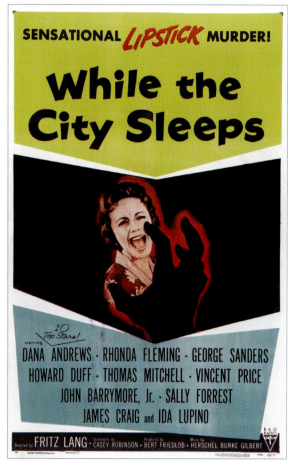

THE BIG CAPER

Another type of crime film that enjoyed popularity during the 1950s concerned the planning and execution of elaborate heists, frequently carried out in broad daylight and generally having unforeseen consequences that result in chaos and carnage. The decade began with two long-acknowledged classics of this type: *Gun Crazy* and *The Asphalt Jungle* (both 1950). The former added understated eroticism to its mixture of noir elements; the latter established a pattern according to which most future "caper" films were cut. Both have proved enormously influential, although *Asphalt Jungle* was by far the bigger critical and commercial success. It certainly inspired a young filmmaker named Stanley Kubrick, whose 1956 thriller *The Killing* employs *Jungle*'s basic plot but adds several clever twists and alters its structure to create a more disjointed and unnerving viewing experience. Caper films adhering to the basic lines of these early suspense dramas were still being made as late as the 1980s. Their posters often relied on catchy blurbs to establish the picture's theme (as in *Armored Car Robbery*'s "Spectacular Stick-Up Stuns Nation").

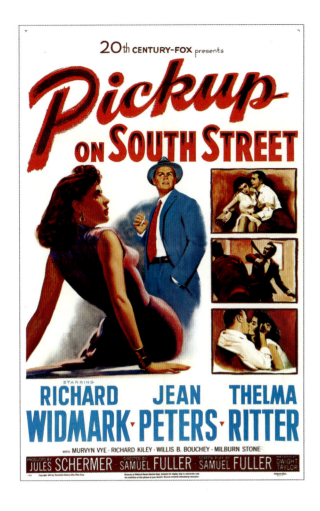

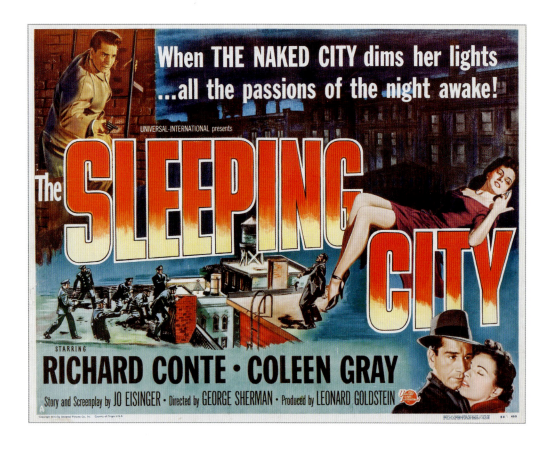

TOUGH COPS, CROOKED AND OTHERWISE

The scrappy private eyes and gentlemen adventurers of '30s B movies rapidly fell from favor after World War II, just as the coming of film noir rang the death knell for whodunits of the Charlie Chan variety. But policemen remained prominent figures in crime movies, finally escaping the constraints of old stereotypes and becoming fully realized characters. Some were scrupulously honest, some were irredeemably corrupt, and some were a little bit of both. Of all the major studios, RKO in particular evinced an appreciation for tough but honest cops willing to sacrifice everything—including their lives, if need be—in the pursuit of justice. *The Racket* (1951) and *The Narrow Margin* (1952) are exemplary examples of the studio's commitment to this ideal. But the new emphasis on realism in cinematic storytelling compelled filmmakers to make movies about bad cops, such as Kirk Douglas's psychopathic plainclothesman in *Detective Story* (1951), or the corrupt police protagonists of *Vicki* (1953), *Rogue Cop*, *Pushover* (1954), and, above all, *Touch of Evil* (1958).

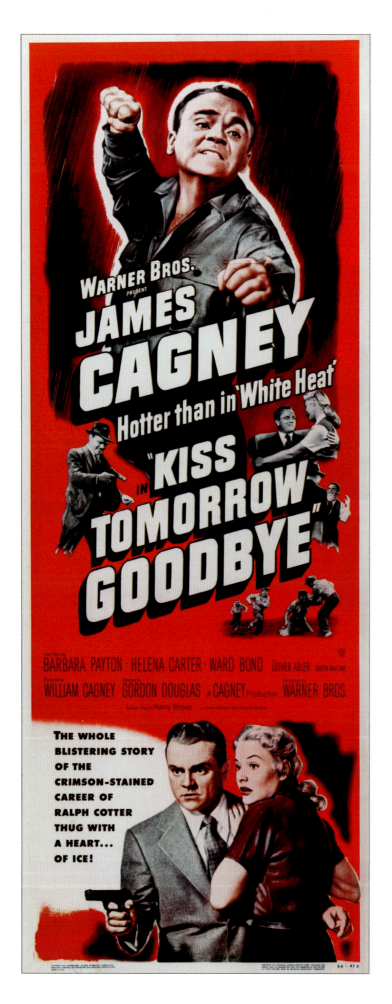

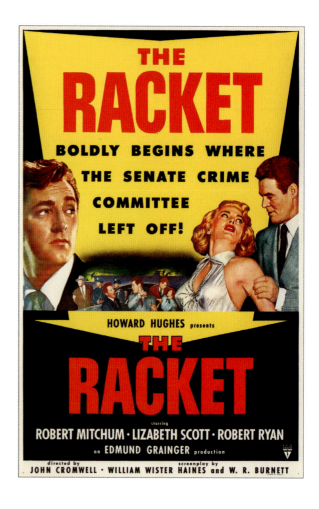

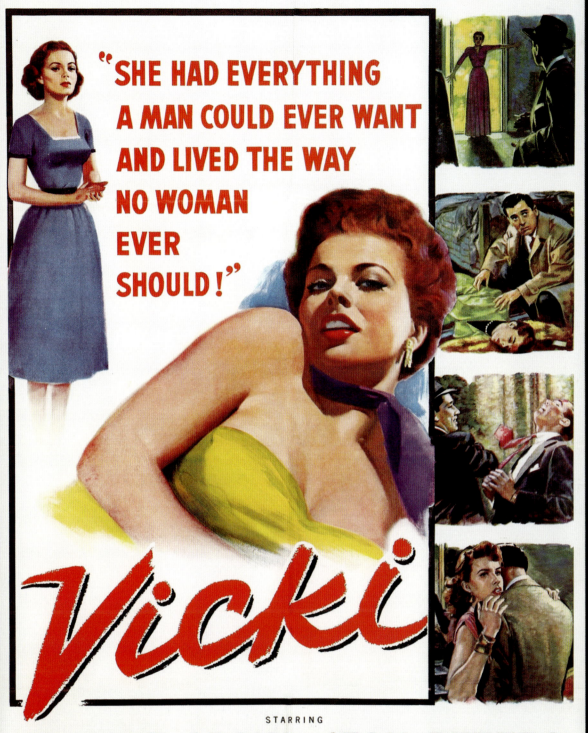

"SHE HAD EVERYTHING A MAN COULD EVER WANT AND LIVED THE WAY NO WOMAN EVER SHOULD!"

Vicki

STARRING

JEANNE CRAIN ☆ JEAN PETERS

WITH ELLIOTT REID · RICHARD BOONE · CASEY ADAMS · ALEX D'ARCY · CARL BETZ · AARON SPELLING

PRODUCED BY LEONARD GOLDSTEIN · DIRECTED BY HARRY HORNER · SCREEN PLAY BY DWIGHT TAYLOR · 20th CENTURY-FOX

BASED ON A NOVEL BY STEVE FISHER

Tough Times, Tough Cities

THE EXPOSÉS

This unique strain of crime cinema flourished in the '50s but had died out by decade's end, succumbing to excess and repetition. There had already been several paperback books devoted to exposés of America's sin cities, but these were—at least in intent—journalistic tomes. Unless they're making documentaries, of course, filmmakers require narratives, so—notwithstanding claims that such blatantly exploitative motion pictures were largely true—fictional and semifictional characters and events were grafted onto the stories. *Slightly Scarlet* (1956) shares plot elements with the exposés but is actually an adaptation of James M. Cain's novel *Love's Lovely Counterfeit*. (It's also considered a noir film despite having been shot in Technicolor, almost certainly to exploit the beauty of its gorgeous, red-headed stars, Rhonda Fleming and Arlene Dahl, who play sisters.) You'll notice that the posters for many of these films are copy heavy; clearly, it was felt they needed some extra promotional oomph in the form of explanatory text and testimonials.

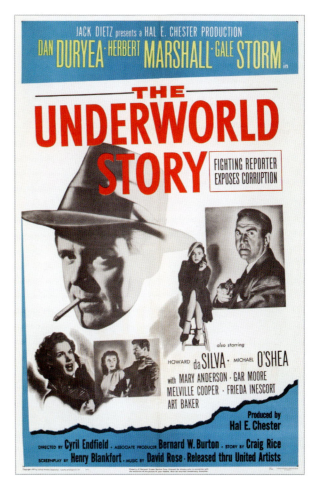

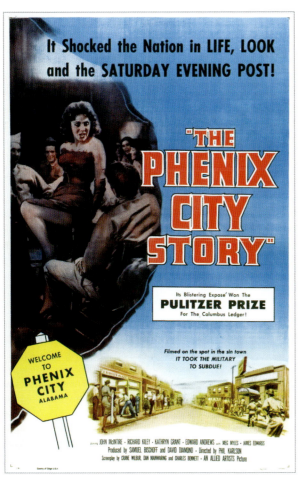

you'll be tense with suspense and limp from excitement!

dan duryea
jayne mansfield
martha vickers

in **the burglar**

with peter capell · mickey shaughnessy

Screen Play by DAVID GOODIS · From the Original Novel
Produced by LOUIS W. KELLMAN · Directed by PAUL WENDKOS
A COLUMBIA PICTURE

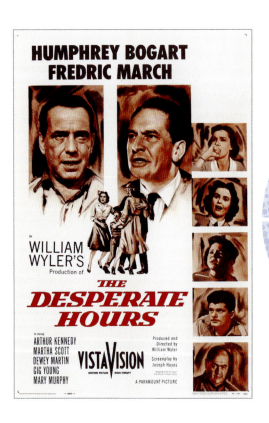

HUMPHREY BOGART
FREDRIC MARCH

WILLIAM WYLER'S
Production of

THE DESPERATE HOURS

Co-starring
ARTHUR KENNEDY
MARTHA SCOTT
DEWEY MARTIN
GIG YOUNG
MARY MURPHY

VISTAVISION
MOTION PICTURE HIGH FIDELITY

Produced and Directed by William Wyler
Screenplay by Joseph Hayes

A PARAMOUNT PICTURE

GINGER ROGERS   VAN HEFLIN   GENE TIERNEY   GEORGE RAFT

Someone Will Kill This Girl Tonight!

20th CENTURY-FOX presents

Black Widow

CinemaScope

with PEGGY ANN GARNER   COLOR by De Luxe   PRODUCED DIRECTED and SCREEN PLAY BY
REGINALD GARDINER · OTTO KRUGER   NUNNALLY JOHNSON

Property of National Screen Service Corp. Licensed for display only in connection with the exhibition of this picture at your theatre. Must be returned immediately thereafter. Country of origin U.S.A. Copyright 1954 · 20th Century-Fox Film Corp.   54-473

CUTTHROAT COMPETITION, ON-SCREEN AND OFF

The noir influence continued to dominate crime and mystery movies during the 1950s, with filmmakers continually testing the Production Code's limits by ratcheting up the sex and violence. Hollywood was well aware that television was eating into its audience, and the major studios felt competitive pressures more keenly after selling off their theater chains (as mandated by the federal government). Without guaranteed venues for their product, M-G-M, Fox, Paramount, and others had no alternative but to fight for every booking. For their part, exhibitors urged the studios to give them films with more mature content—the type of material that was not allowed on television, which had already been designated a family medium. Crime films increasingly stretched the boundaries of acceptability, with physical violence that formerly could only be suggested now shown in graphic detail: when men were shot they *bled*. Previously "taboo" topics such as extramarital affairs and sexual perversion were deemed permissible if they were covered in a tasteful manner. Hollywood movies were growing up, and crime movies especially reflected the new maturity.

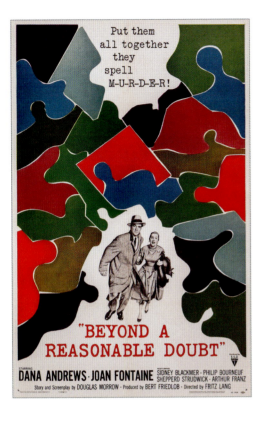

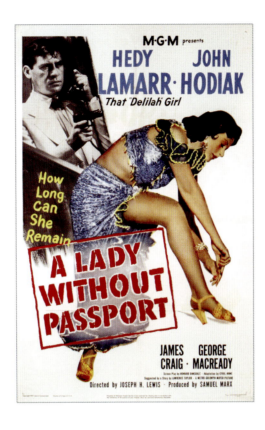

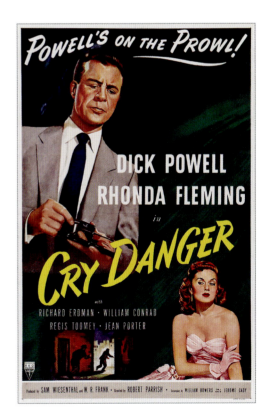

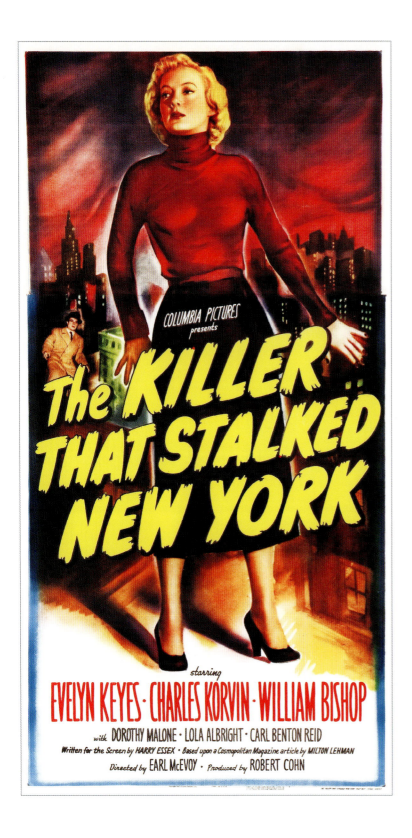

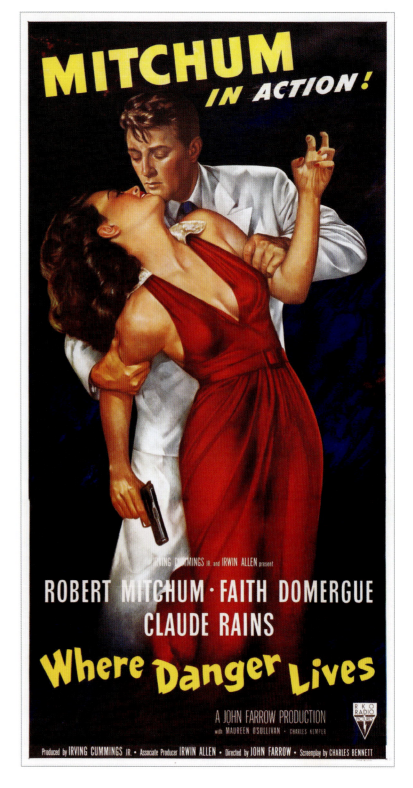

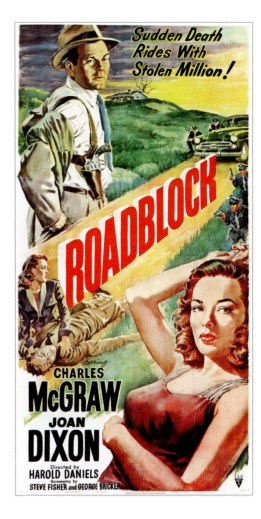

A GENRE GOES POSTMODERN

The '60s and '70s have proven to be tumultuous decades for the entire world, with American citizens in particular buffeted by rising crime (especially in urban areas), racial strife, political corruption, protests against the Vietnam War, economic turmoil (recession and inflation), and any number of societal problems that seep into the popular culture. As confidence in "the system" plummets, Hollywood more fulsomely embraces movie protagonists—cops, vigilantes, private detectives—who openly disregard the law and mete out justice of their own . . .

By 1960, film noir had pretty much flamed out, its tropes rendered impotent by endless repetition. Some of its narrative themes and visual flourishes remained in use but were now packaged differently, updated to maintain relevance as crime films evolved during the decade. Irony and cynicism pervaded the movies of the '60s and '70s, and not just topical ones. The nation's antiestablishment mood was reflected in westerns and historical epics as well, although it was most pronounced in thrillers set in the present day.

As this period began, television still provided the American public with a steady diet of crime and detective programs—police procedurals, private-eye romps, and even series devoted to the exploits of government operatives, secret agents, and the occasional suave crook or two. But the producers of these shows were constrained by strict, inviolable rules imposed on them by the networks' Standards and Practices divisions, created to ensure that program content steer clear of anything that might offend any member of the public. Advertisers insisted on lowest-common-denominator storytelling and impossibly virtuous characters, lest a consumer somewhere get his or her dander up and blame a program's sponsor for a producer's lapse of taste.

Consequently, crime and mystery fans craving stronger stuff turned to their local movie houses. During the previous decade, the Production Code Administration's stranglehold on filmmakers had gradually loosened, as picture patrons expressed increased willingness to see movies that bore at least passing resemblances to reality. The Catholic Church's Legion of Decency, another

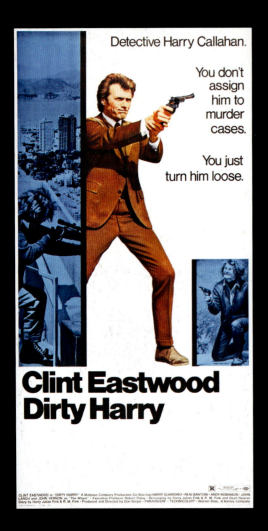

ABOVE: Clint Eastwood was still regarded as a horse-opera star and remembered primarily as "The Man with No Name" from Sergio Leone's trio of spaghetti westerns when he got the opportunity to play tough-as-nails San Francisco cop Harry Callahan in *Dirty Harry* (1971).

longtime bastion of public morality, likewise found its influence diminishing—especially as its dreaded "Condemned" rating was applied to such sober, high-quality films as *8½*, *Of Human Bondage*, and *The Pawnbroker*, to name just a few.

Throwing off shackles that had bound them for decades, members of Hollywood's creative community tackled mature subjects and injected realism into them. By the late '60s, it was not unusual to attend mainstream films containing nudity, sex, profanity, and explorations of previously hot-button topics such as race, religion, corruption, homosexuality, and, above all, the Vietnam War. To be sure, producers at the shallow end of Hollywood's talent pool used their newfound freedom solely for exploitation purposes. But younger filmmakers rejoiced at the chance to make substantive movies with something to say.

Of course, Hollywood remained governed by cycles: if one film about motorcycle gangs proves to be a huge moneymaker, you can bet ten more just like it will be on screens within months. So it was, in the '60s and '70s, with the gangster film. But the new members of the species weren't like the trigger-happy malevolent mobsters of Depression-era sagas such as *Public Enemy* and

ABOVE: Clint Eastwood jokes with director Don Siegel on the set of *Dirty Harry*. Having gotten his start directing montages for Warner Bros. in the late 1930s, Siegel graduated to short subjects, two of which won Oscars in successive years. He began directing feature films in 1946, establishing a reputation for working quickly and economically. He had already worked with Eastwood in *Coogan's Bluff* (1968), and he knew how to get the best out of him.

ABOVE LEFT: Sean Connery shows off to Ursula Andress on a Jamaica beach during location shooting for *Dr. No* (1962), the first of the James Bond spy thrillers. Connery had been a boxer and a bodybuilder in his salad days, and he prided himself on keeping in top physical condition—which helped him when it came to performing vigorous action for the Bond films.

ABOVE RIGHT: Gregory Lee with author Harper Lee, perusing the script of *To Kill a Mockingbird* (1962), based on her bestselling book about murder and race hatred in Depression-era Alabama. More a character study than a crime thriller, the Robert Mulligan–directed drama remains one of the most perfectly realized adaptations ever committed to celluloid.

Little Caesar. They were smarter, slicker, smoother. They planned and executed complicated capers. They generated audience sympathy by taking the form of popular stars: Sean Connery (*The Anderson Tapes*), Steve McQueen (*The Thomas Crown Affair*, *The Getaway*), Michael Caine (*Gambit*).

Another '60s innovation was the "true crime" film, an offshoot of the previous decade's "exposé" thrillers. In fact, Hollywood had dabbled in this sub-subgenre since the '30s but had always changed names, dates, and places to avoid getting involved in litigation with offended relatives of the criminals or their victims.

The passage of years reduced those concerns. In 1932, *Scarface* could be made only by referring to the Al Capone character as Tony Camonte; by 1959, Rod Steiger openly played Capone in a still greatly fictionalized biopic. That legendary criminal couple of the '30s, Bonnie Parker and Clyde Barrow, came to the screen in the glamorous forms of Faye Dunaway and Warren Beatty. But *Bonnie and Clyde* (1967), for all its romanticism, didn't shy away from realistically depicting the lovers' grisly demise, riddled with bullets fired from G-men's guns.

In Cold Blood (1966), based on Truman Capote's bestselling book covering the heinous crimes committed by ex-cons Perry Smith and Dick Hickock, demonstrated just how effective—and affecting—true-crime films could be when written, directed, and acted with taste and sensitivity. *The Boston Strangler*

(1968) was slightly more exploitative but ultimately redeemed by Tony Curtis's magnificent portrayal of real-life strangler Albert DeSalvo.

Another big development in crime films of the '60s was the rehabilitation of the private eye. Ross MacDonald's Lew Archer, a more sensitive version of Sam Spade and Philip Marlowe, debuted in a 1949 novel titled *The Moving Target*, which was adapted with surprising fidelity but for one major change: Paul Newman played Archer but insisted the character be renamed Harper. Why? Mere superstition. Newman's previous two films, both hits—*Hud* and *The Hustler*—had *H* in their titles. He wanted to keep the string going, just for luck, ergo *Harper* (1966). (His next film, in case you were wondering, was *Hombre*.)

Frank Sinatra brought his old scooby-dooby-doo to a wisecracking shamus in the whodunits *Tony Rome* (1967) and *Lady in Cement* (1968). The latter's most interesting body wasn't a corpse but, rather, bikini-clad Raquel Welch, and her prominent placement in advertising materials, including the poster, accounted for a good deal of the film's success.

Given the advent of "blacksploitation" cinema in the late '60s and early '70s, it was inevitable that a tough African American private eye would make the scene. Richard Roundtree played the eponymous investigator in *Shaft* (1971), several sequels, a short-lived TV series, and a 2000 remake. The Big Apple's coolest cops, "Coffin" Ed Johnson and "Grave Digger" Jones, created by novelist Chester Himes, plied their trade none too gently in *Cotton Comes to Harlem* (1970), impersonated by Godfrey Cambridge and Raymond St. Jacques.

No crime-busting cop was tougher, or faster on the draw, than Clint Eastwood's Harry Callahan, the San Francisco–based dick introduced to moviegoers in *Dirty Harry* (1971). He returned several times, although each sequel was a little weaker than the previous one. The same could be said of the *Death Wish* series, based on a book by Brian Garfield. Its leading character, New York architect Paul Kersey (played in the movie by Charles Bronson), turns vigilante after his wife is murdered and his daughter viciously assaulted by street punks. The original 1974 film, a box-office smash, was well done in every aspect, but the inevitable sequels so debased the original premise that the last, made twenty years later, descended into self-parody.

The final major innovation of this period—which began, of course, with the Cold War threatening to heat up—was the advent of the suave secret agent epitomized by Ian Fleming's James Bond, the British operative with a government-granted license to kill. Bond wasn't much of a detective, but his adversaries, such as Goldfinger and Doctor No, were flamboyant supercriminals not unlike the Iron Claws and Hooded Terrors of the Pearl White serials. Little-known Scottish actor Sean Connery fit the part like a glove and attained international stardom as a result of his work in the '60s equivalents of what would come to be known as "popcorn movies"—breathtaking rollercoaster rides one sits back and enjoys without having to think too much about them. Connery's Bond inspired a slew of campy imitators, the most popular being James Coburn's Derek Flint and Dean Martin's Matt Helm, but none came close to filling 007's shoes.⚙

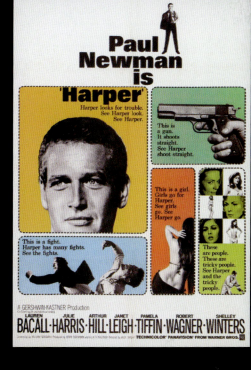

ABOVE: This one-sheet for *Harper* (1966) demonstrates how much movie posters had evolved since Hollywood's golden age. It's a fine example of graphic design, using pieces of black-and-white photographs against color backgrounds rather than painted illustrations, and is heavily reliant on text of the "Dick-and-Jane" type to explain the facets of Harper's character.

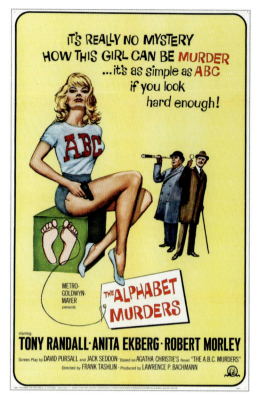

THE AGATHA CHRISTIE REVIVAL

Perhaps the most surprising development in crime films during the 1960s and '70s was the resurgence of whodunits—specifically, those based on novels written by the doyenne of mystery fiction, Agatha Christie. Elderly British character actress Margaret Rutherford charmed nostalgia-minded moviegoers with her eccentric portrayal of Miss Marple, Christie's spinster sleuth, in a quartet of madcap mysteries beginning with *Murder She Said* (1963). Posters for that film carried more or less traditional crime-movie art showing a woman being throttled, but the sequels were illustrated with cartoony caricatures that suggest a lighthearted approach to murder. Christie's insufferably smug detective Hercule Poirot, played by Austin Trevor in several early British talkies, returned to the screen in 1965's *The Alphabet Murders*, which emulated the comedic approach of the Marple pictures. That same year, independent producer Harry Alan Towers proffered the first of his three remakes (the others being released in 1974 and 1989) of Dame Agatha's best-known novel, *Ten Little Indians*. Poirot's shining hour was *Murder on the Orient Express* (1974), with an all-star cast headed by Albert Finney as the braggadocious Belgian.

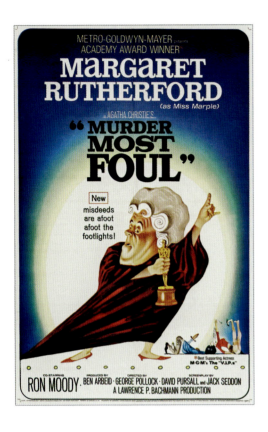

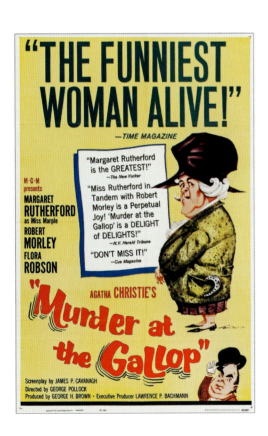

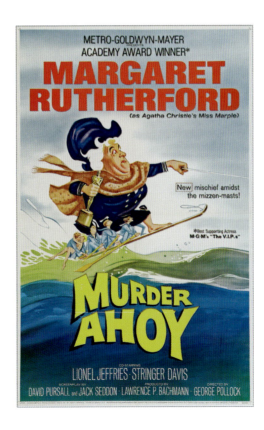

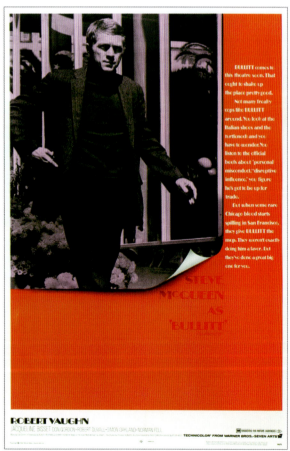

A NEW BREED OF COP

During Hollywood's golden age, police detectives were often portrayed (especially in B pictures) as honest but plodding cops with low IQs and stunted imaginations. That all changed in the '60s. *In the Heat of the Night* (1967) stars Sidney Poitier as Virgil Tibbs, a brilliant Black police detective from Philadelphia—a role Poitier reprised in *They Call Me Mister Tibbs* (1970). Steve McQueen plays the title role in *Bullitt* (1968), set in San Francisco and featuring a hip, stylish, and nonconformist cop. *Cotton Comes to Harlem* (1970) introduced audiences to African American detectives Coffin Ed Johnson (Raymond St. Jacques) and Grave Digger Jones (Godfrey Cambridge), who are only marginally less lethal than the miscreants they pursue. In *The French Connection* (1971), Gene Hackman wears a porkpie hat to distinguish his angry, profane Popeye Doyle from the other, more genteel detectives, but he was a cream puff compared to Clint Eastwood's *Dirty Harry* (also 1971), a laconic but diamond-hard San Francisco police inspector who meted out justice with his .44 Magnum revolver. A few years later, John Wayne traded his horse for a speedy cop car—temporarily, anyway—as *McQ* (1974) and *Brannigan* (1975).

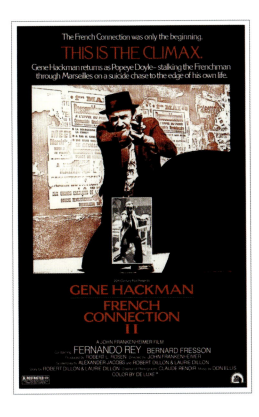

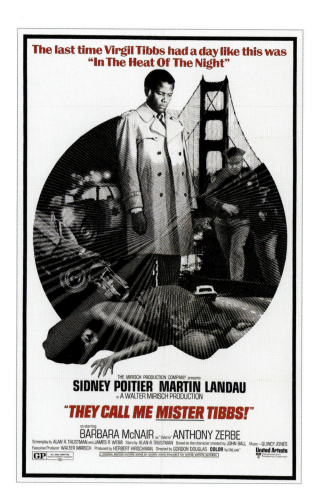

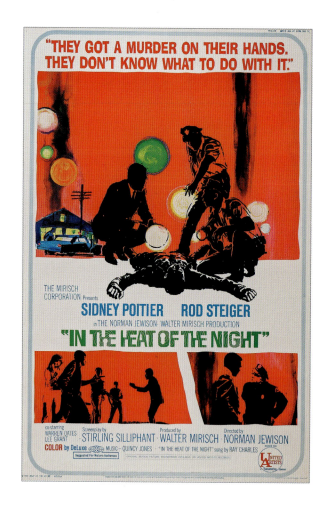

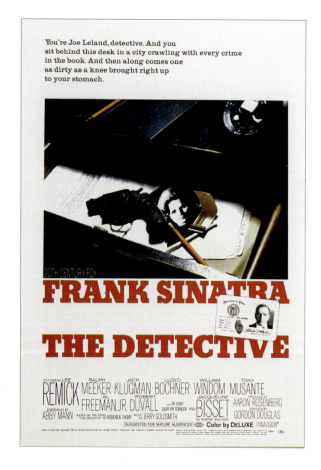

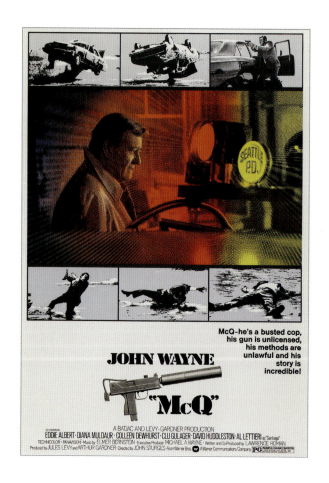

The mob wanted
Harlem back.
They got Shaft...
up to here.

SHAFT's his name.
SHAFT's his game.

You liked it before,
so he's back with more,

SHAFT's BACK IN ACTION!

SHAFT's BIG SCORE!
a brand new caper.

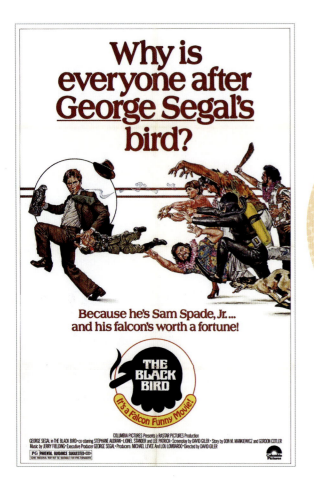

Why is
everyone after
George Segal's
bird?

Because he's Sam Spade, Jr....
and his falcon's worth a fortune!

THE BLACK BIRD
It's a Falcon Funny Movie!

PRIVATE EYES AND VIGILANTES

It wasn't just the police detective that got an image makeover during the Swinging Sixties: the private eye, who had largely fallen out of favor with the coming of noir, was dusted off as well. Turns out he would fit in perfectly with the Vietnam era's cynicism and disdain for authority. Ross Macdonald's Lew Archer, the literary progeny of Sam Spade and Philip Marlowe, reached theater screens in the person of Paul Newman. *Harper* (1966) and *The Drowning Pool* (1975) changed the surname of Macdonald's protagonist but still capture his essence. The former's one-sheet poster utilizes multiple images of Harper accompanied by text written in the style of a child's primer—an inexplicable design choice. Elsewhere, Frank Sinatra got into the act as the aging, eponymous gumshoe of *Tony Rome* (1967) and *Lady in Cement* (1968). In addition to a predilection for pithy wisecracks, the new breed of private eyes shared enormous capacities for physical punishment, as demonstrated by Jack Nicholson in *Chinatown* (1974), a brilliant elegy for the traditional hard-boiled dick. This period of cinema also gave rise to yarns about vigilantes such as Charles Bronson's aggrieved architect in *Death Wish* (also 1974).

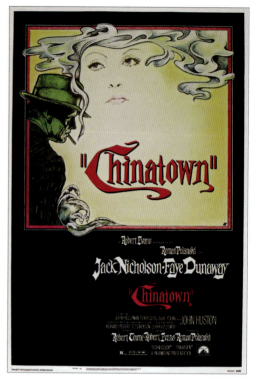

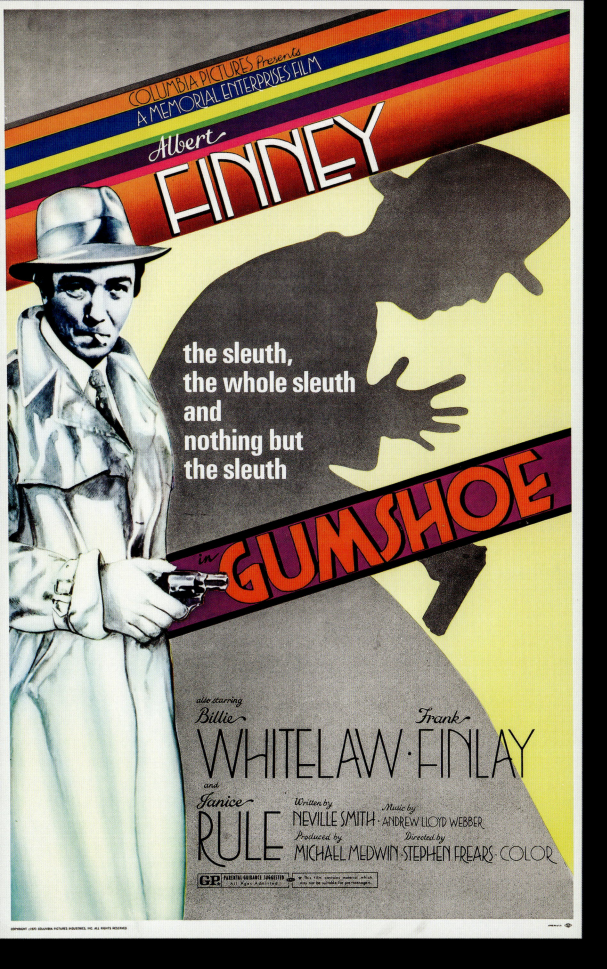

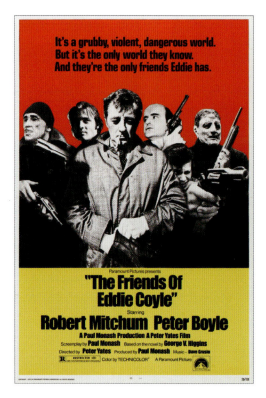

CROOKS AND CAPERS

With the Production Code's influence waning, filmmakers once again felt emboldened to tell stories glamorizing lawbreakers. The most noteworthy of these was *Bonnie and Clyde* (1967), inspired by the Depression-era depredations of a young midwestern couple. It looks like great fun up to the picture's climax, in which Faye Dunaway and Warren Beatty meet the same grisly fate as their real-life counterparts. Nonetheless, audiences frequently gravitated to movies built around crooks and killers, especially those who could be depicted as antiheroes rebelling against the Establishment. Caper films whose principal characters rip off big corporations were especially well received. It helped when these figures were played by popular stars, such as Steve McQueen in *The Thomas Crown Affair* (1968) and Sean Connery in *The Anderson Tapes* (1971). The fascination with stories about charismatic criminals reached its zenith with Francis Ford Coppola's *The Godfather* (1972) and *The Godfather Part II* (1974), which remain two of the best-remembered and oft-quoted gangster films of all time.

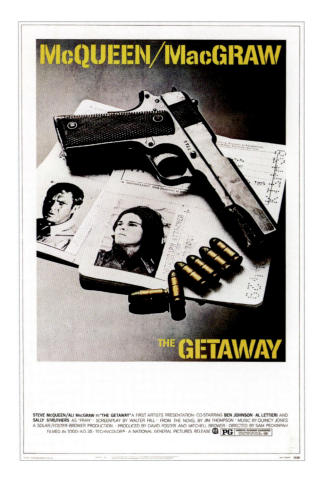

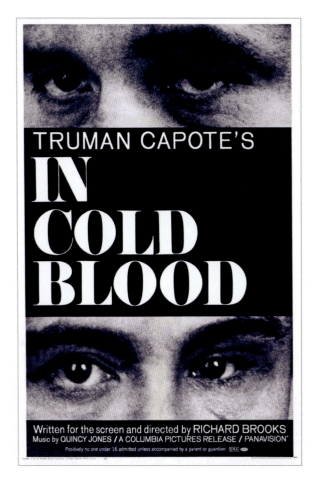

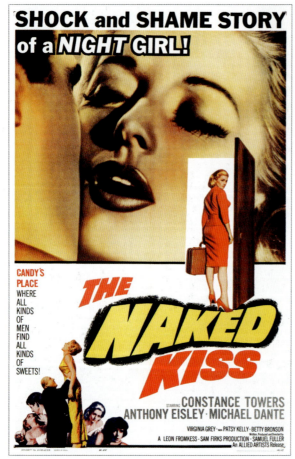

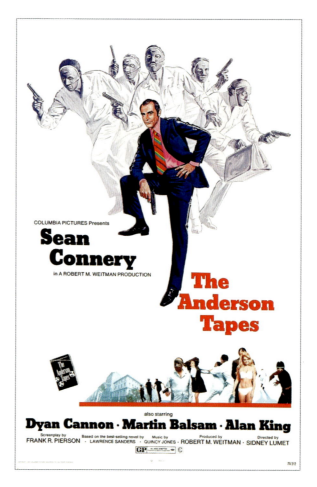

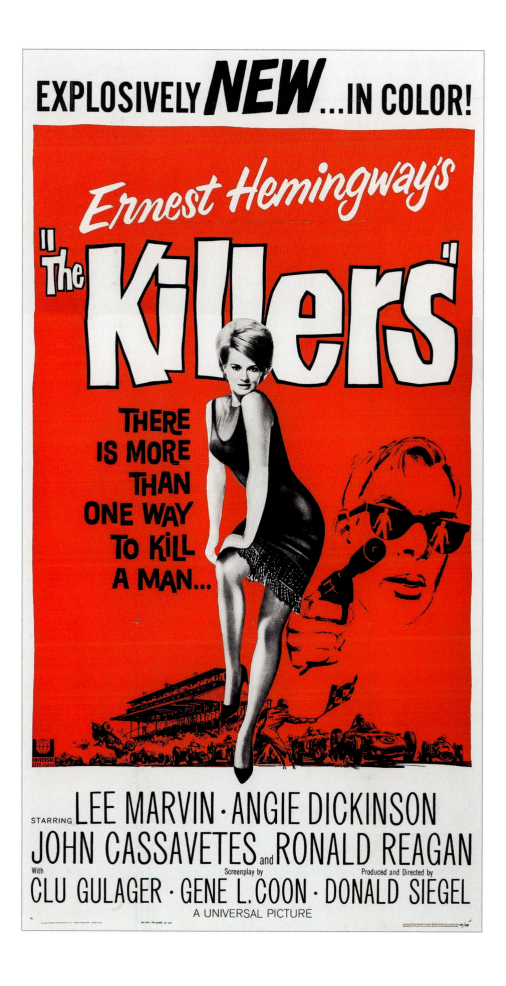

THE SUSPENSE IS KILLING ME

Caper films, comedic whodunits, and trigger-happy cop movies eventually became so numerous and so predictable that watching them took on a ritualistic aspect. Audiences knew what to expect, and filmmakers *knew* that audiences knew what to expect. For that reason, '60s and '70s thrillers that eschew formula and defying expectations were among the most effective crime films of the period. *Peeping Tom* (1960), in which a sexually repressed photographer kills his models one by one, horrified and revolted many moviegoers at the time, but today it is regarded as a masterpiece of erotic suspense. Slightly less provocative but equally spine-chilling were such killer-on-the-loose shockers as 1962's *Cape Fear* and *Experiment in Terror*. Later, *Sleuth* (1972) and *The Last of Sheila* (1973) would treat murder as a suspenseful cat-and-mouse game. By this time, movie posters had begun to employ a combination of painted images and tinted photographs; they often relied heavily on quantities of text to better explain the type of film they were promoting.

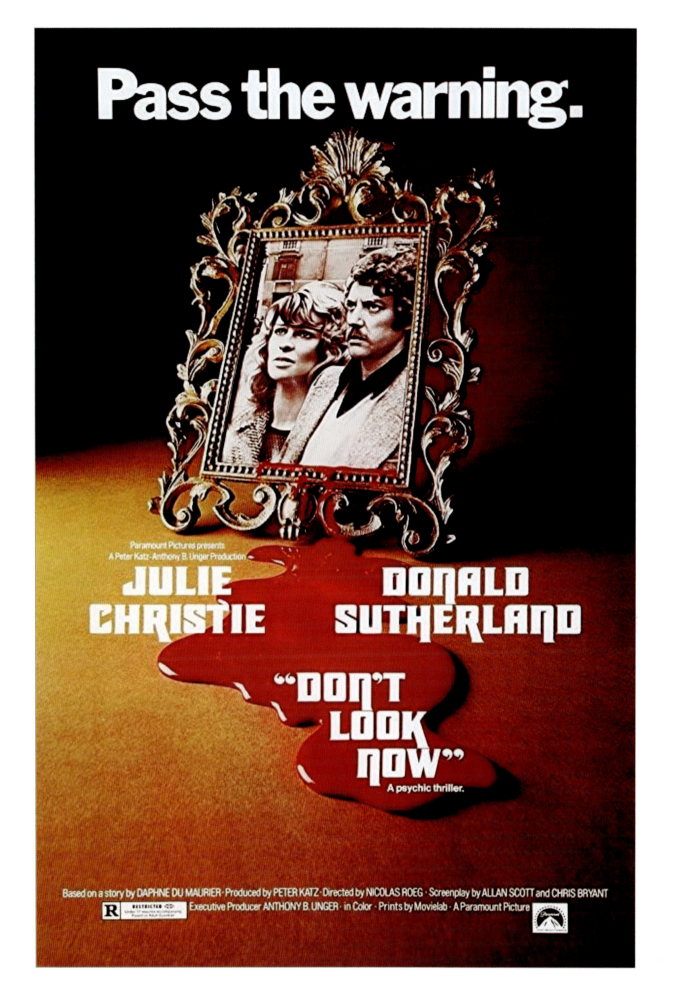

CARY Grant ★ Audrey Hepburn

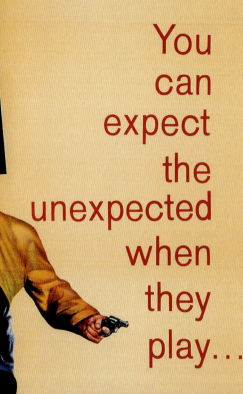

You can expect the unexpected when they play...

"Charade"

a STANLEY DONEN production
in TECHNICOLOR®

UNIVERSAL
CITY STUDIOS

Walter Matthau
James Coburn   Screenplay by PETER STONE
Produced and Directed by STANLEY DONEN   Music · HENRY MANCINI   A UNIVERSAL RELEASE

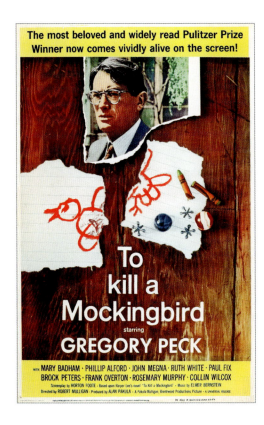

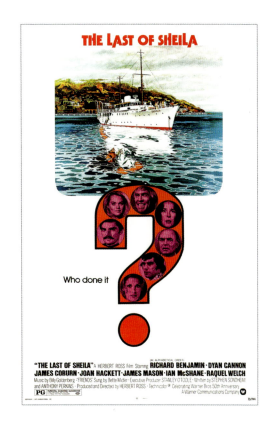

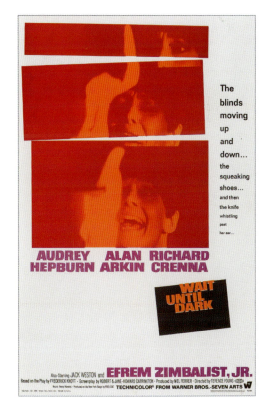

BOND AND FRIENDS

Ian Fleming's novels about the British secret agent James Bond, which began appearing in 1953, were modern-day equivalents of American pulp magazines and British boy's story papers. But it was nearly a decade before 007—the operative with a license to kill—was committed to celluloid by independent producers Harry Saltzman and Albert "Cubby" Broccoli. Their first production, *Dr. No* (1962), was relatively modest in scope, but its surprisingly robust box-office performance enabled the partners to turn out progressively lavish sequels that would make Fleming's character a pop-culture institution. Even the posters became more elaborate, although certain design elements were almost invariably repeated. The painted image of a tuxedo-clad Bond, arms folded and right hand gripping a gun pointed in the air, was used in most of them. Occasionally, the "7" in 007 becomes the handle of a pistol. And, of course, one could always count on beautiful women posing languidly about. These stylistic trademarks were carried over when Roger Moore replaced Connery in 1974. There were numerous Bond imitators, including James Coburn's Derek Flint and Dean Martin's Matt Helm.

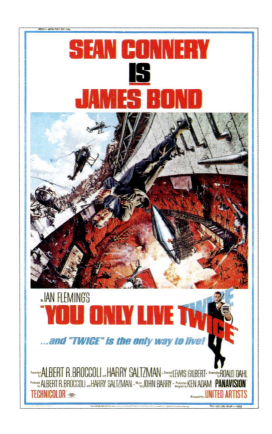

AFTERWORD

The movie business is nothing if not cyclical, and several once-popular genres had fallen out of favor by the mid- and late 1970s, among them the musical, the western, and the screwball comedy. Horror films were big, but the Gothic stylization that dominated 1930s and '40s shockers from Universal was considered old hat. The relaxation of Production Code strictures ushered in a new era characterized by increased levels of sex and gore, while the twin 1977 successes of *Star Wars* and *Close Encounters of the Third Kind* elevated science fiction—long considered fodder for drive-ins and Saturday matinees—to box-office primacy . . .

Crime and mystery films retained their popularity throughout this tumultuous period, but they too changed to reflect the interests of audiences, which skewed younger than ever before. The older folks increasingly preferred to stay home and watch television. And why not? Movie lovers who had faithfully followed the Depression and wartime exploits of Charlie Chan, Sherlock Holmes, Ellery Queen, and the like now had a plethora of detectives—police and private alike—flashing across TV screens on a weekly basis. One of the most popular was Peter Falk's Columbo, who first appeared in a 1968 made-for-TV movie and was given his own series in 1971. He introduced viewers to the "inverted" type of detective tale, in which the criminal's identity was known from the outset and the fun was derived from watching a detective accumulate enough clues to identify and apprehend him.

The late '60s trend toward private eyes, which had produced such long-running favorites as *Ironside* and *Mannix* (both debuting in 1967), extended to the next decade with the likes of *Cannon* (1971) and *The Rockford Files* (1974). Cop shows also proliferated during this period, with *Streets of San Francisco* (1972), *Kojak* (1973), and *Baretta* (1975) among the most popular. Hit series with female detective protagonists included *Police Woman* (1974) and *Charlie's Angels* (1976).

BELOW: *Against All Odds* (1984) was an updated remake of an early noir classic, *Out of the Past* (1947), with Jeff Bridges essaying the role taken by Robert Mitchum in the original but, unlike his predecessor, eschewing fedora hats and belted trench coats. Luscious Rachel Ward plays the femme fatale to a fare-thee-well.

For the most part, TV crime and mystery shows eschew the orthodox whodunit formula developed and codified in Depression-era feature films. In fact, many of them avoid plots revolving around murders in favor of capers concerning kidnappings, jewel thefts, and bank robberies. The narratives rarely (or only superficially) require deductive ability from their detectives; instead, they depict extended pursuits of miscreants on the basis of simple clues left at crime scenes. But they proved quite successful nonetheless.

Meanwhile, on the big screen, old-fashioned whodunit conventions were affectionately spoofed in such all-star romps as *Murder by Death* (1976) and *The Cheap Detective* (1978), conclusively demonstrating that films harking back to the days of Charlie Chan et al. were no longer to be taken seriously, except perhaps by die-hard devotees watching them on late-night local TV.

The 1980s were a mixed bag for crime and mystery lovers, but as always the success of a few key movies launched cycles of imitations that stretched into the early and mid-'90s. Film noir made a flamboyant comeback with two smash releases in 1981: Bob Rafelson's remake of James M. Cain's *The Postman Always Rings Twice*, starring Jack Nicholson and Jessica Lange, and writer/director Lawrence Kasdan's stylish *Body Heat*, with William Hurt and Kathleen Turner. The first was a period piece and the second a contemporary thriller, but both owed a great deal of their effectiveness to their directors' adherence to classic noir tropes.

As a result, the next fifteen or so years saw a veritable parade of updated remakes of noir hits from the '40s and '50s, many bearing the original titles: *I, the Jury* (1982), *Against All Odds* (1984, reworking *Out of the Past*), *No Way Out* (1987, reworking *The Big Clock*), *D.O.A.* (1988), *The Narrow Margin* (1990), *Cape Fear* (1991), *A Kiss before Dying* (1991), and *Kiss of Death* (1995). While none of them improved upon the earlier versions, most possessed considerable merits—not the least of which were big stars and impressive production values—and scored dramatically at the nation's box offices.

Noir's revival and Hollywood's determination to fully exploit it led producers searching for story material to option the screen rights to obscure novels—almost all of them originally published as cheap paperbacks rather than mainstream hardcovers—by authors who'd written them in the '50s for meager advances. Among the most highly regarded (if only by the pulp-fiction cognoscenti) was Jim Thompson; the 1974 adaptation of his novel *The Getaway* was a smash, while a 1976 version of his far-superior *The Killer Inside Me* went virtually unnoticed by theatergoers. But Thompson had written the kind of bleak, cynical yarns that filmmakers now unhampered by Production Code restrictions were dying to bring to the screen. *The Grifters* (1990) was a film festival darling that received phenomenally favorable reviews; earned respectable grosses, given its limited distribution; and made a star of third-billed newcomer Annette Bening. Consequently, producers gobbled up the rights to other Thompson novels that appeared on screen over the next few years: *The Kill-Off*, *After Dark My Sweet* (both 1990), and a remake of *The Getaway* (1994). The author's equally obscure

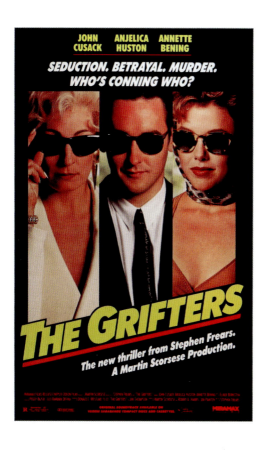

ABOVE: Director Stephen Frears described his 1990 adaptation of Jim Thompson's sleazy 1963 novel as "pulp fiction meets Greek tragedy." Produced by Martin Scorsese and scripted by crime novelist Donald E. Westlake, *The Grifters* was a smash that revived interest in Thompson, whose other noirish works were brought to the screen in quick succession.

contemporaries, such as Charles Williams and Charles Willeford, also found their all-but-forgotten works committed to celluloid: the former's *Hot Spot* and the latter's *Miami Blues* both hit the big screen in 1990. These and other films of their type were eventually dubbed "neo-noirs."

A variation of the neo-noir conflated crime with carnality, putting its emphasis on graphic sex scenes and letting the plot fend for itself. Such pictures were marketed as "erotic thrillers." This subgenre, extremely popular in the '80s and '90s, could trace its origin to *Body Heat*, which had featured some extremely steamy couplings between William Hurt and Kathleen Turner. But two 1987 offerings, *Black Widow* and *Fatal Attraction*, forcefully demonstrated how blatant eroticism could enhance otherwise predictable narratives. And they were relatively tame compared to what would follow. To take the most notorious example, *Basic Instinct* (1992) titillated audiences with a view of leading lady Sharon Stone's nether region, deliberately exposed during an interrogation by the police in a bid to distract her questioners. Her effect on detective Michael Douglas is obvious when he arrives home and violently forces himself on his startled wife (Jeanne Tripplehorn).

Erotic thrillers often relied on the machinations of a glamorous femme fatale who employed her sexuality to manipulate the hapless men in her orbit. They were produced by the dozens, many of them released direct to cable TV or the burgeoning home video market (or both). The more explicit the obligatory sex scenes, the less likely erotic thrillers were to attract top talent. Relatively well-known mainstream actresses such as Sean Young and Joan Severance occasionally worked on these films, as did former TV stars such as Tanya Roberts and Heather Thomas, but mostly their leading ladies included former *Playboy* models and exploitation-film regulars such as Shannon Tweed, Erica Eleniak, and Kathy Shower. Eventually, the erotic-thriller craze burned out, a victim of market oversaturation.

Another neo-noir variation relied on nostalgia and set its narratives during the '30s or '40s. Often filmed in black and white, these period pieces frequently dramatized investigations of real-life crimes. The cycle could be said to have started with *The Two Jakes* (1990), Jack Nicholson's sequel to *Chinatown*, but it attained full flower with *The Public Eye* (1992), *Mulholland Falls* (1996), and *L.A. Confidential* (1997).

Several new filmmaking talents emerged during the '90s, the most impressive being Quentin Tarantino, whose approach to crime thrillers is about as far from cinematic orthodoxy as could possibly be imagined but has resulted in some of the most memorable genre specimens in recent decades, among them *Reservoir Dogs* (1992), *Pulp Fiction* (1994), and *Kill Bill* (2003). Perhaps his most conventional—and therefore most easily accessible—crime film is *Jackie Brown* (1997), a brilliant adaptation of Elmore Leonard's novel *Rum Punch*.

As these words are being written, we're fully one-quarter into the twenty-first century, and the popularity of crime and mystery films shows no signs of abating. The variations of style and substance are more numerous than ever.

ABOVE: Although it came relatively late in the neo-noir cycle, Curtis Hanson's *L.A. Confidential* (1997) was a critical and commercial success, inspiring several knockoffs (made for big screens and small) that didn't come close to achieving its excellence. It was nominated for nine Academy Awards, winning two, and would have received others but for stiff competition from *Titanic*.

Old-fashioned whodunits still pop up now and then, mostly in the form of Agatha Christie remakes—*Murder on the Orient Express* (2001 and 2017), *The ABC Murders* (2018), *Death on the Nile* (2022), etc.—but quite spectacularly in the dazzlingly intricate *Knives Out* (2019). The special-effects-laden exploits of comic-book crime busters such as Batman, Daredevil, and Spider-Man account for a substantial number of recent offerings, and even that venerable genre standby, Sherlock Holmes, has been revived in the person of Robert Downey Jr. (although his interpretation of the character is hardly acceptable to Conan Doyle purists).

TV screens during this century have glowed with countless crime and mystery series, from police procedurals (*CSI*, *FBI*, *NYPD Blue*, *Criminal Minds*) to programs built around malefactors (*Dexter*, *Hannibal*, *The Sopranos*, *Breaking Bad*). And there's no sign of any letup. ✺

ABOVE: A studio publicity portrait for *Goodfellas* (1990), arguably the most influential gangster film in the genre's history, after the first two *Godfather* movies. Thirty-five years after its original theatrical release, it still shines brightly in America's pop-culture firmament. *Left to right*: Ray Liotta, Robert De Niro, Paul Sorvino, Martin Scorsese, and Joe Pesci.

INDEX

CONTRIBUTORS

ED HULSE is a journalist and pop-culture historian who covered the home-video and motion-picture industries for more than thirty years. His work has appeared in *Premiere*, *Variety*, *Playboy*, *Entertainment Weekly*, the *New Yorker*, the *New York Times*, and numerous trade publications. Between 1986 and 1990, he edited *Video Review's Previews*, a monthly magazine spotlighting new video releases. In the late eighties, his articles and movie reviews were syndicated to newspapers by the Washington Post Writers Group. In 1993, he coedited with Packy Smith a greatly expanded version of *Don Miller's Hollywood Corral: A Comprehensive B-Western Roundup*, considered by most aficionados to be the definitive work on the genre. Since 2002, Hulse has edited and published the award-winning journal *Blood 'n' Thunder*, which covers vintage pulp fiction and related pop-culture media. His books include *The Blood 'n' Thunder Guide to Pulp Fiction*, *The Wild West of Fiction and Film*, *Filming the West of Zane Grey*, *Distressed Damsels and Masked Marauders*, and most recently *Wage Slaves in the Dream Factory*. In 2017, he coedited *The Art of the Pulps* with Doug Ellis and the late Robert Weinberg. Four years later, he edited *The Art of Pulp Fiction: An Illustrated History of Vintage Paperbacks*. Under his Murania Press imprint, Hulse has published forty books and monographs covering various aspects of American pop culture from the late nineteenth and early twentieth centuries. His website is muraniapress.com.

Born in Fort Lee, New Jersey, **GLENN KENNY** was a senior editor and the chief film critic of *Premiere* magazine from 1999 to 2007; he currently contributes reviews to the *New York Times*, RogerEbert.com, and other publications. He also creates supplements to physical media editions by the Criterion Collection, Arrow Video, Powerhouse, and other boutique labels. He is the author of *Robert De Niro: Anatomy of an Actor* (Phaidon / Cahiers du Cinema, 2014), *Made Men: The Story of Goodfellas* (Hanover Square Press, 2020), and *The World Is Yours: The Story of Scarface* (Hanover Square Press, 2024). He lives in Brooklyn, New York.